Lecture Notes
in Business Information Processing   196

Series Editors

Wil van der Aalst
Eindhoven Technical University, The Netherlands

John Mylopoulos
University of Trento, Italy

Michael Rosemann
Queensland University of Technology, Brisbane, Qld, Australia

Michael J. Shaw
University of Illinois, Urbana-Champaign, IL, USA

Clemens Szyperski
Microsoft Research, Redmond, WA, USA

Chihab Hanachi
Frédérick Bénaben
François Charoy (Eds.)

Information Systems for Crisis Response and Management in Mediterranean Countries

First International Conference, ISCRAM-med 2014
Toulouse, France, October 15-17, 2014
Proceedings

 Springer

Volume Editors

Chihab Hanachi
Université Toulouse 1
IRIT Laboratory
Toulouse, France
E-mail: hanachi@univ-tlse1.fr

Frédérick Bénaben
Ecole des Mines d'Albi-Carmaux
Centre de Génie Industriel
Albi, France
E-mail: benaben@enstimac.fr

François Charoy
Université de Lorraine
B038 LORIA
Vandoeuvre-lès-Nancy, France
E-mail: charoy@loria.fr

ISSN 1865-1348   e-ISSN 1865-1356
ISBN 978-3-319-11817-8   e-ISBN 978-3-319-11818-5
DOI 10.1007/978-3-319-11818-5
Springer Cham Heidelberg New York Dordrecht London

Library of Congress Control Number: 2014949406

© Springer International Publishing Switzerland 2014
This work is subject to copyright. All rights are reserved by the Publisher, whether the whole or part of the material is concerned, specifically the rights of translation, reprinting, reuse of illustrations, recitation, broadcasting, reproduction on microfilms or in any other physical way, and transmission or information storage and retrieval, electronic adaptation, computer software, or by similar or dissimilar methodology now known or hereafter developed. Exempted from this legal reservation are brief excerpts in connection with reviews or scholarly analysis or material supplied specifically for the purpose of being entered and executed on a computer system, for exclusive use by the purchaser of the work. Duplication of this publication or parts thereof is permitted only under the provisions of the Copyright Law of the Publisher's location, in ist current version, and permission for use must always be obtained from Springer. Permissions for use may be obtained through RightsLink at the Copyright Clearance Center. Violations are liable to prosecution under the respective Copyright Law.
The use of general descriptive names, registered names, trademarks, service marks, etc. in this publication does not imply, even in the absence of a specific statement, that such names are exempt from the relevant protective laws and regulations and therefore free for general use.
While the advice and information in this book are believed to be true and accurate at the date of publication, neither the authors nor the editors nor the publisher can accept any legal responsibility for any errors or omissions that may be made. The publisher makes no warranty, express or implied, with respect to the material contained herein.

Typesetting: Camera-ready by author, data conversion by Scientific Publishing Services, Chennai, India

Printed on acid-free paper

Springer is part of Springer Science+Business Media (www.springer.com)

Preface

We welcome you to the proceedings of the International Conference on Information Systems for Crisis Response and Management in Mediterranean countries (ISCRAM-med), held in Toulouse, France, October 15–17, 2014.

The aim of ISCRAM-med was to gather researchers and practitioners working in the area of Information Systems for Crisis Response and Management, with a special but not limited focus on Mediterranean crises.

Many crises have occurred in recent years around the Mediterranean Sea. For instance, we may mention political crises such as the Arabic Spring (Tunisia, Libya, Egypt, etc.), economic crises in Spain and Greece, earthquakes in Italy, fires in France and Spain, riots in French suburbs or even the explosion of the chemical plant AZF in France (Toulouse). Some of them even had a domino effect leading to other crises. Moreover, history shared by Mediterranean countries, the common climate, and similar geo-political issues have led to solidarity among people and cross-country military interventions. This observation highlights the importance of considering some of these crises in this region at a Mediterranean level rather than as isolated phenomena. If researchers are working on crises that occurred in only one of these countries or involving a single class of crises, it is now appropriate to exchange and share information and knowledge about the course and management of these crises and also to get the point of view of stakeholders, practitioners and policy makers.

By organizing the conference in the southwest of France, given the proximity of Toulouse to North Africa, we have attracted researchers from many south Mediterranean countries and provided the ISCRAM community with the opportunity to create new links with researchers and practitioners from these regions.

The main topics of ISCRAM-med 2014 conference focused on the preparedness and response phases of the crisis lifecycle. The topics covered were: supply chain and distribution, modeling and simulation, training, human interactions in the crisis field, coordination and agility, as well as the social aspects of crisis management.

We received 44 papers from authors in 16 countries and 3 continents. Each submission received at least three review reports from Program Committee members. The reviews were based on five criteria: relevance, contribution, originality, validity, and clarity of the presentation. Using these, each reviewer provided a recommendation and from these we selected 15 full papers for publication and presentation at ISCRAM-med. Accordingly, the acceptance rate of ISCRAM med 2014 for full papers was about: 34%. In addition, these proceedings also include four short papers that were presented at ISCRAM-med 2014.

Furthermore, invited keynote presentations were given by Alexis Drogoul (from UMMISCO laboratory, Can Tho, Vietnam) on "geo-historical modeling of past crisis", Laurent Franck (from Telecom Bretagne school, France) on "emergency field practices versus research activities", and Sihem Amer-Yahia (from CNRS LIG laboratory Grenoble, France) on "task assignment optimization in Crowdsourcing".

Acknowledgments

We gratefully acknowledge all members of the Program Committee and all external referees for the work in reviewing and selecting the contributions.

Moreover, we wish to thank the scientific and/or financial support of: the IS-CRAM Association, IRIT laboratory of Toulouse, all the Universities of Toulouse, University of Lorraine, École des mines d'Albi-Carmaux, and the Région Midi-Pyrénées.

For the local organization of the conference, we gratefully acknowledge the help of Hadj Batatia, Françoise Adreit, Sebastien Truptil, Stéphanie Combettes, Eric Andonoff, Benoit Gaudou, Thanh Le, Sameh Triki, Ines Thabet, Mohamed Chaawa, Saliha Najlaoui and Michele Cuesta.

Finally we would like to thank for their cooperation Viktoria Meyer and Ralf Gerstner of Springer in the preparation of this volume.

October 2014   Chihab Hanachi
                                                    Frédérick Bénaben
                                                    François Charoy

Organization

General Chair

Chihab Hanachi   University Toulouse 1 Capitole – IRIT, France

Co-chairs

Frédérick Bénaben   École des mines d'Albi-Carmaux, France
François Charoy   University of Lorraine, France

Program Committee

Andrea Omicini	Università di Bologna, Italy
Athman Bouguettaya	RMIT University, Melbourne, Australia
Carlos Castillo	Qatar Computing Research Institute, Qatar
Elyes Lamine	Centre Universitaire Jean-François Champollion, France
Emilia Balas	Aurel Vlaicu University of Arad, Romania
Lamjed Bensaïd	ISG Tunis, Tunisia
Francis Rousseaux	University of Reims, France
Gerhard Wickler	University of Edinburgh, UK
Ghassan Beydoun	University of New South Wales, Australia
Hamid Mcheick	University Québec at Chicoutimi, Canada
Julie Dugdale	Université Pierre Mendès France, France
Laurent Franck	Telecom Bretagne, France
Ling Tang	Beijing University of Chemical Technology, China
Lotfi Bouzguenda	University of Sfax, Tunisia
Marouane Kessentini	University of Michigan, USA
Matthieu Lauras	École des mines d'Albi-Carmaux, France
Mohammed Erradi	ENSIAS, Rabat, Marocco
Monica Divitini	Norwegian University of Science and Technology, Norway
Muhammad Imran	Qatar Computing Research Institute, Qatar
Narjes Bellamine Ben Saoud	University of Tunis, Tunisia
Nadia Nouali-Taboudjemat	CERIST, Algeria
Paloma Diaz Perez	Universidad Carlos III de Madrid, Spain
Pedro Antunes	University of Lisboa, Portugal
Ricardo Rabelo	Federal University of Santa Catarina, Brazil
Rui Jorge Tramontin Jr.	Santa Catarina State University, Brasil
Sanja Vranes	Institute Mihajlo Pupin, Belgrade, Serbia

Selmin Nurcan	University Paris 1, France
Serge Stinckwich	IRD, France
Shady Elbassuoni	American University of Beirut, Lebanon
Yiannis Verginadis	National Technical University of Athens, Greece
Youcef Baghdadi	Sultan Qaboos University, Oman

External Reviewers

Abdel-Rahman Tawil	University of East London, UK
Anne-Marie Barthe-Delanoë	École des mines d'Albi-Carmaux, France
Benoit Gaudou	University of Toulouse 1 Capitole, France
Bogdan Pavkovic	Institute Mihajlo Pupin, Serbia
Eric Andonoff	University of Toulouse 1 Capitole, France
Hai Dong	RMIT University, Melbourne, Australia
Houda Benali	RIADI laboratory, Tunsia
Ines Thabet	University of Jendouba, Tunisia
Jason Mahdjoub	University of Reims, France
Jôrne Franke	DHBW Mannheim/DB Systel GmbH, Germany
Marco Romano	Universidad Carlos III de Madrid, Spain
Sajib Kumar Mistry	University of Dhaka, Bangladesh
Sebastien Truptil	École des mines d'Albi-Carmaux, France
Sergio Herranz	Universidad Carlos III de Madrid, Spain
Teresa Onorati	Universidad Carlos III de Madrid, Spain
Valentina Janev	Institute Mihajlo Pupin, Serbia

Keynotes

Simulating the Past to Better Manage the Present: Geo-Historical Modeling of Past Catastrophes in the ARCHIVES Project

Alexis Drogoul

IRD, UMI 209 UMMISCO (IRD & UPMC)
32 av. H. Varagnat,
93143 Bondy Cedex
Tel: +33 (0)1 48 02 56 89
Fax: +33 (0)1 48 47 30 88

Can Tho Univ., DREAM Team
CICT, 1 Ly Tu Trong street,
Can Tho, Vietnam

alexis.drogoul@gmail.com

Abstract. It is now widely accepted that the adaptation of human communities to natural hazards is partly based on a better understanding of similar past events and of the measures undertaken by impacted groups to adapt to them. This "living memory" has the potential to improve their perception of the risks associated to these hazards and, hopefully, to increase their resilience to them. However, it requires that: (1) data related to these hazards are accessible; (2) relevant information can be extracted from it; (3) "narratives" can be reconstructed from these information; (4) they can be easily shared and transmitted. This is classically the task of archivists and historians to make sure that these conditions are fulfilled. The goal of ARCHIVES is to propose a methodology that would enable to fulfill them in a systematic and automated way, from the analysis of documents to the design of realistic geo-historical computer models. Our aim is that, using these models, users can both visualize what happened and explore what could have happened in alternative "what-if" scenarios. Our claim is that this tangible, albeit virtual, approach to historical "fictions" will provide researchers with a novel methodology for synthesizing large corpuses of documents and, at the same time, become a vector for transmitting lessons from past disasters to a contemporary audience. The broad applicative context of ARCHIVES is the study of floods management in Vietnam over the past centuries, which is still a crucial question because these events can be devastating. Opposite strategies have been used in the two deltas that structure the country: while the North has put the accent on the construction of dykes to stem the Red River, the South has adapted by digging a dense network of canals in the Mekong River delta. And, despite the political upheavals undergone by the country in the last centuries, during the Nguyễn dynasty (1802-1945), the French colonization (1865-1954), the independence (1955) or (đổimới, 1986), the reform policy these strategies have remained virtually unchanged. Their permanence raises the question of the social and environmental determinants that led to their design and how they are understood by contemporary stakeholders, heirs of radically different choices made centuries ago. In order to evaluate the feasibility of the whole project, the French and Vietnamese partners of ARCHIVES have worked on a limited case study from January to July 2013, part of the preparation of the "Tam Dao Summer School" (http://www.tamdaoconf.com), during which a one-week training session was delivered on "Modeling the past to better manage the present: an initiation to the geo-historical modeling of past risks". The case study concerned the flooding of the Red River in July 1926 and its impact on Hanoi. Our work was based on (1) the analysis of the colonial archives stored in Hanoi, (2) previous historical researches carried out on this event, (3) the reuse of hydrodynamic and social models developed by partners, and (4) the use of GAMA to build simulation prototypes. This first attempt demonstrated the potential of this approach for historians and users of the model, allowing them to not only visualize this event in a new way, but to also explore fictional scenarios, which helped them in gaining a deeper understanding of the social and environmental dynamics of the flooding.

Revisiting the Möbius Strip: Where Emergency Field Practices and Research Activities Meet

Laurent Franck

Télécom Bretagne - site de Toulouse
10 Avenue Edouard Belin BP44004
F-31028 Toulouse Cedex

`laurent.franck@telecom-bretagne.eu`

Abstract. In this keynote, we will discuss about emergency communications both from field practitioner and researcher standpoints. We'll see how these two stances may contradict. Field practitioners tend to be conservative, for the sake of effectiveness. Researchers, by definition, push forward new telecommunication paradigms, calling to revisit current practices in order to improve them (or so, they believe). In this battle between the "keep it simple" and the "make it better", we will fight our way taking as study case the use of satellite communications during emergencies. What are the current practice? What are the opportunities and the possible implementations? How to strike the right balance between operational constraints and technological advances?

Task Assignment Optimization in Crowdsourcing and Its Applications to Crisis Management

Sihem Amer-Yahia

Laboratoire d'Informatique de Grenoble (LIG)
681 rue de la passerelle
38401 Saint-Martin d'Hères - France
Building D – Office D308
Tel: +33 4 76 82 72 76

Sihem.Amer-Yahia@imag.fr

Abstract. A crowdsourcing process can be viewed as a combination of three components worker skill estimation, worker-to-task assignment, and task accuracy evaluation. The reason why crowdsourcing today is so popular is that tasks are small, independent, homogeneous, and do not require a long engagement from workers. The crowd is typically volatile, its arrival and departure asynchronous, and its levels of attention and accuracy variable. In most systems, Mechanical Turk, Turkit, Mob4hire, uTest, Freelancer, eLance, oDesk, Guru, Topcoder, Trada, 99design, Innocentive, CloudCrowd, and CloudFlower, task assignment is done via a self-appointment by workers. I will argue that the optimization of worker-to-task assignment is central to the effectiveness of a crowdsourcing platform and present a uniform framework that allows to formulate worker-to-task assignment as a series of optimization goals with different goals including addressing misinformation and rumor in crisis reporting.

Table of Contents

Coordination and Agility

Social Aspects in Crisis Management

A Location-Allocation Model for More Consistent Humanitarian Supply Chains

Matthieu Lauras[1,*], Jorge Vargas[1,2], Lionel Dupont[1], and Aurelie Charles[3]

[1] University Toulouse – Mines Albi, Industrial Engineering Department, Albi, France
[2] Pontifical University Catholic of Peru, Department of Engineering, Lima, Peru
[3] University of Lyon II, DISP Laboratory, Lyon, France
jorge.vargas@pucp.edu.pe, {lauras,dupont}@mines-albi.fr,
a.charles@univ-lyon2.fr

Abstract. During the preparedness phase, humanitarians plan their relief response by studying the potential disasters, their consequences and the existing infrastructures and available resources. However, when the disaster occurs, some hazards can impact strongly the network by destroying some resources or collapsing infrastructures. Consequently, the performance of the relief network could be strongly decreased. The problem statement of our research work can be defined as the capability to design a consistent network that would be able to manage adequately the disaster response despite of potential failures or deficiencies of infrastructures and resources. Basically, our research work consists in proposing an innovative location-allocation model in order to improve the humanitarian response efficiency (cost minimization) and effectiveness (non-served beneficiaries minimization) regarding the foreseeable network weaknesses. A Stochastic Mixed Integer Program is proposed to reach this goal. A numerical application regarding the management of the Peruvian earthquake's relief network is proposed to illustrate the benefits of our proposition.

Keywords: Location-allocation, humanitarian supply chain, design scenarios, stochastic programming, consistency.

1 Introduction

Humanitarian Supply Chains (HSC) have received a lot of attention over the last fifteen years, and can now be considered a new research area. The number of scientific and applicative publications has considerably increased over this period and particularly over the last five years. Reviews in humanitarian logistics and disaster operations management have allowed bringing out trends and future research directions dedicated to this area [1]. These authors show that the HSC research projects are mainly based on the development of analytical models followed by case studies and theory. As for research methodologies, mathematical programming is the

---

* Corresponding author.

C. Hanachi, F. Bénaben, and F. Charoy (Eds.): ISCRAM-med 2014, LNBIP 196, pp. 1–12, 2014.
© Springer International Publishing Switzerland 2014

most frequently utilized method. But we must notice that few or no humanitarian organizations go as far as using optimization-based decision-support systems. This demonstrates that a real gap exists between the research work proposals and their application on the field.

One main reason of this difficulty is the inconstancy of the HSC design. Actually, in many cases, roads or infrastructures could have been destroyed or damaged. Consequently, the expecting performance of the network could be considerably degraded. During the Haiti's earthquake in 2010 for instance, a post scenario faced the humanitarian practitioners to figure out a lot of barriers to achieve an effective response solving failure in the relief chain due to many vital transportation, power, and communication infrastructures stayed inoperative: The Toussaint Louverture International Airport stayed inaccessible, many highways and roads were blocked and damaged due to fallen fragments, roughly 44 km linear national roads and four bridges was damaged, Port-au-Prince harbour was seriously affected, the North dock was destroyed and the South dock severely damaged [2].

During the preparedness phase, humanitarians plan their response (distribution) by studying the existing infrastructures and available resources [3]. However, when the disaster occurs, some hazards can impact strongly the network by destroying some resources or collapsing infrastructures. Consequently, the response could be disturbed and the demand can drastically change (in terms of source and/or volume). Therefore, if a sudden change of demand or supply occurs during an ongoing humanitarian operation, a complex planning problem results which includes decisions regarding the relocation of stocks and the transportation of relief items under an uncertainty environment [4].

Consequently the problem statement can be defined as the capability to design a consistent network that would be able to manage adequately the disaster response despite of potential failures or deficiencies of infrastructures and resources. Basically, our research work consists in proposing an innovative location-allocation model in order to improve the humanitarian response resiliency regarding the foreseeable network weaknesses.

The paper is structuring as the following. In a first section, a brief literature review on usual location-allocation models is proposed in order to justify our scientific contribution. Then, the core of our contribution is developed. Finally, a case study on the design of a supply chain dedicated to the Peruvian earthquakes' management is proposed.

2   Background

A thorough logistics network analysis should consider complex transportation cost structures, warehouse sizes, environment constraints, inventory turnover ratios, inventory costs, objective service levels and many other data and parameters. As discussed before, these issues are quite difficult to gather in humanitarian world. But as humanitarians evolve in a very hazardous environment, the academic works must consider the uncertainties they face with [1]. Nevertheless, a great majority of the current research works is deterministic and just few of them propose stochastic or fuzzy approaches [5]. One issue is the environment that changes so quickly and so unpredictably after a disaster occurs. Despite all, as [6] affirm, humanitarians could benefit a lot from the use of optimization-based decision-support systems to design a highly capable HSC.

Moreover there is a consensus among field experts that there are many lessons and practices from the commercial world that could be used in the humanitarian world. It can be stated that although humanitarian logistics has its distinct features, the basic principles of business logistics can be applied [6]. Consequently, we have decided to back up each step of our approach with some analysis of business best practices.

Location-Allocation problems were traditionally developed with well-established deterministic models [7] such as: weighted networks [8], branch-and-bound algorithms [9], projections [10], tabu search [11], P-Median plus Weber [12], etc. Some hybrid algorithms were also suggested, such as the simulated annealing and random descent method, the algorithm improved with variable neighborhood search proposed by [13] or the Lagrange relaxation and genetic algorithm of [14].

But decisions to support humanitarian logistics activities for disaster operations management are challenging due to the uncertainties of events. The usual methods to deal with demand uncertainty are to use a stochastic or a robust optimization model [7]. Stochastic optimization uses probabilities of occurrence and robust optimization uses various alternatives, from the most optimists to the worst-case scenarios. Stochastic optimization models optimize the random outcome on average. According to [15] "this is justified when the Law of Large Numbers can be invoked and we are interested in the long-term performance, irrespective of the fluctuations of specific outcome realizations". In our case, the impact of those "fluctuations" is on human lives and can be devastating. As for robust location problems, according to [16], they have proven difficult to solve for realistic instances. If a great majority of the published research works is deterministic, more and more humanitarian researchers propose now stochastic models in order to better consider uncertainty on demand. A majority of these models are inspired of previous research works already developed for traditional business supply chains such as: the stochastic incapacitated facility location-allocation models, the multiple fuzzy criteria and a fuzzy goal programming approaches [17], the classical p-median problem [18], the fuzzy environment models [19], the model with chance-constrained programming with stochastic demands [20], the Lagrange relaxation and stochastic optimizations, or the capacitated multi-facility with probabilistic customer's locations and demands under the Hurwicz criterion [21], so on. Recently, risks were considered in a multi-objective setting to solve supplier selection problems in [22] and some robust optimization models were proposed for studying the facility location problem under uncertainty [16].

Nevertheless, these models are limited because they do not consider the fact that disaster relief operations often have to be carried out in an disrupted environment with destabilized infrastructures [23] ranging from a lack of electricity supplies to limited transport infrastructure. Furthermore, since most natural disasters are unpredictable, the demand for goods in these disasters is also unpredictable [23]. We think that a HSC design model should include these both dimensions of uncertainty to be accurate and relevant for practitioners. It has been proposed some approaches regarding the problem of demand on uncertainty environments [24]. This paper only focuses on the problem of consistency of HSC design regarding the potential environment disruptions.

3   Modeling Principles

Our objective is to provide management recommendations regarding the design of supply networks in the context of disaster relief (location, number and size of warehouses). The aim of the proposed model is thereby to determine which network configuration and design enable to send all the required products at the required times in the most efficient way, even if the infrastructure has been partially or totally damaged during the disaster. The main originality of our proposal consists in guaranteeing effectiveness of the response despite potential disturbances on the infrastructure while maximizing efficiency (by minimizing the costs). Humanitarian practitioners insisted that the problem is to know about how to achieve a given level of effectiveness in the most cost efficient way, whatever the disturbances related to a disaster are [24]. Actually, our added value is both to complement existing disaster relief facility location studies and to take into account the specifications of the humanitarian practitioners.

To reach this goal, the proposed model should minimize the unsatisfactory of beneficiaries on one hand, and minimize the logistic costs on the other hand. The model has been formulated in order to combine usual facility location problem with the possibility that potential locations may be affected by a disaster (partially or completely). In our approach, we have considered that there are two main ways to modify the logistic environment following a disaster:

- By a limitation of the transportation capabilities;
- By a limitation of the response capabilities of the warehouses.

These two factors should be more or less sensitive function of the vulnerability of the concerned territory. Regarding the first limitation we have proposed to consider a parameter that expresses the maximum throughput between a source and its destination. Regarding the second limitation we have introduced a parameter that expresses the percentage of useable capability of a given warehouse.

As discussed previously, the proposed model is a Stochastic Mixed Integer Program (SMIP). Its principle consists in optimizing risk scenarios in order to evaluate the best locations to open and their associated capabilities. Risk scenarios should consequently be determined to instantiate the model. Although the scenario approach generally results in more tractable models [16], several problems must be solved such as: how to determine the scenarios, how to assign reliable probabilities to each scenario, and how to limit the number of scenarios to test (for computational reasons).

Several options have been proposed in the literature to cope with these topics and to design plausible and realistic scenarios [25] [26]. Our approach consisted in developing scenarios characterized by: a disaster event and its consequences in terms of logistic and human damages. Those scenarios should be established through historical database, forecasting models (if exist) and interviews of experts. In [27], the authors have proposed a concrete methodology to define such scenarios. Then a probability of occurrence should also be determined by experts or forecast models (if exist). Based on this, a probabilistic risk scenario is deduced in which the following information are defined: demand forecast by regions, associated quantity of products needed, delivering transport capacity inter regions (nominal), and disruptions propagation following a category of disaster (% throughput, % warehouse capability).

4   The Mixed Integer Stochastic Program

Following the principles described previously, we have proposed the following MISP to resolve our problem statement:

Indexes
i: demand indexes
j: index of potential warehouses
s: scenario

Unchanged parameters
a_j: maximum capacity of warehouse j
b_j: minimum capacity of warehouse j
cg: overall storage capacity
f_j: implementation cost of the warehouse
nw: maximum amount of warehouses
s: cost of non-fulfillment demand
t_{ij}: transport costs between i and j
v_j: variable cost of warehouse management

Scenarios parameters settings
d_{is}: demand to be satisfied at i
h_s: Scenario probability for s
m_{ijs}: maximum flow between i and j
p_{js}: percentage of usable capacity

Unchanged variables
C_j: capacity warehouse j
Y_j: 1 if the warehouse is located in j, 0 otherwise

Variables of scenarios
R_{is}: i demand not satisfied in scenario s
X_{ijs}: relief provided by j to i in scenario s

Then the objective function is defined by the following equation that consists in minimizing the unsatisfactory delivery (regarding beneficiaries needs) and in minimizing the total logistics costs:

$$\min = s. \sum_i \sum_s hs.Ris + \sum_j (fj.Yj + vj.Cj) + \sum_i \sum_j \sum_s hs.tij.Xijs$$

The following constraints are included in our approach.

Equation 1 ensures that a warehouse j is open only if it delivers some relief to beneficiaries.

$$(1) \ \forall j, \sum_i Xij \leq Yj.MaxDmde$$

Equation 2 expresses that the demand at i is satisfied by the opened warehouses or unsatisfied.

$$(2) \ \forall i, \forall s \sum_j Xijs + Ris = dis$$

Equation 3 guarantees that a warehouse cannot deliver more product than its residual capacity.

$$(3) \ \forall j, \forall s \sum_i Xijs \leq pjs.Cj$$

Equation 4 indicates that if a warehouse is open then its capacity is between aj and bj, if not its capacity is null.

$$(4) \ \forall j, \ aj.Yj \leq Cj \leq bj.Yj$$

Equation 5 shows that the flows between i and j are limited.

$$(5) \ \forall i \forall j \forall s, \ Xijs \leq mijs$$

Equation 6 limits the total number of warehouses.

$$(6) \ \sum_j Yj \leq nw$$

Equation 7 indicates that the total capacity of the warehouses is cg.

$$(7) \ \sum_j Cj \leq cg$$

5   Case Study

5.1   Context

In this section, we present a numerical application case in order to illustrate the benefits of our contribution regarding the management of earthquake disasters in Peru. Analysis of historical data on Peruvian earthquakes shows clearly that the small and medium size earthquakes' occurrences are globally recurrent in frequency and intensity. Consequently, the Peruvian authorities seek to optimize their relief network in order to maximize their efficiency and effectiveness in case of disaster. The current application tries to contribute to resolve this question.

5.2   Scenario Definition

As presented before, our model needs some realistic scenarios to be implemented. Although this part of the research work is not developed in this paper, some elementary information should be explained to well understand the following. Notably, the principle of scenario generation and the principle of damages' impacts assessment have to be exposed.

Scenario generation

Based on the Peruvian historical earthquakes and on the works of the Geophysical Institute of Peru (IGP, http://www.igp.gob.pe), we generated through the methodology developed in [27], 27 risk scenarios that should be occurred following a given probability (as shown on the following table). All these scenarios (see. Table 1) get a magnitude equal or greater than 5,5 M (under this limit, the potential impact is not enough to be considered as a disaster) and a region of occurrence. The database used to generate those scenarios was recorded by the seismographs' network of the IGP. 2200 records were analyzed corresponding to the period from 1970 to 2007.

Table 1. The risk scenarios studied

No	Location	Scenarios by regions	Standarized magnitude	Probability	No	Location	Scenarios by regions	Standarized magnitude	Probability
1	Amazonas	6	7,5	2,1%	15	Lima	4	8,5	1,3%
2	Ancash	25	8,5	8,3%	16	Loreto	10	6,5	3,3%
3	Apurimac	2	6,5	0,6%	17	Loreto	3	7,5	1,0%
4	Arequipa	7	8,5	2,3%	18	Madre de Dios	6	5,7	2,0%
5	Ayacucho	4	6,5	1,4%	19	Madre de Dios	7	6,5	2,3%
6	Cajamarca	2	7,5	0,5%	20	Pasco	5	5,7	1,7%
7	Cusco	1	7,5	0,3%	21	Piura	6	6,5	2,0%
8	Huancavelica	1	6,5	0,5%	22	Piura	7	7,5	2,3%
9	Huanuco	5	5,7	1,7%	23	San Martin	6	6,5	2,0%
10	Ica	14	8,5	4,7%	24	San Martin	7	7,5	2,3%
11	Junin	2	7,5	0,7%	25	Tacna	20	8,5	6,7%
12	La Libertad	14	7,5	4,7%	26	Tumbes	34	7,5	11,3%
13	Lambayeque	2	6,5	0,7%	27	Ucayali	4	6,5	1,4%
							301		100,0%

Damages' impacts assessment

As discussed before, when an earthquake occurs, this has an impact on the network capacity. Consequently we defined with earthquake's experts (from IGP and from the Peruvian Civilian Defense Institute) the expected consequences of each scenario in terms of beneficiaries' needs and logistics' damages (warehouses' capacities, roads' capacities). As indicated earlier, this phase is not developed in this paper but to be more concrete, we propose the following example: Let's consider an earthquake of 7,5 M. If the epicenter region belongs to a Seismic Zone SZ (by opposition to Non Seismic Zone NSZ), the associated warehouse will lose 60 % of their nominal capacity. At a same time, the warehouses capabilities that are in the border regions will lose between 10% and 30% function of the distance and the vulnerability of the region. The following table shows this result (see [27] for more information on this subject).

Table 2. Resume scenarios of reduction capacities

Magnitude	% Reduction of capacity storage			% Reduction of capacity flow transport		
	Epicenter SZ / NSZ	Border SZ	Border NSZ	Epicenter SZ / NSZ	Border SZ	Border NSZ
5,5	0%	0%	0%	0%	0%	0%
	0%	0%	0%	0%	0%	0%
6,5	40%	20%	5%	10%	5%	1%
	20%	20%	5%	5%	5%	1%
7,5	60%	30%	10%	30%	15%	5%
	40%	30%	10%	15%	15%	5%
8,5	80%	40%	20%	70%	35%	15%
	60%	40%	20%	35%	35%	15%
9,5	100%	60%	40%	100%	65%	35%
	80%	60%	40%	65%	65%	35%
10,0	100%	80%	60%	100%	80%	60%
	100%	80%	60%	100%	80%	60%

5.3   Model Execution

The objective of this section is to show that the model can be solve realistic problems and to illustrate how it can be used for supporting decisions about strategic planning humanitarian networks.

Data and parameters
The data and parameters used for this numerical application were gathered from the Peruvian Civilian Defense Institute [28].

In 2011, the current earthquake's Peruvian network gets enough items (kits) to serve 100,000 victims (1 kit per person). This network is composed of 12 regional warehouses.

During the period 1993 to 2014, the number of earthquakes' victims has increased by 333%. Considering that this trend will be maintained, we can roughly estimate that the Peruvian network capacity will be able to store more than 333,333 kits by 2022. Hence, the warehouse capabilities should be respectively, minimum stock 9,000 kits (100,000/12) and maximum 28 000 kits (333,333/12).

The following costs have been considered for the numerical application: a fixed cost due to management of warehouses of $10,000, a variable cost due to buying and possession kits of $100, a variable cost due to non-delivering kit (shortage) of $100, a variable cost due to freight fees for transportation proportional to distance among regions have been estimated (see Table 3), considering that some regions as Ucayali and Loreto have to be supply by air as they are very far and inaccessible.

Table 3. Cost of transportation among Peruvian regions

Regions	Amazonas	Ancash	Apurimac	Arequipa	Ayacucho	Cajamarca	Cusco	Huancavelica	Huanuco	Ica	Junin	LaLibertad	Lambayeque	Lima	Loreto	Madre de Dios	Moquegua	Pasco	Piura	Puno	SanMartin	Tacna	Tumbes	Ucayali
Amazonas	0	704	1794	2154	1479	288	1983	1394	923	1326	1266	577	419	1021	10000	2412	2261	1023	477	2370	1079	2440	765	10000
Ancash	704	0	1193	1498	879	465	1383	821	322	790	665	350	555	485	10000	1812	1606	423	768	1775	883	1785	1054	10000
Apurimac	1794	1193	0	550	322	1546	190	508	876	519	527	1320	1524	884	10000	619	693	767	1738	573	1756	885	2023	10000
Arequipa	2154	1498	550	0	846	1799	456	990	1374	707	1059	1573	1777	1021	10000	756	106	1268	1991	285	2190	372	2276	10000
Ayacucho	1479	879	322	846	0	1240	512	146	561	503	212	1004	1209	610	10000	941	958	452	1423	898	1441	1137	1708	10000
Cajamarca	288	465	1546	1799	1240	0	1745	1183	684	1088	1027	228	236	783	10000	2174	1903	785	449	2073	841	2083	753	10000
Cusco	1983	1383	190	456	512	1745	0	699	1067	710	718	1510	1715	1074	10000	429	517	958	1928	387	1947	710	2214	10000
Huancavelica	1394	821	508	990	146	1183	699	0	505	304	210	948	1153	554	10000	1127	1096	396	1366	1085	1385	1275	1652	10000
Huanuco	923	322	876	1374	561	684	1067	505	0	664	346	658	862	359	10000	1493	1479	104	1076	1450	884	1658	1361	10000
Ica	1326	790	519	707	503	1088	710	304	664	0	442	917	1121	364	10000	1138	766	611	1335	935	1534	945	1620	10000
Junin	1266	665	527	1059	212	1027	718	210	346	442	0	790	994	395	10000	1146	1169	235	1208	1104	1225	1349	1493	10000
LaLibertad	577	350	1320	1573	1004	228	1510	948	658	917	790	0	204	556	10000	1936	1676	662	418	1846	853	1856	703	10000
Lambayeque	419	555	1524	1777	1209	236	1715	1153	862	1121	994	204	0	768	10000	2261	1888	874	214	2057	1058	2067	500	10000
Lima	1021	485	884	1021	610	783	1074	554	359	364	395	556	768	0	10000	1499	1127	255	978	1296	1177	1306	1262	10000
Loreto	10000	10000	10000	10000	10000	10000	10000	10000	10000	10000	10000	10000	10000	10000	0	10000	10000	10000	10000	10000	10000	10000	10000	10000
Madre de Dios.	2412	1812	619	756	941	2174	429	1127	1493	1138	1146	1936	2261	1499	10000	0	803	1387	2356	559	2376	882	2641	10000
Moquegua	2261	1606	693	106	958	1903	517	1096	1479	766	1169	1676	1888	1127	10000	803	0	1377	2100	246	2300	235	2385	10000
Pasco	1023	423	767	1268	452	785	958	396	104	611	235	662	874	255	10000	1387	1377	0	1081	1342	985	1559	1365	10000
Piura	477	768	1738	1991	1423	449	1928	1366	1076	1335	1208	418	214	978	10000	2356	2100	1081	0	2273	1274	2284	287	10000
Puno	2370	1775	573	285	898	2073	387	1085	1450	935	1104	1846	2057	1296	10000	559	246	1342	2273	0	2334	324	2555	10000
SanMartin	1079	883	1756	2190	1441	841	1947	1385	884	1534	1225	853	1058	1177	10000	2376	2300	985	1274	2334	0	2476	1556	10000
Tacna	2440	1785	885	372	1137	2083	710	1275	1658	945	1349	1856	2067	1306	10000	882	235	1559	2284	324	2476	0	2564	10000
Tumbes	765	1054	2023	2276	1708	753	2214	1652	1361	1620	1493	703	500	1262	10000	2641	2385	1365	287	2555	1556	2564	0	10000
Ucayali	10000	10000	10000	10000	10000	10000	10000	10000	10000	10000	10000	10000	10000	10000	10000	10000	10000	10000	10000	10000	10000	10000	10000	0

Results

The model was used to design an optimized network (number, localization and capacity of warehouses) regarding the efficiency (total cost of operation (CT)) and the effectiveness (percentage of non-served beneficiaries (BNA)). To reach this goal, we defined a service efficiency indicator (RS) defining by the ratio BNA/CT, which should be used as comparison criteria for decision-making. The lower the ratio is the better the network configuration is. The following table shows the main results obtained regarding this ratio for an experiment plan that considers from 6 to 12 the maximum number of warehouses that could be opened.

Table 4. Ratio of service versus number of warehouses

Number warehouses	$RS_{cw = 28\,000}$	$RS_{cw = 56\,000}$	$RS_{cw = 84\,000}$
12	8,5%	7,6%	7,5%
10	9,1%	7,6%	7,5%
8	9,9%	7,7%	7,6%
6	10,7%	8,0%	7,7%

The results showed that the worst results are for a maximum warehouse capacity of 28,000 kits because the effectiveness is really damaged. On the other hand, the service ratio remains equivalent for values of maximum storage capacity of 56,000 and 84,000 kits. The best solution in terms of both efficiency (total cost) and effectiveness (number of delivered beneficiaries) is obtained for 11 warehouses characterized as described on the following table.

Table 5. Optimal distribution warehouse to Peruvian humanitarian supply chain

No	Regions	Capacity warehouse
1	Apurimac	9000
2	Arequipa	41584
3	Ayacucho	56000
4	Cajamarca	11349
5	Cusco	56000
6	Huancavelica	22767
7	Ica	49930
8	Junin	12349
9	Loreto	56000
10	Piura	9000
11	SanMartin	9353

The current Peruvian network is composed of 12 warehouses but with a very different geographical distribution and inventory balance. For instance, majority of the relief inventories are nowadays stock in the Lima region because it is probably the most vulnerable (due to the concentration of population). But if an earthquake occurs in this region, the response should not be very effective as a majority of the aid could be unusable. Our approach allows avoiding this trap by distributing the relief stocks quite differently. Nevertheless, within the proposed optimal solution, the total cost is quite similar at the expected one if the current Peruvian network was used (see Table 6). To summarize our proposition can be considered globally equivalent on a financial point of view, but probably more consistent as the model has considered potential failures of the environment in case of disaster.

Table 6. Ratio of service versus number of warehouses

Models	Number warehouses optim.	Total cost HSC network
HSC proposal using MISP	11	60 343 461 [1]
Current HSC in Peru	12	62 218 512 [2]

[1] Using a maximun warehouse capacity of 56 000 kits.

[2] Based on state reports (INDECI, 2011) and rate exchange NS/$: 2,75

6   Conclusions and Future Works

In this paper we have proposed a methodology able to manage the inconsistency of current humanitarian supply chain design models. Actually, majority of the previous propositions did not consider potential damages on infrastructures and resources following a disaster. Consequently, network solutions that should be effective and/or efficient to manage relief operations would become inefficient.

Our research work have tried to reach a triple goal in terms of disaster management performance: (i) agility for a better responsiveness and effectiveness; (ii) efficiency for a better cost-control; (iii) consistency for a better deployment even if some infrastructures are not available any more. These three points have been recently point out by [29] as of prime importance for future research in disaster management.

Based on extent literature, our proposal consists in developing a location-allocation model through a Stochastic Mixed Integer Program (SMIP) that considers potential failures on warehouses capacities and on road capacities. This model optimizes risk scenarios in order to evaluate the best locations to open and their associated capabilities. The risk scenarios should de defined in order to be as realistic as possible (as discussed in [27]).

This proposition was applied to the Peruvian earthquakes situation in order to support future strategic thoughts on inventory pre-positioning. Discussions are ongoing with national authorities in order to validate the relevance of our approach regarding their operational objectives.

Although our proposal is a significant first step towards solving the problem of consistency in Humanitarian Supply Chain Design, several limitations remain, that we propose to study in future research works. They should assess the realism of the input scenarios. To do so, experiments are carried out over several past disasters (particularly in the case of past Peruvian earthquakes) to validate our approach. Other perspectives concern the sensitivity analysis of the model regarding the different parameters. Last but not least, complementary studies on the Peruvian application case should be done in order to obtain more robust results able to support more concretely the decision-making.

Acknowledgement. Authors thank to Dr. Hernan Tavera, research scientist at the Geophysical Institute of Peru (IGP), who provided the database that has been used to elaborate the scenarios.

References

1. Van Wassenhove, L.N.: Humanitarian aid logistics: supply chain management in high gear. Journal Operations Research Society 57(5), 475–489 (2006)
2. APNRDH. Action Plan for National Recovery and Development of Haiti; Immediate Key Initiatives for the Future, Government of the Republic of Haiti (2010), http://whc.unesco.org/uploads/activities/documents/activity-651-5.pdf (October 10, 2013)
3. Duran, S., Gutierrez, M.A., Keskinocak, P.: Pre-Positioning of Emergency Items for CARE International. Interfaces-The INFORMS Journal on the Practice of Operational Research 41, 223–237 (2011)
4. Rottkemper, B., Fischer, K., Blecken, A., Danne, C.: Inventory relocation for overlapping disaster settings in humanitarian operations. Operations Research Spectrum 33(3), 721–749 (2011)
5. Peres, E.Q., Brito Jr, I., Leiras, A., Yoshizaki, H.: Humanitarian logistics and disaster relief research: trends, applications, and future research directions. In: Proc. of the 4th International Conference on Information Systems, Logistics and Supply Chain, pp. 26–29 (2012)
6. Kovacs, G., Spens, K.M.: Humanitarian logistics in disaster relief operations. International Journal of Physical Distribution and Logistics Management 37(2), 99–114 (2007)
7. Bagher, M., Yousefli, A.: An application of possibilistic programming to the fuzzy location-allocation problems. The International Journal of Advanced Manufacturing Technology 53(9-12), 1239–1245 (2011)
8. Hakimi, S.: Optimum distribution of switching centers in a communication network and some related graph theoretic, problems. Operations Research 13, 462–475 (1964)

9. Kuenne, R.E., Soland, R.M.: Exact and approximate solutions to the multisource Weber problem. Mathematical Programming 3, 193–209 (1972)

10. Bongartz, I., Calamai, P.H., Conn, A.R.: A projection method for norm location-allocation problems. Mathematical Programming 66, 283–312 (1994)

11. Ohlemuller, M.: Tabu search for large location-allocation problems. Journal of the Operational Research Society 48, 745–750 (1997)

12. Hansen, P., Jaumard, B., Taillard, E.: Heuristic solution of the multisource Weber problem as a p-median problem. Operations Research Letters 22, 55–62 (1998)

13. Brimberg, J., Hansen, P., Mladenovic, N., Taillard, E.D.: Improvements and comparison of heuristics for solving the uncapacitated multisource Weber problem. Operations Research 48, 444–460 (2000)

14. Gong, D., Gen, M., Yamazaki, G., Xu, W.: Hybrid evolutionary method for capacitated location-allocation problem. Computers and Industrial Engineering 33, 577–580 (1997)

15. Shapiro, A., Dentcheva, D., Ruszczynski, A.P.: Lectures on Stochastic Programming. BPR Publishers, Philadelphia (2009)

16. Snyder, L.V.: Facility location under uncertainty: a review. IIE Transactions 38(7), 537–554 (2006)

17. Bhattacharya, U., Rao, J.R., Tiwari, R.N.: Fuzzy multicriteria facility location problem. Fuzzy Sets and Systems 51, 277–287 (1992)

18. Canós, M.J., Ivorra, C., Liern, V.: An exact algorithm for the fuzzy p-median problem. European Journal of Operations Research 116, 80–86 (1999)

19. Zhou, J., Liu, B.: Modeling capacitated location-allocation problem with fuzzy demands. Computers & Industrial Engineering 53, 454–468 (2007)

20. Zhou, J., Liu, B.: News stochastic models for capacitated location- allocation problem. Computers & Industrial Engineering 45, 111–126 (2003)

21. Mehdizadeh, E., Reza, M., Hajipour, V.: A new hybrid algorithm to optimize stochastic-fuzzy capacited multi-facility location-allocation problem. Journal of Optimization in Industrial Engineering 7, 71–80 (2011)

22. Bilsel, R.U., Ravindran, A.: A multiobjective chance constrained programming model for supplier selection under uncertainty. Transportation Research Part B 45, 1284–1300 (2011)

23. Cassidy, W.B.: A logistics lifeline, p. 1. Traffic World (October 27, 2003)

24. Charles, A.: PhD Thesis, Improving the design and management of agile supply chain: feedback and application in the context of humanitarian aid, Toulouse University, France (2010)

25. Azaron, A., Brown, K.N., Tarim, S.A., Modarres, M.: A multi-objective stochastic programming approach for supply chain design considering risk. International Journal of Production Economics 116, 129–138 (2008)

26. Klibi, W.,, M.: A Scenario-based supply chain network risk modeling. European Journal of Operational Research 223, 644–658 (2012)

27. Vargas-Florez, J., Charles, A., Lauras, M., Dupont, L.: Designing Realistic Scenarios for Disaster Management Quantitative Models. In: Proceedings of Annual ISCRAM Conference, Penn-State University, USA (2014)

28. INDECI, National Institute of Civil Defence, Chief Resolution 059-2011-INDECI (2011), http://sinpad.indeci.gob.pe/UploadPortalSINPAD/RJ%20N%C2%BA%20059-2011-INDECI.pdf (October 15, 2013)

29. Galindo, G., Batta, R.: Review of recent developments in OR/MS research in disaster operations management. European Journal of Operational Research 230(2), 201–211 (2013)

Towards Large-Scale Cloud-Based Emergency Management Simulation "SimGenis Revisited"

Chahrazed Labba[1], Narjès Bellamine Ben Saoud[1,2], and Karim Chine[3]

[1] Laboratoire RIADI-Ecole Nationale des Sciences de l'Informatique, Univ. Manouba, Tunisia
[2] Institut Supérieur d'Informatique, Univ. Tunis El Manar, Tunisia
[3] Cloud Era Ltd. Cambridge, UK
chahrazedlabba@gmail.com,
narjes.bellamine@ensi.rnu.tn,
karim.chine@cloudera.co.uk

Abstract. Large-scale Crisis and Emergency Management Simulations (CEMS) often require huge computing and memory resources. Also a collaborative effort may be needed from researchers geographically distributed to better understand and study the simulated phenomena. The emergence of the cloud computing paradigm offers new opportunities for such simulations by providing on demand resources and enabling collaboration. This paper focuses on the scalability of emergency management simulation environments and shows how the migration to cloud computing can be effectively used for large-scale CEMS. Firstly, a generic deployment approach on a cloud infrastructure is introduced and applied to an existing agent-based simulator. Secondly, a deep investigation of the cloud-based simulator shows that the initial model remains stable and that the simulator is effectively scalable. Thirdly, a collaborative data analysis and visualization using Elastic-r is presented.

Keywords: Emergency Management, Agent-Based Simulation, Cloud Computing, Scalability, Reuse, Deployment.

1   Introduction

Natural and man-made disasters are unavoidable, cannot be prevented and can cause irrevocable damages. Therefore efficient intervention solutions are required to mitigate the harmful effects of such hazardous. Due to the unpredictable scale of many disasters large-scale simulation is required to represent real-life situations. Although there are many circumstances where partial simulations suffice to understand the real world phenomena, there exists a number of problems that cannot be adequately understood with limited scale simulations [1]. Scalability remains an effective research issue and large-scale simulations are becoming more then ever a necessity. Also, nowadays and more than ever, the study of complex systems and related problems requires the collaboration of various members with different knowledge and expertise in order to be solved. Allowing collocated as well as geographically distributed researchers to communicate and collaborate is becoming a

C. Hanachi, F. Bénaben, and F. Charoy (Eds.): ISCRAM-med 2014, LNBIP 196, pp. 13–20, 2014.
© Springer International Publishing Switzerland 2014

realistic way of work. Similarly, for crisis and emergency management there is an increasing interest in the collaboration aspect to minimize the harmful effects of disasters [2, 3]. In addition users are increasingly demanding unlimited resources, with better quality of services and all that with reduced costs. Cloud computing emerges as the most adequate solution today for simulations by providing limitless resources on demand, also by enabling collaboration and increasing accessibility for users located anywhere.

In this work we are interested in studying the benefits of cloud computing for agent-based CEMS by developing cloud-based collaborative and large-scale agent-based crisis and emergency simulation environments. Our work consists in using the cloud environment for: 1) dealing with the scalability issue of an existing agent-based rescue simulator; 2) supporting collaboration during the process of analyzing the data generated by simulations; 3) Investigating the stability of an "old" agent-based simulator after deporting its execution on the cloud.

After a synthetic literature review in section 2, sections 3 and 4 describe our case study by providing an overview of the simulation environment, the migration process to the cloud as well as the new experiments and their related results.

2   Related Work

Agent-Based Systems (ABS) are powerful tools to model and simulate highly dynamic disasters. However, based on a recent survey [4] which investigates the usage of ABS for large-scale emergency response, scalability is a key issue for such systems. The authors mention that the use of a single core machine is unsuitable for large-scale ABS, since it may result in an unpredictable and unreasonable execution time as well as an overrun in memory consumption. To overcome the issue of limited resources, other solutions focus on using distributed computing environments such as clusters [5, 6], and grid computing [7, 8]. Although, the use of clusters and grids may provide an appropriate solution for running large-scale distributed agent-based simulations, such environments are not within the reach of all researchers and organizations.

Using cloud computing for computationally intense tasks has been seen in recent years as a convenient way to process data quickly [9]. In [9], a generic architecture was proposed to deport a desktop simulation to a cloud infrastructure. In fact, a parameter sweep version should be performed before deployment on the cloud. A case study of migrating the City Cat software to the cloud environment shows that "adaptation of an application to run is often not a trivial task" [9]. While [10] introduces the Pandora Framework dedicated to implement scalable agent-based models and to execute them on Cloud High Performance Clusters (HPC), this framework cannot be adapted to agent-based systems that are not implemented on a distributed infrastructure. In [11], the authors present the Elastic-JADE (Java Agent Development Framework) platform that uses the Amazon EC2 resources, to scale up and down a local running agent based simulation according to the state of the platform. Combining a running local JADE platform to the cloud, can enhance the scalability of multi-agent systems, however the proposed solution is specific only to the JADE platform.

3   From SimGenis to LC2SimGenis : Reuse for Deployment and Interfacing

In this section, we focus on the process leading to an effective Large-scale Cloud-based and Collaborative Simulator, which is Generic and interactive, of rescue management (called LC2SimGenis). Reuse for deployment and interfacing are our main activities. Consequently this section is structured as follows:1)presentation of Amazon EC2, Elastic-r and SimGenis;2) description of the deployment approach of SimGenis on the cloud.

3.1   Target Cloud Environments and SimGenis

Amazon Elastic Compute Cloud (EC2) is a web service that provides variable computational capacity in the cloud on pay-as-you go basis [12]. Through the use of shared tokens provided by Elastic-r [13], several types of ec2-instances (micro, small, medium and large…) are available. Indeed Elastic-r [13] is a mixture of the most popular scientific computing software such as R, python, Scilab, mathematica. These software are available in one single virtual environment making their usage even simpler on the cloud.

SimGenis [14] is a generic, interactive, cooperative simulator of complex emergency situations. It is an agent-based simulator developed to design new rescue approaches by enabling the test and assessment of 'what-if' type scenarios. This simulator is developed as a desktop application, composed of three layers: 1) the Graphical User Interface (GUI) which provides configuration and control panels, 2) the storage in files and in databases (Access Database) to keep track of all the stages of its execution (output results, events and agent status over time), 3) the agent-based model, the core of the simulator, where mainly victims and rescuers co-evolve in the accident fields. The rescuers (doctors, firefighters, paramedics) collaborate to rescue (evacuate) the maximum number of alive victims in the minimum period of time. SimGenis is implemented using the Java Agent Development Framework (JADE). JADE [15] is a software framework to develop multi-agent applications based on peer-to-peer communication and in compliance with the FIPA specification [16].

3.2   Deployment Approach: SimGenis as a Service on Amazon EC2

As a first attempt to deploy SimGenis on Amazon EC2 via Elastic-r, we proceeded with a manual deployment approach, as shown in figure 1, with the simulator as a black box without modifying its source code. However, we have chosen to only replace the Microsoft Access database with the open source Apache Derby database [17] for reasons of portability, easy installation, deployment characteristics and the increased functionalities present in such a modern database. The approach for having an operational LC2SimGenis on the cloud is as follows: 1) **Pre-deployment phase** that consists in preparing all the necessary elements for running the simulator properly on the cloud. Specifically, the source code of the application as a whole was encapsulated with the necessary libraries as a service. 2) **Deployment phase** consists in connecting to the platform Elastic-r, configuring and launching the Tokens. When an ec2-instance is ready (within 3 minutes) all the prepared elements, including the executable, the script shell and the database, are uploaded to the working directory MyS3. Indeed, MyS3 is a storage area consisting of an Amazon S3 bucket mounted automatically on the ec2-instance and accessible as a folder. These activities only need to be performed once. Then the execution step can be performed which consists in running and using the simulator: a secure shell connection to the launched ec2-instances is established (Putty SSH client is used here), then a shell script is executed to configure, launch and manage the simulator.

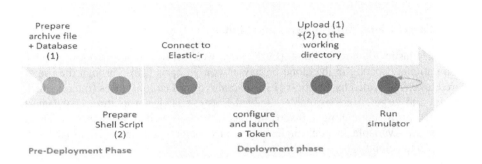

Fig. 1. Deployment approach of SimGenis as a service on Amazon EC2 via Elastic-r

The user can consequently launch the simulator as much as required. The adopted deployment approach is generic and can be applied to any kind of agent-based system and simulator. However, the user may experience some technical problems related to the graphical user interface for configuring and launching the simulation. This issue can be solved by using scripts to perform configurations.

4   Experimentation

After the deployment on the cloud, and in order to concretely test LC2SimGenis in use, we designed a set of virtual experiments to assess the impacts of portability of an old simulator to the cloud and to study effective large scale rescue management.

4.1   Scenarios and Configurations

According to [14] each simulated virtual environment is designed by combining the following aspects: 1) the simulated environment can be limited to one incident field or several that cover the city. 2) the rescue organization strategy may be centralized or distributed 3) the incident field may be considered as one area or divided into sub zones; 4) the rescuers actions may include exploration or may prioritize evacuation 5) each doctor may organize her/his actions according to the distance to, or the severity of, the victims. Therefore, similar to [14], we consider four categories of scenarios:

- Experiment 1: centralized strategy, incident field considered as one zone; evacuate the nearest victims; use of paper forms to record medical assessment.
- Experiment 2: similar to experiment 1 but uses electronic devices instead of paper forms.
- Experiment 3: distributed strategy, incident field considered as four sub-zones; evacuate the nearest victims; paper forms.
- Experiment 4: same as experiment 3 but uses electronic devices instead of paper forms.

Each configuration is defined by the triplet (number of victims, number of alive victims, and number of rescuers). By combining these four experiments classes and the configuration, we design eight what-if scenarios, and then simulated each one at least ten times. The Global Evacuation Time (GET i.e. the simulated time at which the last victim has been evacuated from the disaster field) is used to compare the simulations and study the various effects of the model on the rescue performance.

Concerning the hardware configuration, for the local PC version, a Pentium 4, with 3 Giga Hertz and 512 M RAM was used in 2006; for the cloud based version, experiments are carried out on m1.large ec2-instance with 4 cores (2 cores x 2 units), 7.50 GB memory, Linux Operating System, and $0.24 hourly cost.

4.2   First Results

The assessment of the SimGenis simulator in [14] was carried out on a relatively small scale. The maximum number of agents that could be simulated was 290 agents. The new experiments, on m1.large ec2-instance, allowed us to test old as well as new configurations reaching thousands of agents within the same instance. For example, as illustrated in figure 3, we tested 3000 agents by using only one large ec2-instance.

Given the promising first scalability results reached on a single virtual machine, by deploying the simulator as a monolithic service, we think that deploying a distributed version should improve scalability even more.

Deep simulations of LC2SimGenis showed the stability of SimGenis. In fact, by simulating, on the ec2-instance, exactly the old scenarios (same experiments as well as configurations), comparable behaviors have been observed and similar results have been drawn both on small-scale and large-scale experiments (see figure 2). Also, by analyzing the different tested configurations for each of the four experiments, as shown in figure 3, we confirm that the GET value is still related, in the same way as in [14], to the numbers of living victims and rescuers. Furthermore, the use of electronic devices combined with the centralized strategy shows better results than using them with a distributed strategy. Electronic devices have more influence on the evacuation process than distribution. We conclude again that for large-scale emergency management simulations, determining the "best" rescue plan depends highly on the initial configuration.

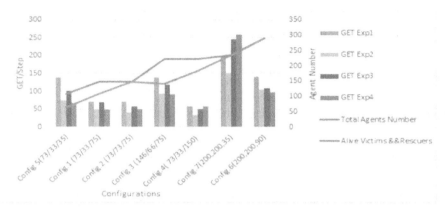

Fig. 2. Global Evacuation Time per configuration for each of the four experiments

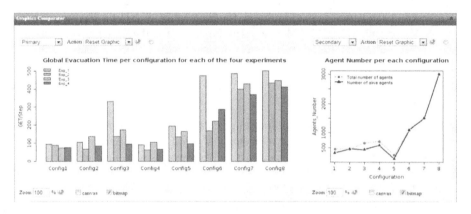

Fig. 3. LC2SimGenis visualization interface

Finally, as expected, all performed simulations prove that using the cloud environment reduces the execution time compared to the local experiments. Figure 4 illustrates this result: the simulations times measured for Experiment1, with each configuration, are smaller using the large ec2-instance than those obtained using a local computer (dual core, 4 GO RAM). However, keeping the simulator GUI after deploying it on the cloud and using an X window server to redirect the interface to a local computer resulted in an important overhead to start the simulation.

4.3   Collaborative Data Analysis and Visualization

In order to analyze and visualize the data generated during a simulation, we used the remote API Elastic-r available for the users to manipulate the platform. A developed project is uploaded to the working directory MyS3. In our case, there are two typical scenarios for performing data analysis and visualization: typical single user scenario and multiple-user scenarios. In the latter case, a user can render the session shared between multiple collaborators geographically distributed. In fact each session has a leader who is responsible for adding, removing, and giving rights to the participants.

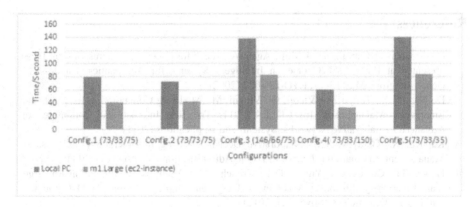

Fig. 4. Comparison simulation-time per configuration using different resources type

5   Discussion and Conclusion

In this paper we investigated to what extent agent-based emergency management simulations can use the cloud environment to improve scalability and achieve collaborative data analysis and visualization.

Our approach to obtain the cloud version is based on the reuse of existing different environments including SimGenis and Elastic-r. It is generic and can be applied for any application which can be used as black-box.

Our present solution proves that cloud computing can be useful for large-scale agent-based simulations in terms of scalability and response time. Given the promising first scalability results reached on a single virtual cloud machine, we believe that using a distributed version of the simulator should improve the scalability even more.

Also the model has shown stability in terms of the results on both small and large scale simulations. In addition, we were able to analyze and visualize the data generated during the simulations by using the collaborative environment Elastic-r for data analysis. Elastic-r provides us with the ability to share an analysis session with multiple geographically distributed users. Therefore, LC2SimGenis can become a useful tool to support effective collaborative decision making in order to assess the rescue plans of realistic disasters, whatever their scale.

As a future work we intend to distribute the agent-based simulator on hybrid cloud resources in order to reach even more scalable simulations. A hybrid cloud is a combination of both private and public clouds. It makes efficient use of the local infrastructure and expands it with public cloud resources. However, distributing an agent-based system on a highly dynamic environment such as the cloud is not a trivial task. The distribution technique should minimize the communication overhead between the used resources, as well as save costs.

References

1. Degirmenciyan-Cartault, I.: A Multi-Agent Approach for Complex Systems Design. Paper presented at RTO AVT Course on Intelligent Systems for Aeronautics, Rhode-saint-Gense, Belgium, May 13-17, RTO-EN-022 (2002)
2. De Nicola, A., Tofani, A., Vicoli, G., Villani, M.: Modeling Collaboration for Crisis and Emergency Management. In: COLLA 2011: The first International Conference on Advanced Collaborative Networks, Systems and Applications (2011)
3. Kapucu, N., Garayev, V.: Collaborative Decision-Making in Emergency and Disaster Management. International Journal of Public Administration 34, 366–375 (2011)
4. Hawe, G.I., Coates, G., Wilson, D.T., Crouch, R.S.: Agent-based Simulation for large-scale Emergency Response: A survey of Usage and implementation. ACM Computing Surveys 45(1), Article 8 (November, 2012)
5. Kalyan, S., Perumalla, K., Brandon, G., Aaby, G., Sudip, K.S.: Efficient simulation of agent-based models on multi-gpu and multi-core clusters. In: SIMUTools, Torremolinos, Malaga, Spain (2010)
6. Cai, W., Zhou, S., Wang, Y., Lees, M., Yoke, M., Low, H.: Cluster based partitioning for agent based crowd simulation. In: Rossetti, M.D., Hill, R.R., Johansson, B., Dunkin, A., Ingalls, R.G. (eds.) Proceeding of the 2009 Winter Simulation Conference (2009)
7. Mengistu, D., Davidsson, P., Lundberg, L.: Middleware support for performance improvement of MABS applications in the grid environment. In: Antunes, L., Paolucci, M., Norling, E. (eds.) MABS 2007. LNCS (LNAI), vol. 5003, pp. 20–35. Springer, Heidelberg (2008)
8. Timm, J., Pawlaszczyk, D.: Large scale multiagent simulation on the grid. In: Proceedings of the Workshop on Agent-based grid Economics (AGE 2005) at the IEEE International Symposium on Cluster Computing and the Grid, CCGRID (2005)
9. Glenis, V., McGough, A.S., Kutija, V., Kilsby, C., Woodman, S.: Flood modelling for cities using Cloud computing. Journal of Cloud Computing: Advances, Systems and Applications 2, 7 (2013), doi:10.1186/2192-113X-2-7
10. Wittek, P., Rubio-Campillo, X.: Scalable Agent-based Modelling with Cloud HPC Resources for Social Simulations. In: 4th IEEE International Conference on Cloud Computing Technology and Science Proceedings, December 3-6 (2012)
11. Siddiqui, U., Tahir, G.A., Rehman, A.U., Ali, Z., Rasool, R.U., Bloodsworth, P.: Elastic JADE: Dynamically Scalable Multi agents using Cloud Resources. In: Second International Conference on Cloud and Green Computing, pp. 167–172 (2012)
12. Amazon EC2, http://aws.amazon.com/ec2/
13. Chine, K.: Open science in the cloud: towards a universal platform for scientific and statistical computing. In: Furht, B., Escalante, A. (eds.) Handbook of cloud computing, pp. 453–474. Springer, USA (2010) ISBN 978-1-4419-6524-0
14. Bellamine Ben Saoud, N., Ben Mena, T., Dugdale, J., Pavard, B., Ben Ahmed, M.: Assessing large scale emergency rescue plans: An agent-based approach. Int. J. Intell. Control Syst. 11(4), 260–271 (2006)
15. JADE, http://jade.tilab.com/
16. FIPA, http://www.pa.org/
17. Apache Derby, http://db.apache.org/derby/

Approaches to Optimize Local Evacuation Maps for Helping Evacuation in Case of Tsunami

Van-Minh Le[1], Yann Chevaleyre[2], Jean-Daniel Zucker[3], and Ho Tuong Vinh[1]

[1] IFI, Equipe MSI IRD, UMI 209 UMMISCO, Institut de la Francophonie pour l'Informatique, Vietnam National University, Hanoi, Vietnam
[2] LIPN, CNRS UMR 7030, Université Paris Nord, 93430 Villetaneuse, France
[3] UMI 209, UMMISCO, IRD France Nord, 93143, Bondy, France

Abstract. Nowadays, most coastal regions face a potential risk of tsunami. Most of researches focus on people evacuation. However, there are always the part of evacuees (e.g. the tourist) who lack information of the city map, we then focus on the solution to guide people in evacuation.

With regards to the guiding system in evacuation, most of the studies focus on the placement of guidance signs. In fact, in panic situation the evacuees can get lost if the they do not receive guidance signs at a certain crossroad or corner. Then, if there are not enough signs at every crossroad or corner on a certain path to the safe places (called shelters), the guidance signs will become useless. In order to give evacuees a complete guidance of evacuation, we propose to place the local evacuation maps which highlight the shortest path from a place (where the panel of the map is placed) to the nearest shelter. At specific places in the city, once this kind of map is perceived, the evacuees should follow the shortest evacuation path to shelters. In this paper, we first present the method to optimize the local evacuation maps by using the genetic algorithm on candidate locations of the maps and the evaluating the percentage survivors as fitness. We then present two approaches to evaluate the fitness: one uses the agent-based simulation and other uses the linear programming formulation. By experimentation, our proposed approaches showed better results the approach of optimizing sign placement in the same scenario.

Keywords: agent-based simulation, linear programming, genetic algorithm, optimization.

1 Introduction

In recent years, whenever we talked about tsunami, we mentioned the terrible destruction and huge casualties (the tsunami from Indian Ocean in 2004 and the tsunami in Tohoku Japan 2011 [1]). Along with the early warning system, the evacuation seems to be one of the most effective mitigation procedures. However, the evacuation of huge population in urgent situation is still complicated, because there are always some people who lack information about the evacuation map (e.g. the tourists). The placement of guidance signs has been taken into account

C. Hanachi, F. Bénaben, and F. Charoy (Eds.): ISCRAM-med 2014, LNBIP 196, pp. 21–31, 2014.
© Springer International Publishing Switzerland 2014

as a solution to minimize the number of victims in case of tsunami (the signs placed in Palabuhanratu, Indonesia [2]).

With regards to the guiding system in evacuation, most of the studies focus on the placement of guidance signs. At some crossroad or corner, signs are placed. When people see the sign, they usually follow the direction of the sign. Figure 1 show a tsunami evacuation sign which is used in New Zealand. In fact, in panic situations the evacuees can get lost if the they do not receive guidance signs at a certain crossroad or corner. Then, if there are not enough signs at every crossroad or corner on a certain path to the shelter, the guidance signs will become useless.

Fig. 1. A tsunami evacuation sign used in New Zealand

In order to give evacuees a complete guidance of evacuation, we propose to place local evacuation maps. A local evacuation map is panel placed in the city usually near the junction (or crossroad). We call such map local because only the surroundings shown including: the nearby safe places (called shelters) where people can evacuate, the shortest path from the current location (where the panel of the map is placed) to the nearest shelter. In figure 2, the map shows: the current location of evacuees, the nearest shelter and the highlighted shortest path to nearest shelter. Once this kind of map is perceived, the evacuees follow the shortest evacuation path to the shelter. We suppose, we have a limited budget which can be proceduced K maps. Our problem is where to place them in city (on which junctions or crossroads) in order to maximize number of survivors in case of a typical tsunami scenario. Of course, people crossing this map are expected to follows the suggested path to safe places. In this paper, we first present method to optimize the placement of local evacuation maps by using a genetic algorithm on candidate locations of the maps and evaluating the percentage survivors as fitness. Then. we present two approaches to evaluate the fitness: one uses the agent-based simulation and other uses the linear programming formulation.

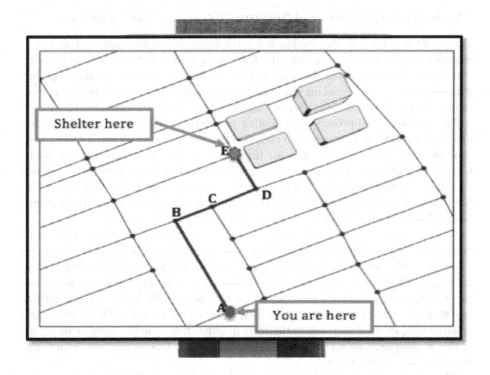

Fig. 2. A proposed local evacuation map

2   Related Work

2.1   Optimization of Sign Placement for Tsunami Evacuation

In recent years, most of studies about solution for guiding people in tsunami evacuation focus on optimizing the guiding sign placement. In 2011, Nguyen et al [3] proposed an approach optimizing of sign placement using linear programming. In this approach, the signs were placed in order to minimize average evacuation time. However, the minimization of average evacuation time was not the same at maximization of survivors. We then focused on another approach that which took number of survivors as its objective function.

In 2013, Le et al [4] proposed an approach to optimizing the sign placement using Genetic Algorithm in which the fitness function was evaluated by a linear programming formulation. After, in 2014, these authors [5] proposed another approach which also used Genetic Algorithm but the fitness was evaluated by Agent-Based Simulation. These two studies motivated us to develop a system optimizing the local evacuation maps by using Genetic Algorithm and evaluating the percentage of survivors as fitness function.

2.2   Estimating Number of Survivors by Agent-Based Simulation

The direct approach to this evaluation is the agent-based simulation. This optimization problem in this case becomes building a model of evacuation simulation (taking the number of survivors as objective function) and then exploring the parameter space (representing the road where to place the sign). The key factor of this approach is how to model the agent behaviors representing evacuees.

The traditional approach for modeling pedestrian behaviors in evacuation is modeling pedestrian movement on the grid. Each step of simulation, a pedestrian chooses one of the neighbor cells for his next location. Although this approach has received much success in simulating the evacuation from the building where the map is really small [6] [7], we argue that it would not be a good choice for the evacuation of tsunami because the evacuation map of a real city is much larger than that of a building.

Another approach proposed in [8] was to model pedestrian behaviors in tsunami evacuation. In this approach, the pedestrian movement was modeled as the transition through the petri-net. With this approach, modeler might add the rules inciting agents to go towards the less crowded road. While this approach provided the way to reduce casualties, we find that it is only suitable for the simulation in which all agents know the map. In fact, since agents normally "observe" what is happening locally, they can make their decision based on the local perception of the environment with the same rules you describe. That is why we do not use this approach in our work.

The Markov Chain Approach seems to be useful to model the simulation in which some people do not know all the map. While the authors in [9] used an evaluation function on every agent to make decision (which distinguishes the knowledge level of agent), the authors in [10] separated agents definitely into two types: one knows all the map, the other does not, which motivates us to use Markov Chain in this paper.

2.3 Evaluating Casualties by Linear Programming Formulation

The Agent-Based Simulation in fact has its own problem of computational speed (the natural trade off for its accuracy). An approach based on linear programming was proposed to speed up this fitness evaluation. In [4], the authors presented a formulation which calculated the percentage of survivors of simulation of pedestrian evacuation in which the agent behaviors were based on Markov Chain approach. From the idea of this study, we propose to reused the formulation to speed up the evaluation of percentage of survivors. However, in order to do this, we have to remodel our problem (which is clearly describe in next section) so that it adapts to this formulation.

3   Formalization of the Optimization Problem

In this paper, we formalize our problem as a typical optimization problem by using Genetic Algorithm. The Genetic Algorithm encodes the set of locations of local evacuation maps as chromosome and takes percentage of survivors as fitness. We also proposed 2 method to evaluate the fitness: The first evaluation is the simulation of evacuation in case of tsunami which takes the crossroads or corner (where the local evacuation map are placed) as the parameters and the percentage of survivors as the objective function. The second one is the linear programming formulation whose inputs are also the location of the local evacuation map and the outcome is the percentage of survivor.

3.1 Fitness Evaluation by Agent-Based Simulation

We build an Agent-Based simulation in which: the environment is modeled from GIS files which describing the roads and the high buildings which are used as shelters. The GIS files are transformed into the graph $G = (V, E)$. The vertices which are nearest to the building (from building GIS files) are denoted as shelter vertices. Next, the pedestrian behaviors in this model are: moving along the edge of the graph, choosing the next target when it arrives a crossroad. If a local evacuation map is perceived, the agent follows the shortest path to reach the shelter, otherwise, it turns randomly. Finally, the outcome of the simulation is the number of survivors which are the number of agents arriving to any shelter vertex within the predefined limited time. Then, we calculate the fitness (in this case is the percentage of survivors) from the number of survivors and initial population.

3.2   Fitness Evaluation by Linear Programming Formulation of Casualties Evaluation of Pedestrian Evacuation

As we mentioned in the related work section, the linear programming formulation is based on Markov Chain approach. In this section, we present a brief description of the Markov Chain which we use in our study.

Modeling Problem as a Markov Chain. Let a graph G = (V, E) represent the map in which V = {1, 2,...,n} is a set of junctions and E ⊆ V × V is a set of edges representing roads connecting vertices. Each edge is associated with a weight c_{ij} representing the required time for an agent to move from vertex i to vertex j. Also, the set of neighbors of vertex i is referred to as N(i) = {j: (i, j) ∈ E}. Let X ⊂ V denote the set of shelters (which represent the high buildings or the high-ground places to which the people evacuate in case of tsunami). If an agent reaches a shelter, then it is considered as out of danger.

A Markov chain is composed of an initial distribution $\mu = \{\mu_i: i \in V\}$ and a stochastic n×n matrix P representing the transition probabilities from one vertex to another. At time t = 0, each agent is randomly placed on the graph with respect to the given distribution μ. At time $t > 0$, an agent positioned on vertex i will move to vertex j ∈ N(i) with the probability p_{ij} such that if (i, j) ∉ E then $p_{ij} = 0$ and such that $\sum_{j \in V} p_{ij} = 1$. Eventually, these probabilities will be estimated using more sophisticated crowd models. Here, we simply use uniform probabilities. Thus, a quadruplet (G, X, μ, P) will completely define the territory and the behavior of agents. We assume that every agent has a threshold of time to evacuate, the optimizing problem becomes to find K vertices (from V) on which to place local evacuation maps such that the number of agents whose evacuation time is above some threshold (e.g. 30 min) is maximized.

Modeling the Placement of Local Evacuation Map. Let vertex i represent the location where a local evacuation map is placed, and vertex j represent the nearest shelter. The modifications of the quadruplet (G, X, μ, P) are described:

1. Add edge (i,j) to E
$$E = E \cup \{(i, j)\} \; (1)$$

2. Set weight of edge (i,j) at weight of the shortest path which is the sum of all belonging edges
$$c_{ij} = \sum_{(h,k) \in ShortestPath(i,j)} c_{hk} \; (2)$$

3. Set the values of the transition probabilities P so that agent always moves to vertex j
$$p_{ij} = 1 \; (3)$$
$$p_{ik} = 0, \forall k \neq j \; (4)$$

Linear Programming Formulation. With the new modified quadruplet (G, X, μ, P), we can totally re-apply the formulation in [4] to evaluate the percentage of casualties. Then, we calculate the fitness (in this case is the percentage of survivors) from the percentage of casualty and initial population.

Original formulation (from [4]) of Casualties Evaluation of Pedestrian Evacuation is following:

$$Percentage\ of\ casualties = \sum_{i \in V} \mu_i q_{i,K} \quad under\ the\ constraints:$$

$$\forall i \in V, \qquad q_{i,0} = 1$$
$$\forall i \in X, \forall k \geq 1, \qquad q_{i,k} = 0$$
$$\forall i \in V \setminus X, \forall k \geq 0,\ q_{i,k} = \sum_{j \in N(i)} p_{ij} q_{j,[k-\hat{c}_{ij}]_+}$$

Here, $q_{i,k}$ is the probability for an agent starting at vertex i to reach the shelter in k step, and $[x]+$ be x if x > 0 or be 0 otherwise.

4   Implementation and Evaluation

4.1   Description of Application Case

In this section, we present the application case so that we can evaluate our proposition. In this case, we simulated the evacuation of pedestrians in the case of tsunami in Danang city in Vietnam. In our simulation we used the real map of this Danang city in Vietnam and simulated 10000 pedestrians with the initial uniform distribution on over the junctions of the map.

The scenario of evacuation in this simulation is the following: there is an earthquake of 8.0 Richter from Manila Trench which causes the tsunami high up to 4 meters. The tsunami propagation time from the source region to Vietnamese coastal area is estimated about 2 hours [11]. However, since it takes time for the local government to consider before declaring evacuation alert and also for spreading information to people, in the worst situation (described more detail in [12]), people have only 30 minutes to evacuate. In such a small amount of time, people have to choose the high building for shelters rather than trying to escape far from the beach.

We created 2 implementations: the first one was the agent-based simulation using GAMA [13], the other was our Linear Programming Formulation of Casualties Evaluation of Pedestrian Evacuation using IBM CPLEX. Both implementations followed strictly the description that we mentioned above and used the same outcome measure: the percentage of survivors, which means that the agent (representing a pedestrian) who arrived shelter within the 900 seconds (30 minutes) is considered survivors. For the optimization phase, we used genetic algorithm provided by ECJ framework [14] and fixed all other coefficients (e.g. selection, crossover, mutation, elistism) by default.

4.2 Evaluation

Consistency of the Evaluation of Casualties through the Linear Program. In the first test case, we evaluated if the formulation and agent-based simulation produce the same result. Since the agent-based simulation is highly stochastic, we consider the linear programming computation as consistent if the percentage of survivors computed by linear is equal in expectation to the average percentage of survivors computed in 100 times of simulation, for any scenario.

In this case, we let both implementations execute 100 times with 120 different scenarios (different signs (number and locations), different thresholds of evacuation time) then we compared the returned number of survivors. The result of all cases of test are almost the same. The figure 3 (result of 100 signs with 30 evacuation minutes) shows that the number of survivors returned from 2 implementations are identical. While the agent-base simulation returns the various results on each execution, the average of these results is almost the same as that given by the linear programming formulation.

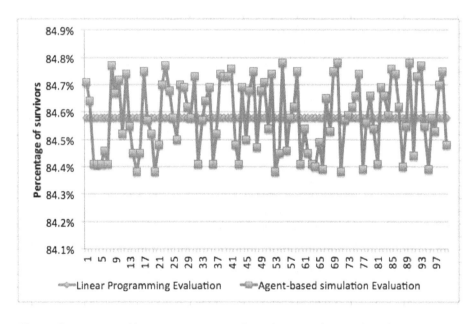

Fig. 3. Consistency of linear programming formulation and agent-based simulation in evaluating fitness

Comparing of Execution Time between Agent-Based Simulation and Linear Programming Formulation. In this test case, we let the two implementations run on the same computer with the same scenario (120 signs, 30 minutes of evacuation) but with different number of agents and then recorded the execution time for each run. In figure 4, while the linear programming evaluation takes the same execution time (less than 10 minutes), the agent-based

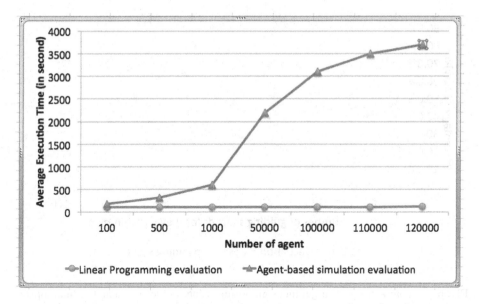

Fig. 4. Comparing the Execution Time in aspect of number of signs (Benmarked on iMac quad-core)

one takes longer and longer with the grow of number of agents. In case 120000 agents, the simulation takes more than 1 hour to run.

Comparing Percentage of Survivors between Guiding Sign Optimization and Local Evacuation Map Optimization. In this test case, we made 2 implementations: The first one was the optimization sign placement (as explained in the related work section) and the second was the optimization of local evacuation map. Since the linear programming formulation and the Agent-Based simulation produced the same result, in order to save time, we chose the linear programming formulation to evaluate fitness in both implementations. We also applied the same genetic algorithm (same kind of evolutionary algorithm with the same coefficient of mutation and crossover) on both implementations. The genetic algorithm of both implementations was run many times on the same computer. Each time, the algorithm took the different number of signs and the total execution time was 24 hours.

The figure 5 shows that local evacuation map optimization prevails guiding sign one. Especially, with 80 maps, the percentage of survivor doubles the result given by the same number of signs. The reason is quite clear: a guiding sign just represents a turn at a certain crossroad and a local evacuation map provides the shortest path including a lot of crossroads which represent a lot of guiding signs.

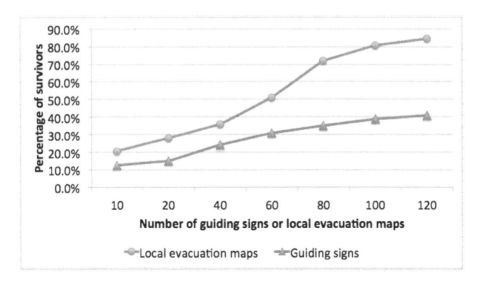

Fig. 5. Comparison between guiding sign optimization and local evacuation map optimization

5   Conclusion

In this paper, we proposed 2 approaches to optimize the local evacuation map in case of tsunami evacuation. The approaches were evaluated and also compared with the optimization of sign placement. The result showed the advantages of the local evacuation map. In the future work, we focus on 4 main directions as follows:

1. Tune a genetic algorithm to get better results: We can calibrate the genetic algorithm to improve the optimizing phase (which type of crossover, which type of mutation, which is the best value for each coefficient in genetic algorithm).
2. Integrate social factor: In fact, people evacuate in group and also share the information to each other. We tent to study on communication factor (which describes how an agent communicates with others for information), leader/follower factor (which means: the people often evacuate in group, the one who does not know the map can follow the other)
3. Integrate guiding signs and local evacuation map: With regarding to the budget, we know that a evacuation map is much more expensive than a guiding sign. We can mix the signs and the maps in the optimization problem to save all the people with minimal cost.

References

1. Suppasri, A., Imamura, F., Koshimura, S.: Tsunami Hazard and Casualty Estimation in a Coastal Area That Neighbors the Indian Ocean and South China Sea. Journal of Earthquake and Tsunami 06(02), 1–25 (2012), doi:10.1142/S1793431112500108

2. Tanioka, Y., Latief, H., Sunedar, H., Gusman, A.R., Koshimura, S.: Tsunami Hazard Mitigation at Palabuhanratu, Indonesia. Journal of Disaster Research 7(1), 19–25 (2012)
3. Nguyen, T.N.A., Chevaleyre, Y., Zucker, J.D.: Optimizing the Placement of Evacuation Signs on Road Network with Time and Casualties in case of a Tsunami. In: 20th IEEE International Conference on Collaboration Technologies and Infrastructures (WETICE 2011), vol. i, pp. 394–396 (2011)
4. Le, V.M., Chevaleyre, Y., Zucker, J.D., Ho, T.V.: Speeding up the evaluation of casualties in multi-agent simulations with linear programming, application to optimization of sign placement for tsunami evacuation. In: 2013 IEEE RIVF International Conference on Computing and Communication Technologies, Research, Innovation, and Vision for the Future, RIVF (2013)
5. Le, V.M., Chevaleyre, Y., Zucker, J.D., Ho, T.V.: A general approach to solve decomposable optimization problems in multiagent simulations settings: application to tsunami evacuation. In: International Conference on Swarm Intelligence Based Optimization (2014)
6. Smith, J.L., Brokow, J.T.: Agent Based Simulation of Human Movements during Emergency Evacuations of Facilities. In: Structures Congress 2008, pp. 1–10. American Society of Civil Engineers, Reston (October 2008)
7. Christensen, K.: Agent-Based Emergency Evacuation Simulation with Individuals with Disabilities in the Population. Journal of Artificial Societies and Social Simulation 11(3) (2008)
8. Minamoto, T., Nariyuki, Y., Fujiwara, Y., Mikami, A.: Development of Tsunami Refuge Petri-Net Simulation System Utilizable In Independence Disaster Prevention Organization. In: The 14th World Conference on Earthquake Engineering, Beijing, China, October 12-17 (2008)
9. Liu, Y., Okada, N., Takeuchi, Y.: Dynamic Route Decision Model-based Multi-agent Evacuation Simulation - Case Study of Nagata Ward, Kobe. Journal of Natural Disaster Science 28(2), 91–98 (2008)
10. Nguyen, T.N.A., Zucker, J.D., Nguyen, M.H., Drogoul, A., Nguyen, H.P.: Simulation of emergency evacuation of pedestrians along the road networks in Nhatrang city. In: 2012 IEEE RIVF International Conference on Computing and Communication Technologies, Research, Innovation, and Vision for the Future (RIVF), pp. 1–6 (2012)
11. Vu, T.C., Nguyen, D.X.: Tsunami risk along Vietnamese coast. Journal of Water Resources and Environmental Engineering (23), 24–33 (2008)
12. Nguyen, H.P., Vu, H.P., Pham, T.T.: Development of a tsunami evacuation plan for urban area of Nhatrang city using GIS. Journal of Earth's sciences (in Vietnamese) (2012)
13. Drogoul, A., Amouroux, E., Caillou, P., Gaudou, B., Grignard, A., Marilleau, N., Taillandier, P., Vavasseur, M., Vo, D.A., Zucker, J.D.: GAMA: Multi-level and Complex Environment for Agent-based Models and Simulations (demonstration). In: The 2013 International Conference on Autonomous Agents and Multi-agent Systems, pp. 1361–1362 (2013)
14. Wilson, G.C., Mcintyre, A., Heywood, M.I.: Resource review: Three open source systems for evolving programs-Lilgp, ECJ and grammatical evolution. Genetic Programming and Evolvable Machines 5(1), 103–105 (2004)

EDIT: A Methodology for the Treatment of Non-authoritative Data in the Reconstruction of Disaster Scenarios

Stefania Traverso[1], Valentina Cerutti[1], Kristin Stock[2], and Mike Jackson[2]

[1] CIMA Research Foundation, Via Magliotto 2,
17100 Savona, Italy
[2] Nottingham Geospatial Institute, Triumph Rd,
The University of Nottingham, Nottingham NG7 2TU, UK

Abstract. EDIT - Extracting Disaster Information from Text – is a methodology for the treatment of textual information extracted from the web, originated by non-expert users and referring to the occurrence of a disaster event. The project was born from a collaboration between CIMA Foundation (Italy) and the Nottingham Geospatial Institute (NGI) (United Kingdom). The methodology addresses the task of integrating unstructured knowledge into operative tools. It focuses on: the semantic analysis of online news and tweets; the automatic extraction of relevant data to enhance knowledge about disasters; the evaluation of reliability of data; the archive into an event-oriented database; the visualization of scenario maps. The study represents the starting point of a new way of approaching disaster scenarios and it is proposed that the approach is taken forward for future large-scale implementation.

Keywords: non-authoritative data, ontology, concept map, disaster scenario, event-oriented database.

1 Introduction

Effective emergency management during disasters requires access to tools that can process data and quickly produce maps to analyze impacted areas and effects: it is vital to read information in a common understanding and in a harmonized environment. In addition to official geospatial data, non-authoritative data, including non-traditional GIS data such as texts, photos, videos and social media messages, can provide an interesting contribution for mosaicking disaster-related information, even if it is necessary to cope with the intrinsic nature of these sources (specifically, that they can be produced by non-expert users, are not homogenous, are not validated and can be misused). It is possible to build dynamic scenarios of risk or damage, complex representations of the effects of extreme events on a target area, relying both on classical geographical information and non-authoritative data.

The EDIT (Extraction of Disaster Information from Text) methodology focuses on the possibility of analyzing a disaster into a multi-perspective reality built with tiles of

C. Hanachi, F. Bénaben, and F. Charoy (Eds.): ISCRAM-med 2014, LNBIP 196, pp. 32–45, 2014.
© Springer International Publishing Switzerland 2014

heterogeneous data. It has been specifically created to extract information from online natural language sources of various types, such as newspaper reports, social networking and blogs. It designs a framework of rules on the specification of data, and creates the representation of footprints of disasters. It is structured in many components and uses an operational tool based on Java for analyzing texts through Natural Language Processing (NLP) techniques, semantics and ontologies.

The objective of EDIT is to manage the knowledge about a disaster with a specific scenario-oriented scheme, with meaningful elements being saved into a formal database. To create the logical base of the process a concept map for disasters-related data has been created.

The semantic analysis is a fundamental step in the process of information extraction from non-authoritative data: it is necessary to move from the natural language to a formal language able to populate the scenario database. Ontologies represent a solution to this semantic heterogeneity: the main aim of the ontology is trying to eliminate, or at least to reduce, conceptual and terminological confusion. In this way, information is filtered with rules necessary to build a scenario table.

Moreover, it is possible to optimize procedures assigning indexes based on the reliability of sources and location accuracy. The study can be performed using different languages and dialects.

The EDIT Project is at the initial implementation phase and is at the moment internally funded: it represents the first research project born from collaboration between CIMA Foundation (Italian Civil Protection, University of Genoa, Liguria Region and Savona Province, Italy) and the Nottingham Geospatial Institute (NGI) of The University of Nottingham (United Kingdom). The methodology has been designed, two case studies have been tested, a first semi-automatic procedure and the filter on reliability have been defined. A more detailed study on location accuracy and a broad phase of test and validation is planned for the next phase of the research.

2   Mapping for Crisis

In all areas related to disaster management, geospatial data and tools have the potential to save lives, provide support to coordinate operations, survey damage, enrich historical archives and design preventive plans.

National and international agencies, local repositories and open geo-data web sources generally provide information containing geospatial data useful to build a disaster scenario. But, in recent years, geography and the production of maps has radically changed. Turner refers to this as Neogeography: it "means new geography and consists of a set of techniques and tools that fall outside the realm of traditional GIS [...]. Essentially, Neogeography is about people using and creating their own maps, on their own terms and by combining elements of an existing toolset. Neogeography is about sharing location information with friends and visitors, helping shape context, and conveying understanding through knowledge of place" [1].

Also the definition of the Web 2.0 indicates a new generation of web interfaces allowing users to share and edit content over the web, interacting in a virtual community through User-Generated Content (UGC), as created in social networks (e.g. Facebook and Twitter), blogs, forums, wikis, videos, photos, media-sharing platform. Users have moved from being a passive public viewing content generated by specialists, to a participatory crowd that shares its knowledge by creating independent information also employing open source and free software.

Focusing on the content of geographic information, a transition from maps generated by professional geographers to Volunteered Geographic Information (VGI) [2] has taken place. The advent of GPS (Global Positioning System), broadcast connections and open and free software has resulted in a large contribution of non-expert users on these topics. Citizens are sensors: they have the knowledge and technologies that permit geo-tagging of content; they are equipped with cheap positioning devices that enable them to determine location with high accuracy; they have access to the Internet and can get free high-resolution imagery. This is participatory GIS (PGIS): it involves people in planning and designing decisions using their collective spatial and real-time knowledge. Recently much attention has focused on social media and Big Data - resources that can help accelerate response efforts with real-time information in Disaster Resource Management (DRM). These new information sources and approaches to data discovery and analysis are crucial to develop more resilient societies. Big Crisis Data refers to the relatively large volume, velocity and variety of raw digital data (e.g. the text of individual Facebook updates) as well as meta-data (e.g. the time and place those updates were posted) [3]. They can accelerate impact evaluations and needs assessment at local level. The rapid identification of risks due to disasters can help affected populations recover more quickly [4]. The Big Crisis Data challenge can be addressed using Human Computing (HC), that includes crowdsourcing and micro-tasking, and/or Artificial Intelligence, that includes natural language processing and machine learning. Big Data are used in the emerging field of crisis mapping. Crisis mapping is an inter-disciplinary field that aggregates crowd-generated input data, such as social media feeds and photographs, with geographic data, to provide real-time, interactive information in support of disaster management and humanitarian relief [5]. Social media and blogs can also be important instruments to communicate crisis information and increase situational awareness when major disasters strike. With the advent of the Internet and Web 2.0 the new media move to a 24-hour cycle that provides immediate access to information. In addition, social media allow citizens to post text, pictures, video, and links to web-sites [6]. The propagation speed, the reaction time and the multidirectional fluxes of new media affect both form and content of traditional communication and question its model, language and priority.

2.1   Advantages and Disadvantages of Non-authoritative Data Usage

Many unconventional data sources are derived from crowdsourcing and come from popular web-based mapping platforms (e.g. OpenStreetMap), websites collecting photos and videos (e.g. Flickr, Youtube), initiatives that collect georeferenced observations of phenomena (e.g. Ushahidi, CrisisMappers). Other types of non-authoritative data can be identified in online news, blogs, social networks. All can be integrated with traditional geospatial data in order to develop more accurate disaster scenarios and improve situational awareness. The combined use of GIS and social media has the potential to create new capacity for community resilience and results in multi-faceted georeferenced landscape, that can be associated with multimedia, such as links to webpages, videos or dynamic data (e.g. webcams). As the number of citizens creating data increases so does the accuracy of disaster impact detection. Such data are cost-effective, can be used to validate global models with local knowledge and have already proved to be able to provide precious information in the application to real cases (e.g. Haiti earthquake, Fukushima event, Philippines Typhoon Haiyan).

On the other hand, the crowd has a broad variation in digital skills and social network users adopt their own languages, especially under stress conditions, and use dialects or idioms difficult to analyze. Several disadvantages are connected to quality, privacy, trust, credibility, accessibility, security, intellectual property; often data are insufficiently structured, documented or validated and contain non-essential information such as unrelated opinions, jokes and off-topic conversation. The variety, complexity, inter-connectedness, and speed of information can be overwhelming for crisis managers [7]. The quality problem is connected to the heterogeneity of expertise and commitment of users, the media formats, the lack of syntactic control, the redundancy and sparseness of users' generated contents. In addition, mobile apps and social media can quickly disseminate false or misleading information.

Security is also a potential issue. Data may be misused to manipulate the public, foment strife and undermine stability. These technologies potentially expose disaster response organizations and the public to inappropriate content, malware threats, and breaches of confidential information. Five potential vulnerabilities in crisis mapping situations have been found [8]: identification of reporters and vulnerable groups; control of communications networks; programming flaws in crisis mapping platforms; identification and infiltration of the digital volunteers; use of unverified reports. It is necessary to underline also other aspects: intellectual property can be violated within the crowdsourced data production process; geo-privacy and ethical issues persist because data remains on the Internet long after a disaster and might be used for other purposes in addition to the possibility of unwanted tracking.

A final consideration is the need to take into account the psychology of the crowd, how people feel in an emergency, how they can be influenced by the content they read on social media and whether they are willing to share their experiences.

3   EDIT

EDIT- Extracting Disaster Information from Text – is a methodology to treat textual information extracted from the web, originated by non-expert users and referring to the occurrence of a disaster event.

The EDIT methodology focuses on the semantic analysis of online news and tweets, the extraction of the relevant data to enhance knowledge about the disaster, the evaluation of the reliability of the data and the visualization of scenario maps representing relevant features. Spatio-temporal information and impact related information can be extracted from text only after the application of standards and techniques that permit rationalization of the contents published online by non-official users. The starting point of the methodology is the web research of online news and tweets using key words. This can be done manually or using a feed reader. The creation of an ontology about a disaster and its consequences is crucial, because it focusses on the definition of a formal model for data processing and reasoning.

EDIT develops a new approach to emergency response applications, integrating a semantic reasoning into an event-based database system with usage of formal domain definitions. The methodology makes it possible to perform a semantic analysis starting from information contained in the web and categorizes results into a PostgreSQL scenario database containing significant disaster-related information (location, time and impacts). Accessing it, users can immediately query and visualize information on maps, for example using a QGIS environment. Data are enriched with the attribute of a semantic reliability index, introduced as a further filter for information.

The main contributions of the method are: the realization of a disaster ontology, the conceptualization of a disaster event into a concept map, the integration of semantic and rule-based reasoning, the creation of a database to handle and select the most relevant event-related information, the application of a semantic reliability data filter and the representation of this information into scenarios through the use of GIS software.

3.1   Related Work

The proposed study is new in its approach to information extraction and elaboration for disaster scenarios representation. Ontology are used by several authors with different purposes. Klien, Kuhn, & Lutz (2006) [9] proposed an approach that combines ontology-based metadata with an ontology based search to solve semantic heterogeneity problems in keyword-based search within a GI web service environment. Wiegand & Garcia (2007) [10] used a task-based Semantic Web model to help automate process of geospatial data sources retrieval and consider only geographic data produced by government agencies. Di Maio (2007) [11] develops an open ontology, an open conceptual and semantic framework, to which developers and users of emergency response systems can reference unambiguously and universally to support emergency response operations. Joshi et al (2007) [12] develop a Disaster Mitigation and Modelling ontology-based approach using OWL, for managing heterogeneous data from different suppliers (individual local, state and federal agencies). Fan & Zlatanova (2011) [13] elaborate an ontology for emergency management using static and dynamic data models.

Research on understanding social media use in disaster to extract useful information is born in last few years when numerous disaster-related messages start to be posted to microblogging sites during crises. Yin et al (2012) [14] use natural language processing and data mining techniques to extract situation awareness information from Twitter. Cameron et al (2012) [15] describe a platform for emergency situation awareness, that detects incidents using keyword detection and classifies interesting tweets using an SVM classier. Imran et al. (2013) [16] automatically identify tweets contributing to situational awareness and classify them according to several types of information. Olteanu et al (2014) [17] create a lexicon of crisis-related terms to improve query methods of relevant tweets.

3.2   Disaster Ontology Definition

An ontology is an explicit specification of a conceptualization [18], or, more specifically, is a formal specification of a shared conceptualization [19]. In simple terms, an ontology is a formal description, in a format that is computer readable, that expresses a set of concepts (e.g. entities, attributes, relationships, values, processes) in a domain of interest [20].

An ontology can be used to solve the problem of semantically heterogeneous descriptions of the same topic: people can express the same ideas with different terms, depending on their needs or background context. The ontology identifies concepts and relationships within a scientific domain, trying to reduce conceptual and terminological confusion, and allowing reasoning about reality through inference rules. Four steps are necessary to realize a disaster ontology:

Specification. The definition of the domain is an answer to the question "how can a disaster be described?". Four classes can be determined, corresponding to four questions: "What is the cause of the disaster?", "Where does it happen?", "When does it happen?", "What is the impact of the disaster on the territory and its elements?".

Conceptualization. A top-down development process can be adopted, main classes are identified by answering the specification questions; then, classes are organized into a hierarchical taxonomy: if a class A is a super-class of class B, then every instance of B is also an instance of A (that is the class B represents a concept that is a "kind of" A). After the definition of classes, it is required to describe the internal structure of concepts and their relations: classes and sub-classes and relative relations are illustrated with a concept map.

In this phase, it is useful to create a list of all terms that can be used to make statements. A glossary of recurring terms for disaster events has been realized in order to build the ontology. Definitions associated to glossary terms have been collected from web sites concerning disaster management. In particular, considering the question "How can a disaster be described?", four domains of interest have been created: the type of natural hazard that triggers the disaster, corresponding to "What is the cause of the disaster?"; the impact of the disaster, in term of magnitude, exposure, vulnerability and damage, corresponding to "What is the impact of the disaster on the territory and its elements?"; the location, referring both to the phenomenon and the position of exposed elements, corresponding to "Where does the disaster happen?"; the time of disaster occurrence, corresponding to "When does the disaster happen?".

These questions correspond to the definition of four main classes related to the leading disaster event concept. For each of these classes a glossary has been created and a thesaurus adopted to recognize and address synonyms and repetition of classes. The use of the thesaurus and the classification of synonyms for the same concept word is very important, especially when textual information written with natural language needs to be analyzed. For example, flood and inundation have a very similar meaning, so both of them are chosen as key-words but only one is chosen to indicate the class. Classification by keywords is a technique that allows us to make an automatic classification. For each class, a set of keywords has been selected by sorting words on their frequency of occurrences in texts.

Formalization and Implementation. This has been realized through the construction of a disaster database, by mapping the concept map to a formal database structure and the realization of a Java code that processes the natural language of web texts and distributes different parts of sentences in corresponding database tables.

Evaluation. This has been realized by applying the ontology to two case studies, where the natural language processing is gathered both manually and automatically.

An additional component to the ontology is the multilingual approach: EDIT has been used to prove that ontologies can be used in similar manners within different languages, so the procedure has been developed both for English and Italian languages in an analogous way.

The disaster-related ontology is in a prototype stage, is not fully specified with OWL format since it is built using the concept map and it is mapped to code lookup tables of database. Until now, the ontology concerns floods and earthquakes, but it will contain other type of natural hazards in the future.

3.3   Concept Map

In order to better analyze and evaluate concepts and relationships, the ontology has been graphically represented as a concept map. A concept map is a graphical tool to organize and structure knowledge. It is a diagram containing concepts, ideas, words and the relationships among them. In general, a concept map is represented by boxes containing keywords connected with labelled arrows in a downward-branching hierarchical structure. The arrows represent taxonomies and sub-classes connections.

Concept maps can be used to communicate complex ideas. Concept mapping can also be seen as a first step in ontology building, as it corresponds to the conceptualization of the domain classes and relations: Fig.1 shows the concept map developed in EDIT. Four main characteristics have been identified to describe the disaster event:

Natural Hazard. The trigger for a disaster, a list, a glossary and a thesaurus have been created, plus the possibility of domino effects;

Location. The exact location (e.g. expression such as "at", "in" followed by the address); geographical coordinates (latitude, longitude and altitude); cardinal directions related to other locations (north, south, east, west, northeast,…); proximity to other elements ("near", "in front of",…);

Time. Exact time (year, month, day and hour), or duration ("for" "in the space of", in less than"), or temporal relations ("before", "during", "after");

Impact. The magnitude of events, plus its impacts on territory (e.g. hit, affect, kill, destroy,…) and affected elements related to the class they belong to.

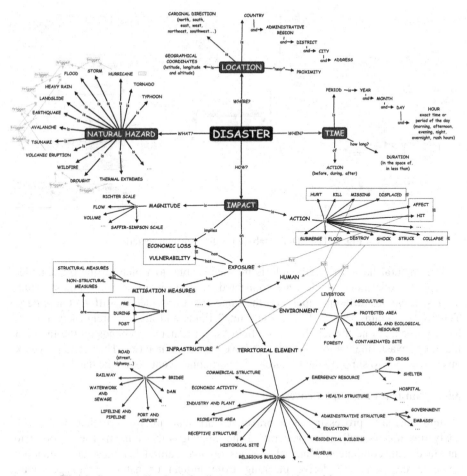

Fig. 1. Conceptualization of a disaster: representation with a concept map

3.4   Database Creation

The logical steps adopted in the process are: building the concept map, building the ontology based on the concept map, mapping the ontology to a database.

An entity-relationship data model has been chosen. Entities are described by at least two attributes: one is a unique identifier (key field) that must be unique for each occurrence of an entity, and the other is a property of the entity (e.g. a name or a number). Different entities can be related through relationships characterized by a cardinality that can be one-to-one, one-to-many, or many-to-many.

Specifications of the properties of classes (or objects) and relations in the database represent metadata of the ontology. The open source object-relational database management system PostgreSQL is chosen to realize the EDIT database for disaster representation: eighteen tables were created in order to contain all the relevant information; six of them are code lookup tables that contain glossary and thesaurus. The general schema of the database is reported in Fig.2.

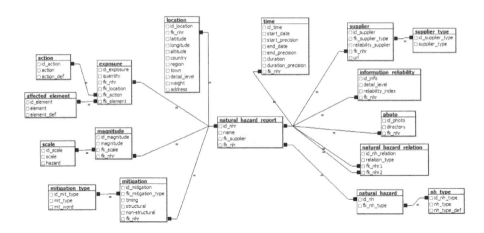

Fig. 2. The EDIT database for disaster representation

The "natural hazard report" table is the main table, to which all the other tables (except for code lookup tables) are connected. It is necessary to adopt this structure because there are different reports on the same event provided by different suppliers. This table contains "id" and "specific name" fields and also a foreign key for the hazard type and one for suppliers. The field "specific name" depends on the fact that the most devastating natural hazards can have a proper name (e.g. Hurricane Katrina): this allows one to simplify the research of a particular event inside the database.

3.5   Natural Language Processing

Natural language processing is a branch of artificial intelligence that deals with analyzing, understanding and generating the languages that humans use, in order to interface with computers. Many challenges involve natural language understanding enabling computers to derive meaning from human or natural language input. Understanding or interpreting language depends on the ability to understand the words used in a domain.

Spatio-temporal information and impact-related information naturally correspond to the textual description of events that occur at a geographic location at a specific time and with consequences on human life and activities.

Generally automatic information discovery requires the use of information extraction techniques, like parsing, tokenizing and POS (Part-of-Speech) tagging.

Parsing is a method to perform syntactic analysis of a sentence, it involves breaking down a text into its component parts of speech with an explanation of the form, function and syntactic relationship of each part.

A natural language parser is a program that works out the grammatical structure of sentences: probabilistic parsers use knowledge of language gained from hand-parsed sentences to produce the most likely analysis of new sentences.

Tokenization divides the character sequence into sentences and the sentences into tokens. Not only words are considered as tokens, but also numbers, punctuation marks, parentheses and quotation marks.

The process of classifying words into their parts of speech and labeling them accordingly is known as part-of-speech tagging, POS-tagging, or simply tagging.

The EDIT methodology enables the extraction of impact-related, temporal and spatial information from documents, typically represented in the form of textual expressions, and the management into a database.

In order to extract relevant information from textual documents Java code has been developed. It synthetizes the process of tokenization and bypasses the POS tagging by comparing words contained in text with a list of keywords (the ones defined in the code lookup tables of EDIT database).

In order to extract relevant information from textual documents, a series of templates were defined that described common sentences and phrases used to report disaster impacts. These templates were defined by manual examination of disaster reports from different sources, and consisted of a combination of parts of speech (for generic words like determiners) and specific lists of words with a particular part of speech. Each word was coded and word categories were created to eliminate synonyms when appropriate.

The spatial information and the geo-localization was realized by comparing sentences with data from OpenStreetMap (OSM) or other repositories of spatial data.

3.6   Twitter

Online conversational text, exemplified by microblogs, chat and text messages, is a challenge for natural language processing. Conversational text contains many non-standard lexical items and syntactic patterns as a result of unintentional errors, dialectal variation, conversational ellipsis, topic diversity, and creative use of language or orthography.

Word segmentation on Twitter is challenging due to the lack of orthographic conventions; in particular, punctuation, emoticons, URLs, and other symbols may have no whitespace separation from textual words and internally may contain alphanumeric symbols that could be mistaken for words. Applying the EDIT Java code to the content of the tweet message it is possible to extract relevant news; in addition, selection of relevant words can be put in evidence considering hash tags. Also, templates that are specific to the Twitter context can be defined.

3.7   Semantic Reliability Index

The literature on the quality of heterogeneous data is broad. The ISO 19113:2002 and ISO 19114:2003 standards define as consensual dimensions of geographic data quality the positional, temporal and thematic accuracy, the logical consistency, the completeness and lineage of data.

In addition to the information extraction process, it is important to create a filter in order to determine if specific information can correctly be added to a scenario or not.

The information filter should consider two main topics: content and position.

A reliability index has been developed in EDIT to detect the quality of the information. Considering the position, a geographic accuracy index could also be developed: this is not part of the present study but it will be considered as a future development. Extrinsic and intrinsic quality can be defined for information reliability:

extrinsic is related to supplier validity, intrinsic to textual, spatial, temporal, measurement validity [21]. The quality assessment can be applied both ex-ante, as a guarantee that the database stores only VGI with a desired minimum level of quality, or ex-post, when a user wants to evaluate if the VGI in a database is of some utility for his purposes.

Focusing on the reliability of data content, some significant factors affect the quality of the information extraction, including: level of detail of the information, accuracy and precision of the information, correctness and completeness of a sentence, conformity to the reality, truthfulness of information, quantity of similar information, characteristics and reputation of the sources, expertise of providers, use of the information, subjectivity of the information [22].

The reliability index is created by taking into account the distinct components of the information: each item is associated with metadata which contain the reliability indicators. Data should be firstly analyzed on the basis of each single criterion expressed linguistically by the decision maker. Then, a global reliability index is created by assigning different weights to each component; different indexes are considered for the different tables in the database: location, time, exposure and supplier; different weights are considered for category of items and different scales for different levels of detail. Weights are assigned according to subjective criteria and classifications.

The total reliability of the information results by the combination of the single reliability indexes: it is important to note that information with location index less than 0.5 are not considered for the scenario creation even if the same information has time, exposure or supplier indexes with high or medium-high reliability. The total reliability index can be described by the following equations:

$$R = 0 \qquad\qquad \text{if } W_{L,M} \, or W_{L,m} < 0,5 \qquad (1)$$

$$R = \frac{W_{L,M} + W_{L,m} + W_E + W_T + I_s}{5} \qquad \text{if } W_{L,M} \, or W_{L,m} > 0,5 \qquad (2)$$

where: $W_{L,m}$ micro-scale location weight; $W_{L,M}$ macro-scale location weight; W_E exposure weight; W_T time weight; I_S supplier weight.

4   Application to Two Case Studies

The EDIT methodology was evaluated by application to two test events with different characteristics. The first case study is an example of manual historical research on a past event, the Christchurch earthquake, New Zealand 2011. The use of semantic analysis on online news to extract relevant information to store in the EDIT database has been performed using the English language. The second case study is the flood of the Secchia River, Italy 2014: near-real-time data reports from online news websites, tweets and photos have been investigated. The semantic analysis and the population of the EDIT database has been realized using the manual and the automatic procedure, a translated version of database tables suitable for the Italian language. The application to two different languages was intended to prove the flexibility of the model and has produced interesting results.

For research on Twitter the second case study has been used also to test the possibility of integration with the AIDR tool[1].

The second case study focuses on the flood which occurred in the municipality of Modena, Bastiglia, Bomporto (Italy) on January 19th, 2014, when the right bank of Secchia river broke after heavy rains.

The collection of news on the Internet using the search keywords 'Alluvione Modena' on the time period January 2014, 19th-22nd was paired with Twitter search for the time period January 2014, 23rd-31st performed by a local installation of the tool AIDR and search keywords #allertameteoER and #alluvioneMO.

The analysis was realized both with a manual procedure and automatic EDIT Java code. Twitter reports started only from January 23th due to the development of the EDIT procedure contemporary to the occurrence of the event: the decision to test possibilities to analyze tweets in real-time with AIDR tool was taken some days after the event struck, so it was necessary to install the tool and let it run. A brief summary of results obtained from the application of EDIT on Secchia flood January 2014 is visible in Fig. 3, where impacts derived from both manual and automatic procedures on online reports and tweets are presented. In both case studies queries and maps have been produced using a QGIS environment, the PgAdminIII interface for handling EDIT database and OSM features as geographical layers.

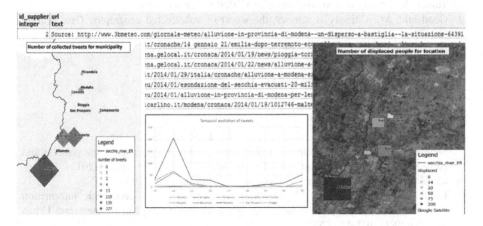

Fig. 3. Output of EDIT research on Secchia flood January 2014 impacts: application of manual and automatic procedures on online reports and tweets

5   Conclusion

Non-authoritative data, such as Big data and social media, can be a powerful instrument both during disaster and post-event phases and can be used to fill in gaps in data: emergency response applications require the handling of large amounts of information in order to provide a wide view of on-going scenarios.

---

[1] The free and open source Artificial Intelligence for Disaster Response (AIDR) platform leverages machine learning to automatically identify informative content on Twitter during disasters. It is under development by Qatar Computing Research Institute [23].

EDIT is a prototype and can be seen as a starting point for further developments; some aspects to be exploited are: an improvement of automatic research and storing processes, the widening to studies on crowd behavior, the definition of a location accuracy index based on geospatial criteria.

However, significant efforts have been spent on designing the methodology and authors believe it provides a strong and well described tool to formalize non-authoritative data processing related to disasters, in particular: the kind of information necessary to build a disaster scenario; the need to change the natural unstructured language into a formal structured language; the integration of semantic reasoning into an event-based database system; the evaluation of reliability of data provided by non-authoritative sources and the usage of open source tools.

In addition, EDIT creates a new point of view in mosaicking the representation of a disaster, the single vision grows more and more depending on quality and quantity of data, and generates from a specific empty 'scenario tables-structure' that can be partially or completely populated during an event and can be used worldwide for a great variety of hazards.

References

1. Turner, A.: Introduction to neogeography. O'Reilly Media (2006)
2. Goodchild, M.: Citizens as sensors: the world of volunteered geography. Geo. Journal (2007)
3. iRevolution Blog, http://irevolution.net/2013/06/27/what-is-big-crisis-data
4. iRevolution Blog, http://irevolution.net/2013/01/11/disaster-resilience-2-0
5. iRevolution Blog, http://irevolution.net/2011/01/20/what-is-crisis-mapping
6. FEMA, http://emilms.fema.gov/is42/BPSM0101020t.htm
7. Shanley, L., Burns, R., Bastian, Z., Robson, E.: Tweeting up a storm - the promise and perils of crisis mapping. Photogrammetric engineering and remote sensing (2013)
8. Chamales, G., Baker, R.: Security crisis maps in conflict zones (2011)
9. Klien, E., Kuhn, W., Lutz, M.: Ontology-based discovery of geographic information services—An application in disaster management. Computers, Environment and Urban Systems 30(1), 102–123 (2006)
10. Wiegand, N., Garcia, C.: A task-based ontology approach to automate geospatial data retrieval. Transactions in GIS 11(3), 355–376 (2007)
11. Di Maio, P.: An Open Ontology for Open Source Emergency Response System (2007)
12. Joshi, H., Seker, C., Bayrak, S., Ramaswamy, S., Connelly, J.: Ontology for disaster mitigation and planning. Society for Computer Simulation International San Diego, CA, USA (2007)
13. Fan, Z., Zlatanova, S.: Exploring ontologies for semantic interoperability of data in emergency response. Applied Geomatics 3(2), 109–122 (2011)
14. Yin, J., Lampert, A., Cameron, M., Robinson, B., Power, R.: Using Social Media to Enhance Emergency Situation Awareness. IEEE Intelligent Systems 27(6), 52–59 (2012), doi:10.1109/MIS.2012.6
15. Cameron, M., Power, R., Robinson, B., Yin, J.: Emergency situation awareness from twitter for crisis management. In: Proc. of WWW, pp. 695–698. ACM (2012)

16. Imran, M., Elbassuoni, S., Castillo, C., Diaz, F., Meier, P.: Practical extraction of disaster-relevant information from social media. In: WWW Companion (2013)
17. Olteanu, A., Castillo, C., Diaz, F., Vieweg, S.: CrisisLex: A Lexicon for Collecting and Filtering Microblogged Communications in Crises. In: ICWSM, Ann Arbor, MI, USA (2014)
18. Gruber, T.: Towards Principles for the Design of Ontologies Used for Knowledge Sharing. In: Formal Ontology in Conceptual Analysis and Knowledge Representation. Kluwer Academic Publishers (1993)
19. Borst, W.: Construction of Engineering Ontologies. University of Tweente. Enschede, Centre for Telematics and Information Technology (1997)
20. Wiegand, N., Garcia, C.: A task-based ontology approach to automate geospatial data retrieval. Transactions in GIS 11(3), 355–376 (2007)
21. Bordogna, P., Carrara, L., Criscuolo, M., Pepe, M., Rampini, A.: A linguistic decision making approach to assess the quality of volunteer geographic information for citizen science. Information Sciences (2013)
22. Meek, S., Jackson, M.J., Leibovici, D.G.: A flexible framework for assessing the quality of crowd-sourced data. In: Proc. AGILE Conference, Castellon, Spain (2014)
23. iRevolution Blog, http://irevolution.net/2013/10/01/aidr-artificial-intelligence-for-disaster-response

Towards a Decision Support System for Security Analysis

Application to Railroad Accidents

Ahmed Maalel[1,*], Lassad Mejri[1], Habib Hadj-Mabrouk[2], and Henda Ben Ghézala[1]

[1] RIADI Laboratory, ENSI, National School of Computer Sciences,
University of Manouba, 2010, Tunisia
{ahmed.maalel,henda.benghezala}@ensi.rnu.tn,
mejrilassad@yahoo.fr
[2] IFSTTAR, French Institute of Science and Technology of Transport,
Planning and Networking, France
habib.hadj-mabrouk@ifsttar.fr

Abstract. The work presented in the context of this paper is to develop a decision support system for security analysis called Adast. Adast is based on Case-Based Reasoning (CBR) and ontologies to help capitalize and exploit the knowledge on railroad accidents from our field of application. The advantage of this approach, based primarily on case-based reasoning and ontologies, lies not only on the capitalization of knowledge from experience feedback, but also on benefit in order to provide assistance to domain experts in their crucial task of analyzing and Improving security. In this paper, we will present the first realized works of Adast.

Keywords: Decision support system, Case-Based Reasoning, Ontologies, Security analysis, Railroad accident.

1 Introduction

Recently, an increasing number of companies and industries have undergone greatly in competition. At the same time, we are witnessing an explosion technological advances and new technologies of information and communication that companies must integrate to achieve the performance that goes far beyond those obtained by conventional practices. However, these constraints are at the origin of the birth of many risks. Sometimes we are witnessing serious and costly failures, accidents and human losses, especially when it is a highly risky area such as railroad transportation (our current case study).

From its beginning, the railroad transportation has a high-risk-level factor, often discovered through realized accidents. Accordingly, all authorities and stakeholders have tried over time to learn from experience feedback through railroad accidents. That is why the experience feedback, and more generally security, has become for many industrial companies (including the field of railroad transport) a major concern

---

* Corresponding author.

C. Hanachi, F. Bénaben, and F. Charoy (Eds.): ISCRAM-med 2014, LNBIP 196, pp. 46–56, 2014.
© Springer International Publishing Switzerland 2014

and an essential element not only for the success of their projects but also for their development, or even their survival. We can note the absence of an explicit methodology for the experience feedback and security analysis. This approach standardizes, for experts of different levels, both the used terminology and vocabulary and the methods used for each step of the experience feedback process. In conclusion, it is essential to build capacity and computational tools not only to model and capitalize knowledge of experience feedback, but also to exploit them in order to propose and derive the know-how which assists and stimulates the domain experts in the task of security analysis.

In our work, the Case-Based Reasoning (CBR), considered as a method of reasoning by analogy in the field of machine learning, is selected in conjunction with ontologies to overcome these challenges. First, the CBR is a relative method of experience feedback. It is considered as a process of solving the problem by starting a recall for similar past situations and continuing through the reuse of information and knowledge available on these situations to develop a new solution to the common problem found by adapting past solutions. Our approach is to combine both ontologies to understand the limitations and shortcomings related to the knowledge representation and the CBR related to addressing the problem of exploiting this knowledge.

This paper describes all stages of the aid decision process. This paper is organized as follows: The first section presents the notion of an accident case and some information on the formalization of the domain knowledge. Section 2 describes our decision support system Adast. The experiments will be the subject of the last section.

2   Formalization of an Accident Scenario

2.1   Notion of an Accident Case

A "case" is a structured story made or imagined as a past performance [1]. According to [2], a case can be defined as a set of contextual knowledge teaching a lesson. The certification experts use the term scenario to express an accident. This concept is richer than the concept of cases we find in the literature. Indeed, an accident brings together three complementary views of a descriptive accident:

— *Descriptors such as "Background"* that define the context of the accident scenario and the framework within which it takes place. They concern some descriptors (event = dreaded collision), (accident area = terminus) (Dangerous elements = operator roaming ...);
— *Descriptors such as "problem"* represent failure categories and related causes to three factors (humans, the system and the environment).
— *Descriptors like "Solution"* represent solutions to maintain or restore the operation of a transportation system, hence inhibiting the consequences of failure.

We adopt in our approach a static characterization of an accident scenario, through a description comprising a set of parameters with several attributes. Each accident scenario is characterized by a membership class.

2.2   Case Model

Our case model is based on the works of [4] and [5]. A case in our system represents an accident experience. It is described by a triplet (problem, solution and class):

- — *Problem:* the description part of the problem (the accident), which includes two families of descriptors; the symptoms and causes of major potential accidents, we can cite as an example the context of the accident, dangerous elements, possible causes, and the dreaded events including the risk level;
- — *Solution:* preventive and remedial measures implemented to prevent the recurrence of the accident;
- — *Class:* the membership class of the accident.

Our case model is based on domain ontology. This ontology describes specifically the area of a railroad accident such as: the type of accident, the geographical area, the principle of railway line, the actors involved and their failure, preventive and protective measures, etc (Fig. 1).

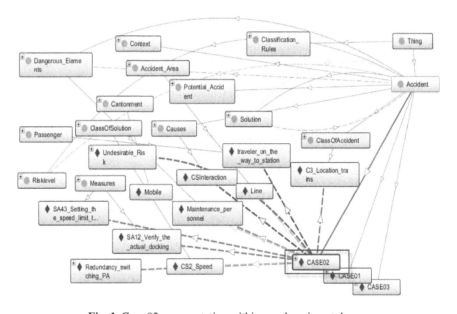

Fig. 1. Case 02 representation within our domain ontology

3   Proposed Approach

Several approaches of the CBR systems have been proposed in the literature. These architectures share more or less the same components. Inspired by these works and architectures, our system [5,6] has two parts: an offline process, and an on-line process (Fig. 2):

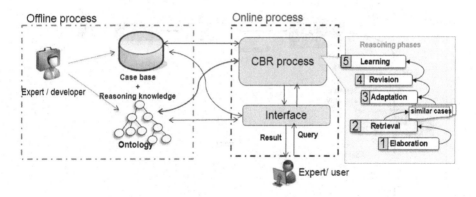

Fig. 2. Functional architecture of the proposed CBR approach

— *The offline process* includes the real-field knowledge and those extracted from the domain experts, the formalization of knowledge related to reasoning, the construction of a knowledge model based on ontologies (domain ontology) and finally the preparation of the case base.

— *The on-line process* includes an interface dedicated to the interaction between the expert / user and the system along the CBR reasoning cycle.

3.1 General Description of the Approach

In this section, we show the different CBR phases and we implement the interactions between the different modules of the proposed system (Fig. 3).

Elaboration Phase

During this phase, the necessary information for the problem formulation is collected and organized so as to constitute a new case (the target case). In this step (1), the system prompts the user through the instantiation of the ontology (presented in the previous section), which will be viewed as a form to fill out. The user/expert characterizes its target case (a railroad accident where looks for a possible solution) by selecting the main concepts of the problem part (Context of the accident, dangerous elements, possible causes, etc.).

If this description (target case) is not initially sufficient, the user/expert will enrich its description in the enrichment phase. The description of the case is not subject to a preset structure (in terms of attributes). It would be useful to help the user/expert during his experience transcription. This assistance comes in the form of a list of relevant concepts to use, derived from the case base. The case base is an important source of help in this phase. To develop this list, we use techniques of data mining, (association rules) by applying the *Apriori* algorithm developed by [7]. The validation of the formulation will be the entrance to the next CBR phase which is the retrieval phase.

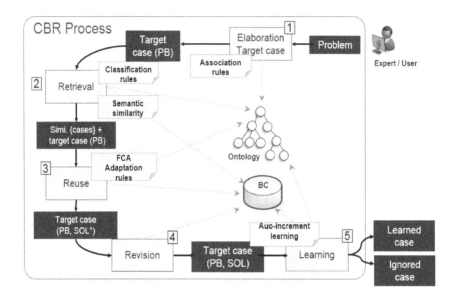

Fig. 3. Articulation of various CBR process phases

Retrieval Phase

Schematically, the retrieval phase explores the whole case base in order to restore (find) similar cases to the target case. In our context, the retrieval phase is optimized because it operates only on cases belonging to the same class. The method of the decision tree that allows achieving from a set of examples (case) learning a tree structure is used to classify a new target case. The classification helps us point to the class membership of the target case before seeking similar cases. Therefore, the similarity is supported only for all of the class membership of the target case. The classification task is a critical one because it has an impact on the downstream steps of reasoning.

Each case is capitalized in the case base as an instance of the domain ontology, thus the calculation of similarity cases related to the calculation of similarity between instances of the ontology. In the literature, several studies on the measurement of the semantic similarity between the ontology concepts have been developed in different contexts. The calculation of similarity between two instances of the ontology consists of two parts: a concept-based similarity and a slot-based one. We do not pretend to define new similarity measurements. We use the measurements described in the literature that suit us best. So, we use the measurements proposed by [8] and [9].

Reuse Phase

We adopt two main steps in the reuse approach. In the first step in which the system generates an adequate adaptation knowledge connected to all the most similar cases found in the retrieval phase. We use the approach of Formal Concept Analysis (FCA) to discover semantic links between given cases, particularly the eligibility of found substitutions to possibly offer the right solution to the target case. In the second step, the system infers the found conditions (substitution rules) to generate a possible solution to the target case under the control of the domain expert.

The approach of the extracting knowledge adaptation takes place in four steps:

— *Step 1*. Separate cases in the case base according to their class of solution [4]. A case may have one or more solutions, and can be found in several solution classes;

— *Step 2*. Construct the formal context of each set of cases. We define the multi-valued formal context $\mathbb{K} = (\mathcal{G}, \mathcal{M}, \mathcal{W}, \mathcal{J})$ where $\mathcal{G}$ is a set of cases with the same class of solution, $\mathcal{M}$ is a set of multi-valued attributes, $\mathcal{W}$ is a set of values attributes, and $\mathcal{J} \subseteq \mathcal{G} \times \mathcal{M} \times \mathcal{W}$ is a ternary relation between $\mathcal{G}, \mathcal{M} \ and \ \mathcal{W}$ such that $g, m, w \in I$ which means that the description (the problem part) case c has the attribute with a w value;

— *Step 3*. Transform each context to a uni-valued context and generate the formal-concept lattice. Formal concepts are the maximum clusters of cases with the same attribute values;

— *Step 4*. Find specific adaptation conditions to each case. Any formal concept leads to a set of matching conditions noted $\mathbb{CA}$, applicable to cases belonging to the extension.

Revision Phase

In this phase, the proposed solution will be evaluated manually by the user/Expert. It may be that the solution proposed by the system is not suitable (it proves to be unable to solve the problem). The user/expert has the opportunity to modify, refine or even reject the proposed solution. The identification of possible causes of this failure can help us improve the adaptation knowledge.

Learning Phase

We have proposed an auto-increment approach for this learning phase in order to solve these problems and maintain the case base.

We consider a target case with the solution part informed and revised case case^*_{target}. Two possibilities are considered as follows:

— *Possibility 1*. There is no solution in the Case Base (CB) which is similar to the solution attributed to the target case. The solution space is not covered by any solutions source belonging to the C_k class: CB $\leftarrow$ CB $\cup$ target case;

— *Possibility 2*. It there is at least one solution that is similar to the target case. We will select a prototype by choosing a case that has the same solution. The case or the subset of the selected cases is the one that has the largest description (on the problem part) relative to the other cases. Since each case base has an instance of the domain ontology, then we do a comparison of problem parts with selected cases. We calculate the degree of the noted D_S semantics through a similarity calculation-based concept: If $DS_{Pb*} > D_s^i$ then CB $\leftarrow$ CB $\cup$ Target case.

3.2   Proposed Decision Support System

Actually, after thirty knowledge extraction sessions [10-13], we have created a database of a historical knowledge of safety analysis of the already certified and approved automated transport systems. This knowledge has been formalized in the case model based on the domain ontology already presented. In the current work, the two modules, acquisition and reasoning, are implemented and are the model of the proposed system feasibility.

Functional Architecture

The architecture of the model feasibility, based on Adast, comprises two main modules: the acquisition module case and the reasoning module. These two modules are interacting with other components making the interface role with the knowledge base and the domain ontology.

Figure 4 shows the functional architecture of the proposed model.

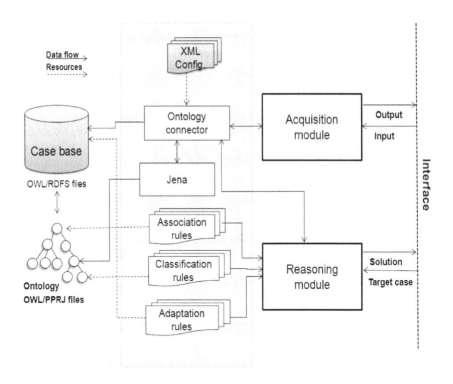

Fig. 4. Functional architecture of the model feasibility based on Adast

The main components of the Adast architecture are:

— *Ontology Connector:* It ensures the communication between the case base and the ontology;

- *Jena:* It is a framework written in Java providing an environment that facilitates the development of applications for the semantic web;
- *Configuration File:* It is an XML file that specifies the necessary configuration settings and operation of Jena and the connection to the ontology;
- *Classification Rules:* These rules are used to detect the target class membership of a new case;
- *Adaptation Rules:* These rules are used to apply the appropriate substitutions for the proposal for a possible solution to the target case;
- *Base Case:* The base case includes all source cases;
- *Ontology:* It is the basic formalism for the description of the accident scenario. It also allows the representation of different inference rules used by the reasoning module.

We present in the following figure (Fig. 5) the main screens of the decision support system:

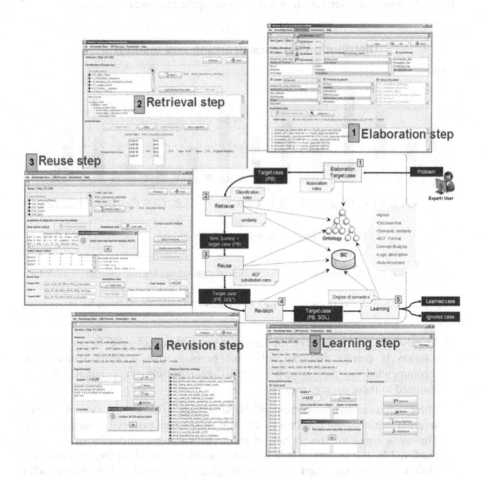

Fig. 5. Feasibility model screens

3.3   Experiments

This paragraph provides an assessment of the system, more precisely, the process of the decision support module and the problem solving. This evaluation will lead to limitations including the prospects arising to improve the proposed approach.

Very schematically, the quality of a system decision support is measured by assessing the validity and usefulness of the produced knowledge. The knowledge is valid if it is appropriate and consistent with what we have already known about the studied area. It is useful if it helps to achieve the defined objectives. Controlling of these two criteria (validity and usefulness) is generally the responsibility of domain experts. To test the representativeness of the results obtained by our system, we have chosen to use test cases from the training sample. This initial sample has been used repeatedly to develop the decision support process. We have agreed to use the part that represents one fifth of the sample. The selected test cases are randomly selected from 11 classes of preset scenarii.

Figure 6 shows the distribution of test cases compared to cases sources.

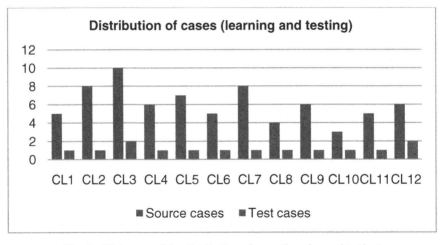

Fig. 6. Histogram of the distribution of cases (learning and testing)

We have tested the various test cases (14 cases) and the results can be interpreted as follows:

— 11 solutions are "consistent" (a percentage roughly equal to 80 % success): the solution is correct and can solve the problem (the accident scenario) as recommended by the domain expert (they represent the original solutions assigned to these source cases;

— Three solutions are "no-consistent" (a percentage of 20%): the system offers a solution that does not conform to the original solution assigned to the test cases. The main cause of this failure stems from the non-conformity of the class predicted by the system, which has led to a calculation similarity in a different class to the one supposed to be the adequate class membership (the classifier that we have adopted in our approach gives a percentage of 87 % success cases).

This may lead to the identification of source cases with a low percentage of similarity where the adaptation rules do not allow solving the target case.

Although this first evaluation of the entire system has shown the validity of our decision support approach, Adast. A more detailed assessment is needed to measure and eventually optimize the system performance. For this, it is imperative to enrich the basis of examples of learning additional cases related not only to the risk of collision but also to other accident risks.

4   Conclusion

We have presented in this paper a new decision support approach to improve security analysis, called Adast. The advantage of this approach, based primarily on case-based reasoning and ontologies, lies not only on the capitalization of knowledge from experience feedback, but also on benefit in order to provide assistance to domain experts in their crucial task of analyzing and Improving security.

First, the CBR is a reasoning paradigm that solves new problems by adapting solutions from past problems that have been solved. The CBR cycle that we have adopted is divided into five phases: elaboration of target case, retrieval, reuse, revision and learning. Each phase has a specific role in solving the problem and involves a specific knowledge. For this purpose, we have also used other types of knowledge underlying the reasoning domain ontology: similarity knowledge, reuse knowledge etc. The Similarity knowledge is used to recall similar cases and the adaptation knowledge is used to reuse the solutions form the remembered cases. The advantage of our decision support system lies not only to the capitalization of knowledge from experience feedback (accident scenarii), but also to benefit in order to provide assistance to domain experts in their crucial task of analyzing and Improving security.

Although the work has been developed to present several contributions; however, a fairly extensive experimentation will be of great use to validate and consolidate all the research work. This is the subject of our ongoing work.

References

1. Aamodt, A.: A Knowledge-Intensive Integrated Approach to Problem Solving and Sustained learning. PhD thesis, University of Trondheim, Norway (1991)
2. Kolodner, J.: Case Based Reasoning, 668 p. Morgan-Kaufmann Publishers, Inc. (1993)
3. Fuchs, B., Mille, A.: Une modélisation au niveau connaissance du raisonnement à partir de cas, L'Harmattan editor, Knowledge Engineering (2005)
4. Abou-Assali, A.: Acquisition des connaissances d'adaptation et traitement de l'hétérogénéité dans un système de RàPC basé sur une Ontologie. Application au diagnostic de la défaillance de détecteurs de gaz. PhD thesis, University of Compiègne, INRIA (2010)
5. Maalel, A., Mejri, L., Hadj-Mabrouk, H., Ghézela, H.B.: Towards a case-based reasoning approach based on ontologies application to railroad accidents. In: Xiang, Y., Pathan, M., Tao, X., Wang, H. (eds.) ICDKE 2012. LNCS, vol. 7696, pp. 48–55. Springer, Heidelberg (2012)

6. Maalel, A., Mejri, L., Hadj-Mabrouk, H., Ben Ghezéla, H.: Toward a Knowledge Management Approach Based on an Ontology and Case-based Reasoning (CBR). In: IEEE RCIS2012, Sixth International Conference on Research Challenges in Information Science, Valencia, Spain, May 16-18 (2012b)

7. Agrawal, R., Srikant, R.: Fast Algorithms for Mining Association Rules. In: Proceedings of the 20th International Conference on Very Large Data Bases, Santiago, Chile (1994)

8. Wu, Z., Palmer, M.: Verbs Semantics and Lexical Selection. In: Proceedings of the 32nd Annual Meeting of the Association for Computational Linguistics, New, Mexico, USA, pp. 133–138 (1994)

9. Zhang, K., Tang, J., Hong, M., Li, J., Wei, W.: Weighted ontology-based search exploiting semantic similarity. In: Zhou, X., Li, J., Shen, H.T., Kitsuregawa, M., Zhang, Y. (eds.) APWeb 2006. LNCS, vol. 3841, pp. 498–510. Springer, Heidelberg (2006)

10. Hadj-Mabrouk, H.: Apprentissage automatique et acquisition des connaissances: deux approches complémentaires pour les systèmes à base de connaissances, Thèse de doctorat en Automatique Industrielle et Humaine, Université de Valenciennes (1992)

11. Hadj-Mabrouk, H.: ACASYA et SAUTREL: Deux mécanismes d'apprentissage d'aide au retour d'expérience. In: 4th International Conference: Sciences of Electronic, Technologies of Information and Telecommunications, March 25-29 (2007)

12. Mejri, L.: Une démarche basée sur l'apprentissage automatique pour l'aide à l'évaluation et à la génération de scenarios d'accidents. Application à l'analyse de sécurité des systèmes de transport automatisés, Université de valenciennes (décembre 6, 1995)

13. Mejri, L., Hadj-Mabrouk, H., Caulier, P.: Un modèle générique unifié de représentation et de résolution de problèmes pour la réutilisation des connaissances de sécurité. In: Revue Recherche Transports Sécurité, LAVOISIER edns., vol. 103, pp. 131–148 (2009)

Crisis Mobility of Pedestrians:
From Survey to Modelling, Lessons
from Lebanon and Argentina

Elise Beck[1,2], Julie Dugdale[3,4], Hong Van Truong[5],
Carole Adam[3,4], and Ludvina Colbeau-Justin

[1] Univ. Grenoble Alpes, PACTE, F-38000 Grenoble, France
[2] CNRS, PACTE, F-38000 Grenoble, France
[3] Univ. Grenoble Alpes, LIG, F-38000 Grenoble, France
[4] CNRS, LIG, F-38000 Grenoble, France
[5] Institut de la Francophonie pour l'Informatique, Hanoi, Vietnam
elise.beck@ujf-grenoble.fr,
{julie.dugdale,carole.adam}@imag.fr,
hongvantruongiph@gmail.com, ludvina@colbeau-justin.net

Abstract. This study aims at developing a generic model of crisis mobility based on two case studies in Lebanon and Argentina. The research is characterised by a strong interdisciplinary cooperation between geographers, psychologists and computer scientists. The objective of the model is to show how appropriate human behaviours can reduce fatalities. The paper presents the methodology used in both case studies, some results of the Lebanese model as well as lessons from Lebanon to be applied to Argentinian study (on-going work). The methodology consists in field studies, model design, development, validation/calibration and simulation. The simulation aims at reproducing survey results as well as investigating new scenarios.

Keywords: pedestrian mobility, earthquake, survey, Lebanon, Argentina, generic model.

1   Introduction and Background

1.1   Objectives

What do people do facing an earthquake? Are these behaviours 'appropriate'? What would happen if all the population knew how to behave correctly or if many people were prone to panic? Although post-seismic surveys help us to understand people's reactions [1], in some contexts such as low magnitude earthquakes or long return period seismicity, it is difficult to observe and analyse the behaviours that were adopted during a crisis. Moreover, although good information campaigns may reduce fatalities, it is difficult to evaluate how much they may ultimately influence people's behaviours in the case of an earthquake. By appropriate behaviour, we mean a behaviour leading to one´s protection and safety. In order to avoid subjectivity, the

C. Hanachi, F. Bénaben, and F. Charoy (Eds.): ISCRAM-med 2014, LNBIP 196, pp. 57–70, 2014.
© Springer International Publishing Switzerland 2014

reference taken to evaluate the adequacy of the adopted behaviour is the official measures suggested by public authorities. This study aims at developing a generic agent-based model of the mobility of pedestrians during a crisis based on two case studies. Both Beirut and Mendoza are located in seismic areas. The urban contexts are slightly different. The city of Beirut is characterized by a heterogeneous urban morphology with a high density of old and modern buildings. In Mendoza, the urbanization is adapted to seismic hazard as buildings are rarely high and the streets are wide. Both cities were destroyed by earthquakes in the past. Spatial and social data accessibility is also different in both countries; consequently different survey methodologies must be used. The paper presents 1) how a first model was developed in the Lebanese context, 2) which lessons from this first model will be used in the on-going work carried out in Argentina, 3) the Argentinian case study and 4) how both models will help developing a future generic model of pedestrians' mobility after an earthquake.

1.2   State of the Art

Several models have been developed to reproduce crises related to hazards. They either focus on organising rescue forces (RoboCup Rescue Simulation, [2]) and evaluating rescue plans (SIMGENIS [3]), or deal with citizens' evacuation [4,5]. Sometimes, models manage to simulate both rescuers and evacuees' behaviours [6, 7]. Our aim focuses on citizens' evacuation, especially modelling pedestrians' behaviours after an earthquake. Data used to build behavioural rules can come from different sources, e.g. video recordings [8]. In our case, for both models we use survey data.

The choice of the scale is also crucial. Whereas many models focus on a small geographic area, such as the evacuation of a building [9], our model covers a larger area, like the district of Sioufi, in Beirut, Lebanon, or the medium-size city of Mendoza, Argentina. In addition we model a larger number of people, up to one thousand. Moreover, we used Geographic Information Systems (GIS) to represent environmental aspects such as the road network, buildings and green spaces.

1.3   Methodology

A first model (called AMEL for "agent-based modelling for earthquake in Lebanon") was developed in the framework of a multidisciplinary project, LIBRIS. The methodology used for AMEL [10] was first described in 1999 [11, 12] and has been used for designing and developing agent-based simulators in several works over the years, for example in [3, 13, 14]. It consists of the following steps:

1. Field studies: this first step covers performing detailed field studies of the real situation in order to assess the human behaviours and their underlying motivations. Behaviours were collected through a survey to assess the social vulnerability of the Beirut population in two districts [15].
2. Model design: this step consists in designing the formal model (for example using UML) of what has been obtained from the analysis of field studies data. In particular it involves defining the environment, conceptualising the agents and behaviours rules.

3. Development: this step corresponds to the computer implementation. Here we use GAMA, an open-source platform [16], which provides high-level primitives and powerful features to integrate spatial data from GIS.
4. Validation and calibration: validation is a central step of our methodology and is strongly dependant on the data provided by field studies. Iteration plays a major role in refining the model.
5. Simulation: this final step covers the definition of scenarios, sensitivity analysis, simulation and experimentation.

2   The AMEL Model

2.1   Description of the Model

The model was created to simulate the movement of pedestrians after an earthquake in the Sioufi district, Beirut, Lebanon. The model consists of six entities: Quake, Street, Building, Green_space, Obstacle and Human. The interactions among them are described in the paragraphs below and illustrated in figure 1.

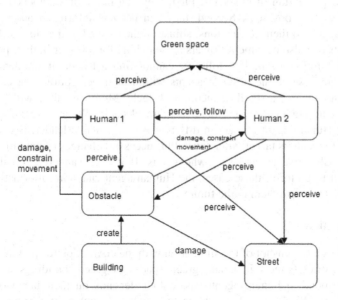

Fig. 1. Interactions among agents in the AMEL model

The Quake agent represents the earthquake, in particular its intensity and the time it happens. Currently, the quake agent has no interaction with others agents.

The Street, Building and Green_space agents represent elements of the infrastructure of the district (streets, buildings and green spaces). Street agents are represented by a weighted graph: each street is an edge and each intersection is a vertex. An additional weight is applied to the street if it is blocked by damage. The graph is used to define each human agent's knowledge (beliefs) of the street network.

Obstacle agents represent the obstacles induced by the earthquake, particularly by the damaged buildings. Based on the damage level of buildings, we can group obstacles into three levels: large, medium and small. For example, buildings completely collapsed cause large obstacles, buildings badly damaged with much falling debris cause medium obstacles, and buildings with some debris cause small obstacles. Obstacle agents have two behaviours: street damage and human damage. First, all streets that are covered by the large obstacles are blocked: no one can pass through these streets. Second, the large obstacles destroy people in those zones. In the zone of medium and small obstacles, people are exposed to the danger: this means that agents in the danger zone have a high risk of being injured. Medium obstacles can slow down the movement of agents in their zones.

The most important agents are Human agents. They represent the people in the Sioufi district. They have three groups of behaviours: movement, imitation (leader - follower) and perception of obstacles. First, they can move on unblocked streets or stay at their current positions. Second, they can become informal leaders who can guide other agents to their destinations, adjusting their speed to the slowest follower. Human agents can also become followers by searching for a leader in their perception zone and then following it. If a follower cannot find a leader, it wanders around. Third, they can observe the obstacle agents within their perception zones. They are exposed in the zone of a small or medium obstacle. Moreover, they will be slowed down when entering in the zone of a medium obstacle. When perceiving a large obstacle, the Human agent can act in different ways. If it is a leader, it will choose another way to reach its target; after several unsuccessful changes of path to its target, it will eventually give up and stay where it is. If it is a wanderer, it will choose another target to go to. In these cases, the Human agent can store information about blocked streets to avoid them in the future.

2.2   Simulation

Figure 2 shows a screenshot of the simulation with the GAMA platform. On the left is shown the district (streets in black, green spaces in green, buildings in yellow). Circles correspond to human agents, the colour depends on their behaviours. The outputs can also be displayed on charts to show the number of victims, exposed people, leaders and followers, and total exposure time. On the right, the user can set up different parameters: distribution of human agents, distribution of their behaviours, and some global parameters. The scenarios are defined in terms of these parameters (Table 1).

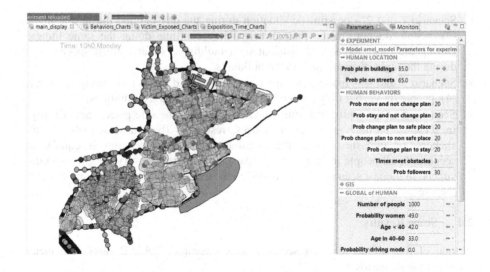

Fig. 2. Screenshot of the simulator

Table 1. Parameter values used to define nine simulation scenarios

Scenario	0	1	2	3	4	5	6	7	8
Prob. people in buildings	100	35	100	35	100	35	35	35	35
Prob. people in street	0	65	0	65	0	65	65	65	65
Prob move and not change plan	12	65	65	0	0	0	0	0	0
Prob stay and not change plan	57	35	35	0	0	0	0	0	0
Prob change plan to safe place	2	0	0	0	0	100	100	100	100
Prob change plan to not safe place	9	0	0	100	100	0	0	0	0
Prob change plan to stay	20	0	0	0	0	0	0	0	0
Nb of people	1000	1000	1000	1000	1000	1000	1000	1000	1000
Prob women	49	49	49	49	49	49	49	49	49
Age <40	42	42	42	42	42	42	42	42	42
Age 40-60	33	33	33	33	33	33	33	33	33
Prob follower	0	30	30	30	30	0	0	0	0

2.3   Simulation Scenarios

The following scenarios are created based on changing the parameter values for human behaviours and human location (Table 1). Each scenario is characterized by different parameter values and represents different situations: the survey results, pessimistic situation (representing 'bad' behaviours in the sense of not following the security advice), and optimistic situation (representing 'good' behaviours where people follow the security advice). The scenarios are designed to show if different behaviours will change evacuation efficiency and human exposure.

- Scenario 0 – reproduction of the survey: parameter values are taken from the survey and advised by experts.

- Scenario 1 and 2 – pessimistic situation during the day (1) and during the night (2): people do not change their activity, they continue doing the same things. During the day, people are distributed in buildings, streets, green spaces, etc; during the night, they are only in the buildings.
- Scenario 3 and 4 – Inadequate situation during the day (3) and during the night (4): people move, but they go to unsafe places (e.g. damaged buildings).
- Scenario 5 to 8 – Optimistic situations: People go to the safe places. Specifically, in scenario 5, they go to green spaces, resources (hospitals, schools, rescue shelters) or into the streets (the distribution between locations is equal). In scenario 6, all people go to the green space. In scenario 7, everyone goes into the streets. In the last scenario, they go to the resources that are truly safe and not into the streets.

2.4   Some Results

A total of five simulations per scenario were executed. Table 2 shows the mean results of the scenarios.

Table 2. Mean results

Scenario	0	1	2	3	4	5	6	7	8
% of victims	23	12	25	14	23	10	9	9	9
% of exposed people	72	59	61	67	59	22	12	38	16
% of people who go out the district	1	0	0	0	0	11	0	24	11
% of people in the safe places in the district	4	28	14	19	18	57	79	29	64

From the scenario results, the evacuation time is between 37 and 50 minutes. A detailed list of evacuation times is shown in Table 3.

Table 3. Evacuation time (in seconds) of five simulations (1-5) and mean evacuation time (in seconds and in minutes) for nine scenarios (0-8)

Scenario	0	1	2	3	4	5	6	7	8
1st simulation (seconds)	2352	3003	2455	2810	2915	2565	2258	2666	2823
2nd simulation (seconds)	2518	2452	2586	2947	2599	2534	2421	3039	2724
3rd simulation (seconds)	2533	2374	2535	2537	1988	2670	1988	3818	3440
4th simulation (seconds)	2329	3020	2543	2673	2763	2802	2192	2679	2612
5th simulation (seconds)	2656	2723	2456	3172	2767	2635	2206	2680	2637
Mean (seconds)	2478	2714	2515	2828	2606	2641	2213	2976	2847
Mean (minutes)	41	45	42	47	43	44	37	50	47

As we can see in table 2, the number of victims in scenarios 0, 2 and 4 are higher than in others (23 – 25%). The reason is that in these scenarios, all people are in the buildings at the moment of the earthquake; there are more people in badly damaged buildings, so the casualty rate is higher. The number of exposed people in the scenarios from 0 to 4 is also high (59 – 72%) because of many reasons. First, more than half the people do not move (scenario 0), instead they stay where they are. In the district with such damaged buildings, it is clear that the number of exposed people is very high. Second, even if they move, most people do not change their activities but continue to move toward their initial destinations (which can be damaged) (scenario 1 and 2) or move to unsafe places (scenario 3 and 4). In these scenarios, we can see many people who are exposed for a long time (top of Figure 3).

Contrary to the previous scenarios, the number of victims and exposed people in the scenarios from 5 to 8 is lower (percentage of victims: 9 – 10%, percentage of exposed people: 12 – 38%) because people go to the safe places. Moreover, there are more people who are exposed for a short time (bottom of figure 3). In addition, by comparing the mean results of optimistic scenarios, scenario 7 (people go into the streets) results in quite high rate of exposed people (38%) because there are lots of damaged streets. So the idea that the streets are usually considered as safe places must be reassessed: the Lorca earthquake that occurred in 2011 in Spain demonstrated the falsity of this idea, as all 9 victims were killed by the fall of non-structural elements while being in the street [17].

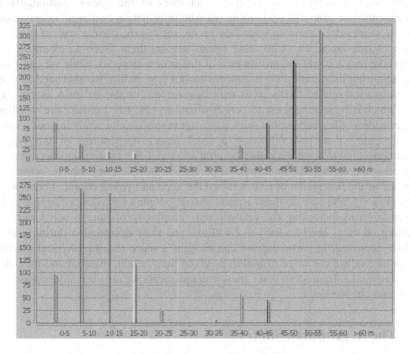

Fig. 3. Top: Exposition_Time_Chart of scenario 3, Bottom: Exposition_Time_Chart of scenario 5. The horizontal axis shows time slot periods and the vertical axis shows the number of exposed people in a corresponding time period. The values of parameters used for these two scenarios are represented in the table 1.

In summary, the location of people during the earthquake affects the number of victims. To reduce death or injury, people should adopt mobility behaviours like changing their initial activities to go to real safe places such as green spaces, schools or rescue centres. The behaviour that people go into the streets is insufficient, as is shown by the relatively high rate of exposed people (38%) in the scenario 7.

2.5   Model Enhancement

We have developed the AMEL prototype that shows pedestrians' movements following different human behaviours after an earthquake. Using GAMA, we were able to incorporate the real map of the neighbourhood in Beirut, including current streets and actual buildings. Furthermore, agents can perceive objects (obstacles, building, other agents) and, as in real life, they only have a limited knowledge of the current state of the road network.

Despite some promising first results, there are several improvements that we can make to the model that will be applied to Mendoza. The first one concerns geographic aspects: for the model to be applicable to other towns and cities, we need to collect spatial data and data on building types (e.g. year of construction, material, number of storeys, etc.) that are specific to the area under consideration, in this case Mendoza. In addition, we can improve the existing behaviours of the agents, particularly the human agents. For example, concerning realistic information exchange, agents should be able to share information on what they know, such as the current state of the roads, location of safe areas, etc. with other agents around them. Such an extension may need to take into account the provenance of the information. So, while we can model agents acquiring information via traditional modes (e.g. radio), we also need to model how information related to the crisis may be received 'on the go' such as via social media, which is increasingly used in crisis situations [18, 19]. Furthermore we should consider adding other behaviours, such as an agent specifically searching out a family member, rather than just following a local leader. Depending on the type of information collected, we may also be able to model the relationship between age, sex, profession, earthquake intensity and perception of risk. For example, what is the difference in the perception of risk between the aged and young people, between men and women, etc. and how do these aspects change people's behaviours during a crisis.

In addition to increasing the realism and complexity of human behaviours, our modelling of static objects, such as buildings and their degradation during a crisis, could be improved. In particular, we can imagine a more realistic physical model of the ground damage coverage of buildings given their height, material and magnitude of the earthquake. In order to make these enhancements we are currently conducting a further study in Mendoza.

3   The Argentinian Survey

3.1   The VUSIM Project

VUSIM stands for *Vulnerabilité aux séismes de Mendoza* (Vulnerability to earthquakes of the city of Mendoza). The project aims at evaluating the territorial vulnerability of the city of Mendoza, Argentina and is divided into 6 tasks: 1) synthesis of risk management procedures; 2) evaluation of social vulnerability, including behaviours adopted in past seismic events; 3) evaluation of physical vulnerability of "critical buildings" (resources in the case of a crisis); 4) evaluation of territorial vulnerability of the city; 5) transfer of the results to civil society ; 6) agent-based modelling of crisis mobility following an earthquake.

The study takes place in the city of Mendoza (the 'Mendoza Capital' department), standing at the foot of the Andes (33°S latitude), and in an area where floods are common. According to the last census in 2010, the city itself has a population of around 115,000 inhabitants [20], with the outer urban area approaching 1,000,000 inhabitants (more than 930,000 in 2010). The area is divided into six sections. The Mendoza Province, as well as the San Juan Province, has the highest level of seismic activity in Argentina. Mendoza was completely destroyed by a strong earthquake in 1861 (Io=IX, 6,000 fatalities, [21]. This event had important consequences for land planning, as the original centre (where a museum stands today as a reminder of the origins of the city) was moved in 1861, 1 km to the north-west, in a process to rebuild the "New City". On the eastern part of the city is the San Martin Park, almost 400 ha., which is an important place for Mendoza's inhabitants, not only for leisure but also because of its safety aspect in the case of an earthquake. The city also has one large (Plaza Independencia) square, surrounded by four smaller ones (Chile, San Martin, Italia and España), all of which represent important open spaces.

Regarding seismicity, the last strong earthquake occurred in 1985 (Io=VIII). The 2010 Chilean earthquake was also well felt in Mendoza but no damage was observed. This means that all people under 35 have not yet experienced a strong earthquake. Finally, concerning prevention, the population is regularly informed about the safety measures to follow. Although posters with safety measures in the case of a fire or an earthquake hang inside every public building they are sometimes hard to understand, assimilate and apply). Schoolchildren also have evacuation exercises several times a year. These different elements may influence the population's knowledge of seismic hazard, risk perception and behaviour adoption.

3.2   The Survey

The sampling method is non-probabilistic and stratified. This method was chosen to ensure representativeness of the random sample, provided by the statistical laws of probability. It consists first in defining the strata (sections in our case), then in identifying the distribution of significant criteria in the reference population (here, age and gender) and finally in applying this distribution to each strata. 70 persons were surveyed in each section.

After a pre-survey with 17 people, the initial questionnaire was modified and the survey was carried out in the Department of Mendoza Capital for 15 days (April 8-23, 2014). The context of the investigation is specific and may have influenced some answers as on April 1st a major earthquake occurred in Chile, as well as in Mexico on April 18th. The survey was conducted by 14 geography students. One section was assigned to each group of 2 or 3. They interviewed people at different times of the day, any day of the week. A survey lasted between 15 minutes and 1 hour for the longest.

The questionnaire was based on former studies aiming at developing a methodology for social vulnerability assessment [15, 22, 23, 24]. Six themes were explored through closed questions, pick lists, and semi-open questions: 1) questions about risk perception allowed us to prioritize people's concerns and assess their knowledge of seismic risk; 2) people's knowledge of safety measures was also explored; 3) former experience of earthquakes allowed us to identify crisis actions and mobility; 4) individual protection against earthquakes, perception of building resistance and individual involvement in one's own protection were also examined; 5) the characteristics of information awareness were identified; 6)socio-demographic characteristics finally allowed us to profile the interviewed person.

In this questionnaire, questions on behaviours are essential and contribute to the vulnerability assessment as well as crisis mobility in the case of an earthquake. Thus, we were interested in gathering operative terms: what are the behaviours and movements adopted during and after the earthquake? What are the places preferentially reached after the earthquake? What are the modes of transport used (foot, car, bicycle, other)? Who are the persons met directly after the earthquake (level of family or social closeness)? These elements were explored through questions and a mental map.

The mental map was associated to the questionnaire. It aimed at collecting the spatial representations of the respondent (Fig. 4). The mental map is here understood as the representation of a real-life space, specific to each person [25]. It allowed: on one hand to display the mobility of the people following an earthquake and to identify the sequences of their movement; and on the other hand, to materialise the perception of zones with highest and lowest vulnerability. A map of the city was shown to each respondent who was then asked to draw his path and circle areas.

Here we present some first results of the survey. 88% of the interviewed people have experienced an earthquake. The different types of behaviours are shown in table 3. It is interesting to observe that almost half of the surveyed persons left their building after the earthquake. However, most of them did not move further than the patio or the street and stayed in front of the building.

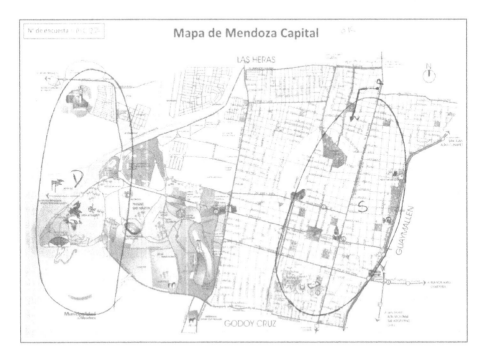

Fig. 4. Example of a mental map. S: safe zone; D: damaged zone; P: departure; L: arrival.

Among those who have already experienced an earthquake, only 13% moved following the earthquake, specifically due to the event (others continued what they were doing). Most of them (42%) used the 1985 earthquake to show how they behaved. Over time, and due to the nature of the event, many people forget what they did and only a few of the surveyed people (around 30) could draw the trajectory they took on the map. As observed in the Lebanese survey, most people tried first to reach family members.

Table 4. Behaviours adopted following an earthquake by the interviewed people of Mendoza (sum greater than 100% because several responses were allowed)

Category of behaviour	%
Continued what he/she was doing	29.4
Escaped from the building	49.2
Took information (radio, telephone)	12.0
Did not move but applied some safety measures (cut gas and electricity, evaluated damages, etc.)	9.5
Other	10.3

3.3   Model Methodology: From Two Case Studies to One Generic Model

The VUSIM model is a further step to achieve a generic model. The AMEL model will be first applied to the Mendoza context, using the same methodology (see section 1.3) and taking into account particularities of the Argentinian context. The final aim is to attain a generic model. The methodology is as follows:

1. Field studies in Mendoza: gathering data on behaviours through a survey, as well as collecting geographical data. This first step will also categorise the different behaviours, by validating the behaviours identified in the Lebanese case and, if necessary, expanding their variety.
2. Model design: based on the model designed for the Lebanese context, the VUSIM model will also aim at improving it. Most changes in the model rules will depend on the survey results. The environment definition, especially regarding building attributes, will depend on the geographic and geophysical (physical vulnerability) data available.
3. Development: the model will be implemented on the GAMA platform. Special attention will be given in trying to reduce the simulation time as much as possible by program optimisation and especially reducing the initialising step.
4. Calibration and validation: the validation step will be achieved progressively, each time that the model is expanded.
5. Simulation: the simulation will be based on scenarios designed with the help of local stakeholders and/or Argentinian colleagues, in order to take into account local particularities and needs regarding risk prevention.
6. Both AMEL and VUSIM models will be compared in order to derive any generic aspects that could be transposed to any other geographic and cultural context. This will lead to the development of a generic model.

The gathering of behavioural data through the survey was carried out in May 2014. The other steps are on-going.

4   Conclusion

We presented a methodology to develop a generic multi-agent model based on two case studies. The model aims at reproducing crisis mobility following an earthquake. The paper aimed to present how lessons from one case study can help enhancing another one, and how both case studies may allow developing a generic model (ongoing work). Reproducing a real situation (survey results) as well as scenarios, the first model applied to one district of Beirut (AMEL model) and developed with the GAMA platform showed that applying safety measures helps decreasing fatalities and exposure to danger. However, the Lebanese case study revealed some possible improvements, especially regarding the interactions between agents, and the modelling of exposure due to damaged buildings. Taking into account these weaknesses, the same methodology will be used to develop a model adapted to the city of Mendoza, Argentina, where gathering social data via a survey has just been completed. The behavioural rules of human agents will be built according to the results of a risk perception survey whose first results show that the distribution of mobility behaviours are very different from the Lebanese study. These two studies represent two major steps in the process of developing a generic model that could be applied to any other geographical context. Finally, this collaboration between geographers, psychologists, and computer scientists highlights how interdisciplinary work is effective and satisfactory in the field of social modelling.

Acknowledgments. The study was made possible thanks to the financial support of the Agence Nationale pour la Recherche (LIBRIS project) for the AMEL model as well as the Université Joseph Fourier, the Institut National Polytechnique de Grenoble (AGIR) and the Centre National de la Recherche Scientifique (PEPS) for the VUSIM project. Julie Dugdale would also like to acknowledge the support of the University of Agder, Norway, to which she is associated. The authors would like to thank Jocelyne Gerard and her colleagues of the *Département de Géographie (Université Saint Joseph*, Beirut, Lebanon) as well as Carine Azam for their support in achieving the LIBRIS survey. Alejandrina Videla and Silvia Quiroga, from the *Centro de Estrategias Territoriales para el Mercosur (Universidad Nacional de Cuyo*, Mendoza, Argentina), Tangui Trémel (Université de Montpellier) and the students of the Geography Department (*Facultad de Filosofía y Letras, Univ. Nacional de Cuyo*) who participated to the VUSIM survey are also acknowledged.

References

1. Juster-Lermitte, S., Beck, E., Bouchon, B., Fournely, F., Juraszek, N., Jomard, H., Lamadon, T., Lavore, V., Poursoulis, G., Rey, J., Sarant, P.-M., Seyedi, D.: Le séisme de L'Aquila (Italie) du 6 avril 2009, AFPS mission report (2009)
2. Skinner, C., Ramchurn, S.: The RoboCup Rescue Simulation platform. In: Proceedings of the 9th International Conference on Autonomous Agents and Multiagent Systems, Toronto, Canada, pp. 1647–1648 (2010)
3. Bellamine-Ben Saoud, N., Ben Mena, T., Dugdale, J., Pavard, B., Ben Ahmed, M.: Assessing large scale emergency rescue plans: an agent based approach. International Journal of Intelligent Control and Systems 11(4), 260–271 (2006)

4. Shiwakoti, N., Sarvi, M., Rose, G.: Modelling pedestrian behaviour under emergency conditions – State-of-the-art and future directions. In: 31th Australasian Transport Research Forum, pp. 457–473 (2008)
5. Anh, N.T.N., Daniel, Z.J., Du, N.H., Drogoul, A., An, V.D.: A hybrid macro-micro pedestrians evacuation model to speed up simulation in road networks. In: Dechesne, F., Hattori, H., ter Mors, A., Such, J.M., Weyns, D., Dignum, F. (eds.) AAMAS 2011 Workshops. LNCS, vol. 7068, pp. 371–383. Springer, Heidelberg (2012)
6. Hawe, G.I., Wilson, D.T., Coates, G., Crouch, R.S.: Stormi: An agent-based simulation environment for evaluating responses to major incidents in the UK. In: 9th International ISCRAM Conference - Vancouver, Canada, (2012)
7. Tsai, J., Fridman, N., Bowring, E., Brown, M., Epstein, S., Kaminka, G., Marsella, S.C., Ogden, A., Rika, I., Sheel, A., Taylor, M., Wang, X., Zilka, A., Tambe, M.: ESCAPES - evacuation simulation with children, authorities, parents, emotions, and social comparison. In: International Conference on Autonomous Agents and Multiagent Systems, AAMAS (2011)
8. D'Orazio, M., Spalazzi, L., Quagliarini, E., Bernardini, G.: Agent-based model for earthquake pedestrians' evacuation in urban outdoor scenarios: Behavioural patterns definition and evacuation paths choice. Safety Science 62, 450–465 (2014)
9. Liu, Z., Jalalpour, M., Jacques, C., Szyniszewski, S., Mitrani-Reiser, J., Guest, J., Igusa, T., Schafer, B.W.: Interfacing building response with human behavior under seismic events. In: Proceedings of 15th World Conference on Earthquake Engineering, Lisbon, 10 p. (2012)
10. Truong, H.V., Beck, E., Dugdale, J., Adam, C.: Developing a model of evacuation after an earthquake in Lebanon. In: Proceedings of ISCRAM (Information Systems for Crisis Response and Management) Vietnam Conference, Hanoi, Vietnam, October 30-November 1, 8 p. (2013)
11. Dugdale, J., Pavard, B., Soubie, J.L.: Design Issues in the Simulation of an Emergency Call Centre. In: Proceedings of the 13th European Simulation Multiconference (ESM 1999), Warsaw, Poland, June 1-4 (1999)
12. Dugdale, J., Bellamine-Ben Saoud, N., Pavard, B., Pallamin, N.: Simulation and Emergency Management. In: Van de Walle, B., Turoff, M., Hiltz, R.H. (eds.) Information Systems for Emergency Management. Advances in Management Information Systems. Sharp (2010)
13. Kashif, A., Binh Le, X., Dugdale, J., Ploix, S.: Agent based framework to simulate inhabitants' behaviour in domestic settings for energy management. In: Proceedings of International Conference on Agents and Artificial Intelligence (ICAART), Rome, Italy (2011)
14. Kashif, A., Ploix, S., Dugdale, J., Binh Le, X.H.: Simulating the dynamics of occupant behaviour for power management in residential buildings. Energy and Buildings 56, 85–93 (2013)
15. Beck, E., Colbeau-Justin, L., Cartier, S., Saikali, M.: Comportements de mobilité en cas de crise sismique à Beyrouth (Liban). In: 8e Colloque de l'Association Française de Génie Parasismique, Ecole des Ponts Paris Tech, September 6-8, 10 p. CD-Rom Proceedings (2011)
16. Grignard., A., Taillandier, P., Gaudou, B., Huynh, N.Q., Vo, D.-A., Drogoul, A.: GAMA v. 1.6: Advancing the art of complex agent-based modeling and simulation, PRIMA (2013)
17. Bertran Rojo, M., Lutoff, C., Beck, E., Schoeneich, P. : L'étude de la vulnérabilité sociale face aux séismes, revisitée par le prisme des mobilités, XIe Rencontres ThéoQuant, Besançon, février 20-22 (2013)

18. Wendling, C., Radisch, J., Jacobzone, S.: The Use of Social Media in Risk and Crisis Communication. In: OECD Working Papers on Public Governance, vol. 25. OECD Publishing (2013)

19. Vieweg, S., Hughes, A.L., Starbird, K.: Palen. L.: Microblogging During Two Natural Hazards Events: What Twitter Contribute to Situational Awareness. In: Proceedings of the ACM Conference on Computer Human Interaction (CHI) (2010)

20. INDEC, Instituto Nacional de Estadística y Censo, Censo, Argentina (2010), http://www.censo2010.indec.gov.ar (last consulted on May 13, 2014)

21. INPRES, Instituto Nacional de Prevención Sísmica, Terremotos Históricos, http://www.inpres.gov.ar/ (last consulted on May 13, 2014)

22. Beck, E., André-Poyaud, I., Lutoff, C., Chardonnel, S., Davoine, P.-A.: Risk perception and social vulnerability to earthquakes in Grenoble (French Alps). Journal of Risk Research 15(10), 1245–1260 (2012)

23. De Vanssay, B., Colbeau-Justin, L.: Social aspects of tsunami risk: institutional and social surveys. SCHEMA Project n°0300963. PCRD 6 (2010)

24. Ipsos Antilles (polling company): Étude Réplik et Séisme du 29 November 2007. Technical report (2008)

25. Lynch, K.: The Image of the City, Cambridge (Mass.). The MIT Press (1960)

Supporting Debriefing with Sensor Data:
A Reflective Approach to Crisis Training

Simone Mora and Monica Divitini

Dept. of Information and Computer Science,
NTNU, Trondheim, Norway
{Simone.Mora,Monica.Divitini}@idi.ntnu.no

Abstract. In this paper we present our exploration into the use of sensor data to promote debriefing after training events simulating work experiences. In this way we address one of the core challenges of crisis training, namely the difficulty to exploit the full potential of training events, e.g. during drills. The paper is theoretically grounded in the theory of reflective learning. The theoretical understanding is used for informing the design of WATCHiT, a wearable device for collecting sensor data during an event, and two applications for promoting debriefing in two different scenarios, CroMAR and Procedure Trainer. CroMAR supports disaster managers during in-situ debriefing after large events, while Procedure Trainer supports a team in reflecting after the simulation of a medical emergency procedure. The evaluation of the two applications shows that sensor data can be successfully used to support debriefing in both scenarios. Based on our experience, we draw lessons learned for the design of systems supporting debriefing in training events.

Keywords: Training, Reflective Learning, Sensor Data, Wearable Computing, Experience-based Learning, Emergency Drill.

1   Introduction

Training for crisis preparedness is challenging because of the complexity of work to be performed, but also for its sporadic and discontinuous nature that makes it difficult to assure that practitioners gain sufficient experience. To compensate for the lack of real experience, drills and field tests recreating realistic crisis experiences are often organized. Drills and field tests are complex activities that promote training of different skills for individual workers, as well as an occasion for organizations to test protocols and their capability to apply them. Though learning from (simulated) experience is recognized as critical, it is expensive and it is important to optimize its impact. To this aim, after simulated events, like for real ones, a debriefing session takes place to understand the critical aspects linked to the intervention. Debriefing sessions might significantly vary in terms of level of detail and people involved. For example, debriefings might be conducted separately by each involved unit or together, if the focus is on coordination. Workers at all levels might be involved, while in other cases only top management is involved to reflect on high-level organizational issues.

C. Hanachi, F. Bénaben, and F. Charoy (Eds.): ISCRAM-med 2014, LNBIP 196, pp. 71–84, 2014.
© Springer International Publishing Switzerland 2014

Effective debriefing are made difficult by the highly distributed nature of crisis work, the co-existence of different partial perspectives on the unfolding of an event, and the lack of data that can complement human memories of the event.

In this paper we investigate how to support debriefing with sensor data collected in the field during training events[1]. Information about the environment and workers is already recognized as critical in crisis response, including e.g. location of workers, number of rescued people, environmental data (temperature, humidity, air quality). Information from (real and simulated) crisis scenes is useful to provide support for decision-making processes along the command chain [1], to support cooperation in the field [2, 3], and to prepare realistic scenarios to be used in training exercises [4]. In our work we focus on information that can be used in debriefing and that can be collected by workers in the rescue field. Collecting information during crisis work is demanding for workers and prone to error. Often collected information gets biased or distorted by factors like attention, impossibility to use tools while doing a rescue activity (e.g. carrying someone on a stretcher). Errors affect both the ability to react timely to events and, critical for our research, the completeness and correctness of logs to be used during debriefing. We therefore focus on the use of sensors worn by field workers to collect data. In this paper we present a device for collecting data, WATCHiT, and two applications used to visualize the collected data supporting two types of debriefing sessions, CroMAR and Procedure Trainer (hereafter Trainer).

The three prototypes are informed by state of the art knowledge on reflective learning and have been developed through a user-centred iterative approach, thanks to the cooperation with an Italian organization for crisis management and preparedness.

The paper is organized as follows. In Chapter 2 we present our theoretical approach. In Chapter 3 we present two scenarios of debriefing and compare similarities and differences. In Chapter 4 we present our approach to data collection in the field through WATCHiT. We then briefly present CroMAR (Ch. 5) and Trainer (Ch. 6). Since the focus is on the overall approach rather than the individual applications, functionalities and evaluation are not described in details. In Chapter 7 we discuss our experience with development and evaluation in order to draw lessons learned about the use of sensor data in crisis training to support debriefing.

2   Theoretical Underpinning

Debriefing is a form of reflection as outlined by Boud et al. [5]. During debriefing, a re-evaluation of experience takes place, with explicit attention to emotions as well as ideas and behaviour. Reflecting on action is critical to learn from past experiences and performing better in the future [5, 6]. Different tools have been developed to support reflection, as an individual or collaborative activity. Generally, these tools provide access to information about past events. This information is important to support reflection not only to complement human memory, but also to allow bringing in multiple perspectives on collaborative processes [7].

---

[1] In the paper, when referring to *events*, unless differently specified, we refer to training events with a high degree of realism and aiming at promoting learning by providing the involved workers with a realistic work experience, like for example in drills and crisis simulations.

The CSRL (Computer Supported Reflective Learning) model identifies fours stages of reflection [8]: *do work*; *initiate reflection session*; *conduct reflection session*; and *apply reflection outcomes*. For each stage, the model specifies relevant sub-steps. For example, *initiate reflection session* includes *decide to reflect* and *frame the reflection session*. The model explains reflective learning as a cycle involving these fours stages. In our domain, a debriefing can be seen as a reflection session on crisis work. For each stage, the CSRL model identifies support that can be provided through technology. For example, in the *do work* phase, technology can be used to monitor work and collect data useful for reflection; in *initiate reflection session* technology to set the objectives for reflection or involve others in the session; in *conduct reflection session* to share work experiences with others; and in *apply reflection outcomes* to decide how the change to work will be implemented. It should be noted that one reflection cycle could also trigger new reflection cycles, for example, when a reflection session identifies as outcome the need to reflect on a specific aspect of work, e.g. how a crisis procedure is applied, with someone at a higher organizational level. In this way, we can look at reflection as a storyline that might involve different actors within the organization [9]. The CSRL model worked as theoretical underpinning for the development of the applications presented in this paper, providing a language guiding our understanding of reflection and requirements for supporting technology.

3   Different Forms of Debriefing

In this chapter we present two scenarios that illustrate the work context for which our applications are designed. The scenarios are based on observational studies conducted by the authors during real and training events in Italy. So, they are realistic, though they do not refer to a specific instance of work.

3.1   Scenario of Use 1

Scenario - A large organization is coordinating a training event simulating a flood over a large area. During the crisis a large number of workers is deployed. People work alone, but more often are grouped in teams and work under the supervision of a coordinator. Different hierarchical levels are identifiable. Workers participate with different roles, e.g. the emergency management team coordinates action; medical units take care of injured; police assures security in the area; Civil Protection prepares sheltering for the population. The simulation lasts from dusk to dawn.

Analysis - Though clear protocols are identified for recurrent situations, each event is unique, requiring adaptation and quick decision-making capabilities. It is therefore important to reflect on an event to learn from it, at the individual, team, and organizational level. Given the highly distributed nature of the work, it is impossible for any of the involved person to get a complete overview of the unfolding of the event, that it involves multiple, sometimes contradicting perspectives.

Supporting Reflection - In this situation, coordinators, who tend to have an overview perspective on the event, might benefit from the detailed and local information of workers in the field, providing different perspectives on how the event has unfolded in a certain area or for a certain team. After the event, we therefore envision enriching the current practices of debriefing by introducing a mobile (tablet-based) augmented reality viewer showing information collected during the event. Reflection is expected to happen at the same physical location of the event. Mobile augmented reality can help to access spatial information that might be relevant to re-think the event. For example, comparing a photo of a square during an event with the real space under normal conditions might help to reconsider actions that have been taken and to identify, e.g. alternative escape routes.

3.2   Scenario of Use 2

Scenario - A small organization of paramedics is providing ambulance services. Their work is performed on a voluntary basis and the management strives for finding the time and resources for the continuous training that is necessary to assure that core procedures are applied correctly and timely. An important procedure is the one for rescuing a traumatized injured, for example after a car accident. The procedure includes a list of actions to load and fasten the patient on a stretcher and get ready for ambulance transportation. Workers need continuous training to be sure they can apply their knowledge correctly. To this aim, the procedure is performed in a classroom by a team of three on a dummy or a real person, trying to recreate a realistic situation. After the procedure is completed, most of the teams are running away because they have to go back to their regular work.

Analysis - Correct implementation of work procedures is a critical factor, with impact on the number of casualties in a crisis. Practitioners don't just need to learn the correct sequence of steps to be taken, but also to perform them as quickly as possible and without making mistakes. The degree of collaboration within a team, their mutual understating and ability to self-asses mistakes during the action (i.e. a procedural step skipped or non correctly implemented) are critical.

Supporting Reflection - Teams can benefit from reflecting on their performance, e.g. their knowledge of procedural steps and their coordination. They might also benefit from benchmarking their performance against others. Sensors could help in this context by collecting time and perceived number of errors. In this setting we envision a lightweight mobile application that promotes reflection using the data captured during the execution of the procedure. Since the availability of voluntary workers is limited, the application must be designed to promote a quick and simple reflection session to be performed right after the completion of the procedure.

3.3   Comparing the Two Scenarios

The two scenarios have been chosen because they represent very different situations. They therefore support us in the exploration of the use of sensor data for fulfilling different needs. Although both scenarios need data to feed the reflection process they pose different requirements for the technology. In scenario 1 the envisioned reflection support is targeting people with an overall perspective of the event, while in Scenario 2 the users are the team members. For Scenario 1 the geographical element (location of operations, environmental data) and integration of multiple data sources is critical, while in Scenario 2 time is the central factor.

The two scenarios also differ in terms of type of data to be captured and user intervention in data acquisition.

The data that is needed in Scenario 1 depends on the specific event. For example, capturing GPS location of teams during work is valuable in highly distributed operations; temperature and noise might be relevant when an event takes place in harsh environments, and so on. The range of datatypes needed in Scenario 2 is more static, being not dependent on the environment.

Data collection is challenging in both cases. In both scenarios it is difficult to collect data by instrumenting the environment. Training events often take place in rural areas that, differently from cities, aren't already equipped with technology to capture the event (e.g. CCTV cameras, sensor stations). Wearable computers, by turning workers themselves into sensors, can provide data about an event.

Also, the traditional automatic sensor approach is not the best option. In fact, in Scenario 2, recording completion time and number of errors using automatic capturing methods is not feasible since the data is connected to a qualitative process for real-time monitoring of own team's. In Scenario 1, though some data could be captured automatically, others might benefit from the intervention of workers making a conscious decision about relevance of certain information at a certain point in time and place. However, capturing data with the intervention of workers requires the user to interact with the capturing tool, whose design might be limited by the protocols themselves. For example touch screens are not a feasible approach when protocols require the workers to wear gloves or to not detract hands from the operations.

In the following section we present WATCHiT a prototype of wearable, sensor-enabled, computer that aims at addressing data capturing in a wide area of scenarios.

4   WATCHiT: Collecting Data from the Field

WATCHiT (Figure 1-a) is a wearable computer embedded in a wristband for non-disruptive sensor data capture during crisis work. Data captured include information from the individual (e.g. stress level or time-on-task) and from the environment (e.g. temperature, noise, location). Data is broadcasted in real-time over radio connections using open standards, allowing integration with third-party information systems; but it can also be stored in the device whereas a wireless networking is not feasible.

The main difference with respect to related sensor-based approaches is that with WATCHiT the users can customize the device using sensor modules; and the users have control over the collection by means of attention-free mnemonic body gestures implemented with RFID tokens (Figure 1-c, d).

Sensor modules enable for transient customization of the types of data capturable: the set of information WATCHiT captures is not defined a priori, but can be customized by plugging sensor modules on the technology-augmented wristband (Figure 2-b); before the deployment of the device for an event. In the current prototype we built modules for sensing location, time, air quality and to read RFID tokens.

A disruption-free user interface allows the user to be in control of the data collection process, it makes use of RFID tokens to be embedded in uniforms or tools (Figure 1-b). Tokens, acting as contactless buttons, are triggered when waved in close proximity to the WATCHiT wristband (Figure 1-c). They can be programmed to control the activation of specific sensors or to bookmark raw data with pre-defined information tags. For example a worker could tag GPS coordinates captured by the location sensor module with labels like *Injured rescued* or *High stress*. Another example, as depicted in Scenario 2, is the use of token as triggers for signaling completion time and report errors during rescue procedure training.

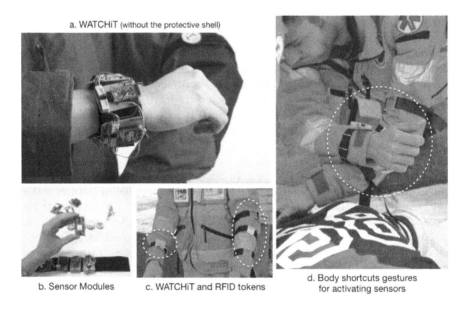

a. WATCHiT (without the protective shell)

b. Sensor Modules   c. WATCHiT and RFID tokens

d. Body shortcuts gestures for activating sensors

Fig. 1. WATCHiT Prototype

WATCHiT doesn't provide capability for displaying the information captured. It serves as a versatile, reconfigurable tool aiming to be as much as possible less intrusive for the wearer. It therefore only implements the first phase of the CSRL model (monitor work). In order to use the data acquired by WATCHiT during debriefings, hence fully implementing the CSLR model, data need to be accessed via applications able to provide tools for visualization and analysis.

Prototypes shown in Figure 1 have been built with the Arduino toolkit[2], Bluetooth 2.1 and RFID low-frequency technology. Protective hard-shell for the modules have been custom designed and 3D-printed.

In the following sections we describe two mobile applications that leverage data captured using WATCHiT to actively support debriefings in scenarios similar to the ones above presented.

5   CroMAR: Supporting in Situ Debriefing on Complex Events

5.1   System Description

CroMAR is an app for iPad that features mobile augmented reality browsing of information captured during a (real or simulated) crisis event [10]. Information is

---

[2] Arduino prototyping platform – http://arduino.cc

intended to support disaster managers in doing post-crisis debriefing, where the event unfolded. Our user studies revealed that often the efficacy of debriefings is impaired by data being reviewed in a context different from the rescue work scene, both for the physical environment (e.g. a meeting room vs. a city square) and for the lack of a holistic view of opinions from the different roles involved (disaster manager, rescue workers, but also citizens). Thanks to CroMAR, we can ground the reflection process in a physical context that helps making sense of the information and reflect on alternative paths of actions. Information displayed in CroMAR comes from multiple sources, including sensor data from WATCHiT, data stored in Response Management Information Systems and social networks (e.g. Twitter). Data captured by field agents during their work (broadcast radio, video feeds, sensor data) is visualized side by side with information crowd-sourced from the public (messages from social networks) and open data (e.g. weather information, maps) (Figure 2). This is intended to provide multiple points of views of the same event. CroMAR is modular and extendible; information sources can be added as plug-in built for specific data sources or organizational needs.

Fig. 2. Different contents and navigation modalities in CroMAR

CroMAR allows for navigating information along the space dimension, via augmented reality and map-based visualizations; and the time dimension via a timeline control. Moreover information is grouped in layers that can be selectively activated, overlapped and compared in real time, to customize the navigation experience. Since debriefings and reflection are collaborative activities, CroMAR allows synchronous collaboration via videoconferencing and asynchronous collaboration via a recommendations text editor and an email sharing of the set of information the user is looking at.

5.2   Evaluation

CroMAR was evaluated during a massive drill arranged by an Italian large emergency organization. Simulated crisis events lasted three days. Scenarios included flooding, earthquake and a massive car jam. Teams of field rescue workers were deployed to find and rescue figurants (made up with fake wounds) in a physical environment that resembled a real emergency (broken trees, debris, cars on fire).

During the events, data about stress levels of workers, their GPS locations, and information about activity was captured by two team leaders wearing WATCHiT, with the goal of supporting post-drill debriefings.

After the simulated events, CroMAR has been used by a senior disaster manager, hereafter quoted as "Mr.G", to conduct an on-site debriefing. The debriefing was observed by one of the authors. During the on-site debriefing Mr.G was able to recall events and decisions taken by the management during the drill. For example, the visualization of one data point triggered Mr.G to reflect on an issue he faced during the simulation: the control room had missed one of the figurants from their counting. This was caused by one agent misreporting the location of the figurant and the information got lost. Standing where CroMAR visualized a "high stress level" warning generated by one team leader (using WATCHiT), Mr.G was able to link the data point to the problem they had, connecting the source of the problem to a specific location and context of the worker (high stress level). This gave him new input to make sense of his experience (as a coordinator) thanks to input from the field. Even if the issue could not be completely clarified with CroMAR, the outcome of the session was a clearer reconstruction of (a problematic aspect of) the experience.

Unexpectedly Mr.G also walked with CroMAR towards spaces where no agent (and thus no data) was supposed to be found, hazardous areas, in order to use the absence of information as a proof that no one had been working in unauthorized areas.

6   Procedure Trainer: Supporting Debriefing on Short Medical Procedures

6.1   System Description

While CroMAR focuses on supporting reflection on organizational issues, Trainer uses sensor data to support reflection on the implementation of protocols (e.g. medical procedures) by workers in the field, immediately after the procedure has been performed. Trainer promotes a quick reflection session with easy triggers that can be done by the worker herself or collaboratively by a team. (A complete description of the application is available in [11]).

Trainer relies on WATCHiT to allow practitioners self-report completion time and errors for each procedure step. To capture those data WATCHiT is configured with three RFID tokens the practitioner can activate by proximity with the wristband to signal (i) the fulfillment of a step, (ii) report errors or (iii) register when a step has to be skipped due to a critical error (Figure 3-a, b).

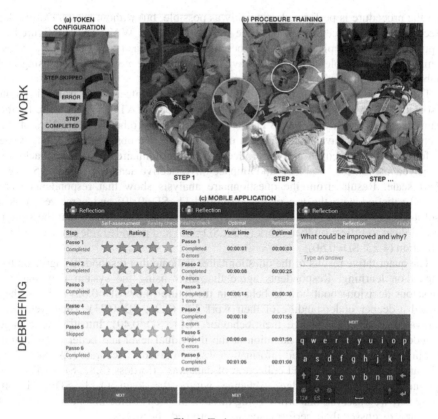

Fig. 3. Trainer app

The reflection session supported by the application is highly structured and users have to go through a set of quick steps that are designed to make people revisit their experience. The app aims at triggering reflection by highlighting possible divergences among the perceived performance (via self-evaluation) and the optimal time provided as best practice. After the procedure is completed, the application shows the time taken to complete each step and prompt the practitioner for rating her performance, then the intervals collected are compared with best practices, finally the user is asked to elaborate the outcome of the debriefing (Figure 3-c). The app also features an editor and database of procedures so the user can be trained on different protocols.

6.2   Evaluation

Trainer was evaluated by voluntary workers of different Italian associations participating in a common training event. During the trial, practitioners were asked to perform the "Soccorso Trauma" procedure: a 6-steps procedure to load the person who got injured on a spinal board and prepare her for ambulance transportation. A team of three members normally executes the procedure. One team member acts as leader and has the responsibility to overview the execution of the procedure and to keep the patient's head immobilized until the procedure is completed. It is important that the procedure is performed as quickly as possible, but without errors. During the execution of the procedure at least one practitioner wore WATCHiT configured to capture time of completion and number of errors for each step. Upon procedure completion, the whole team could navigate through the collected data using the mobile phone with the Trainer app (Figure 3-c).

The system was evaluated with 9 teams of volunteers, all from different associations, for a total of 27 participants. In one group WATCHiT was wore by the team leader, while in the other 8 cases we gave it to the other two members of the team because they have more freedom of movement. We observed the teams while performing the procedure and we collected 27 questionnaires to get feedbacks on perceived usefulness, usability and impact on reflective learning using a 5-levels likert scale. Results from the questionnaire analysis show that respondents were overall satisfied with the use of the system (4.11, SD=0.49) and perceived it as a useful tool for training (4.22, SD=0.62). The respondents also agreed that the system helped them to reflect on their work (4.00, SD=0.6) and provided relevant content for reflection (4.23, SD=0.50).

The quantitative results of the questionnaires indicate that respondents agree on the impact on learning. Respondents agree that after using the system they made a conscious decision about how to behave in the future (4.07, SD=0.62) and that they gained a deeper understanding of their work life (3.96, SD=0.71). They were also motivated to actually change their behavior (4.11, SD=0,49). Intention to change included e.g. need for more attention at the individual level and better coordination within the team. The collected information was perceived as accurate (3,9, SD= 0,6), relevant (4,03, SD=0,50), and collection of data was effortless (3,81, SD=0,47). The system stimulated knowledge exchange within the team (4.11, SD=0.41). In particular, we observed that while going through the steps of the mobile apps some of the teams discussed their performance and continued afterwards.

7   Lessons Learned

In both scenarios, the data collected in the field through WATCHiT has been useful to debrief on the event. In the following we reflect on our experience.

Sensor Data: Strengths and Weaknesses
Sensor data is easy to capture and provides quantitative information that is easy to manipulate, e.g. to provide comparison and different visualizations. However, it is important to be aware that sensor data capture only a dimension of the work practice and one should always consider how to complement sensor data with other sources, to include aspect of the work that can only be assessed in a qualitative way.

One should also be aware that putting the focus on one aspect, others might get neglected. For example, in Trainer, sensors are used to collect the time to perform the steps of a rescue procedure. This might lead to put focus on time to perform the procedure rather than quality. In this perspective, data collected with sensors might put the focus of reflection on "shallow" quantifiable aspects rather than quality of work. It is therefore critical to set the right focus for reflection (*initiate reflection stage* in the CSRL model). In addition, it is important to find the right set of data to collect, one shading light on the different perspectives that one should reflect on.

More data from different types might however result in an increased complexity of the application and/or of the associated debriefing.

Making Sense of Data

Sensor data in their raw form are of a limited use, also because the number of data points collected can quickly grow beyond being manageable by humans. It is therefore important to consider and promote the sense making processes that make data useful. There are two main mechanisms that we have identified: *visualization* and *storytelling*.

Visualization is re-creating a context that helps users to make sense of the data, in this case for debriefing. It is therefore critical to identify the type of visualization that triggers reflection. So, one should consider how to visualize the collected data, but also relate it to e.g. differences with data from other users or a baseline, as in Trainer, or relating the data to other information, e.g. geographical location as in CroMAR. The chosen visualization should also take into account the context of debriefing. For example, Trainer is designed to be used right after the procedure is concluded, taking advantage of the limited time when all the team members are available. We have therefore chosen a simple data visualization and navigation of the data supported by a strict set of steps users have to go through. In CroMAR, where the user is intended to use more time to make sense of the event, the visualization is richer, in terms of both content and navigation possibilities.

Sensor data, since they need to be interpreted, might trigger storytelling and a richer sense making of the experience. We have observed this happening during both the evaluations. Users try to explain to themselves and to others the data, connecting it to their memory of the event. During the evaluation of CroMAR, for example, the coordinator tried to explain a problematic event with the data that he received. While using Trainer, a team was trying to explain their time with how they remembered they had performed the procedure. This sense making process, done individually or collaborative, plays an important role in learning and it should be promoted both in the application and in creating enabling conditions during debriefing, for example providing the appropriate time and space for it.

Rethinking Debriefing

We are aware that the scenarios that we described differ from current practices of debriefing. This does not intend to question the value of traditional debriefing, but rather explore the space of possibility offered by sensor data to promote complementary forms of reflection. One of the strengths of applications like the ones we have presented is to bring debriefing out of the control room and involve different workers at different times. The full benefit can be achieved when creating conditions to promote smooth transition among different reflection cycles, e.g. supporting in situ coaching sessions or sharing of outcomes and data from one in situ reflection session, like the ones with Trainer, for more in depth reflection sessions after the event or at the organizational level. In this way, the whole organization could benefit from the results of reflection at the individual and team level. In this perspective, sensor data could also be used to support traditional debriefing. In our studies we have for example observed the coordinator bringing one of the outcomes of his debriefing with CroMAR into the main debriefing.

Sharing information arises however a number of challenges. In fact, in our evaluation we observed how the memories of the workers are continuously used to make sense of the data. When the data is to be used in a separate context, its interpretation might be challenging. In addition, it is necessary to define criteria to identify which data and reflection outcomes might be useful in different situations.

Focusing on the Collective Nature of Crisis Work

The experience with CroMAR has pointed out the importance of capturing and comparing multiple perspectives on the experience on which to reflect. In the evaluation the coordinator was able to reflect only by using data from the field, the workers and his overall knowledge of the event. Being able to get multiple perspectives on a shared experience is critical, however our evaluation pointed out that capturing relevant perspectives might be challenging. To address this challenge it is necessary to introduce adequate scaffolding mechanisms, but also provide easy modalities of input and, when relevant, connection with applications used for work that might automatically provide complementary data. In addition, this arises the need for specific support to distinguish better and compare input from different users, especially one´s own vs. that of others. This challenge brings along issues connected to visualization, ownership, and privacy [12].

Motivation to collect data should also be considered. When collecting data for one´s own debriefing, like in Trainer, the ones who collects the data also benefit from it. In CroMAR this does not happen. The workers in the field do the work and the coordinator benefit from it. This is a well-known challenge in collaborative settings [13], and it should be addressed when deploying a system.

Requirements for Data Capturing

Our experience allowed us to draw requirements for systems supporting data collection both in real and simulated event, as currently partially implemented by WATCHiT prototype used in our evaluations.

Due to the nature of crises, sensing information with static sensors embedded in the environment is not always a viable solution. Although urban environments are populated with sensors whose data might be useful for crisis debriefing, there are large areas of the world that are not. Since the location a crisis unfolds is often unforeseeable, it is important to complement data from static sensors with mobile ones. The degree of mobility of capture is also important. While rescue vehicles can be equipped with sensors, the highest degree of mobility is achieved with sensors worn by workers.

Being each event almost unique, it is also difficult to define which data might be relevant for debriefing. Relevancy of data is also dependent on the role of the worker, for example firefighters might need a different set of data than ambulance drivers. For these reasons, the capturing device should be customizable with sensors modules for the relevant datatypes in a specific event. The specific set-up of the device should be non-permanent and easy replicable by the workers themselves.

To inform the design of specific sensor modules, our experience reveals three classes of information that could be implemented as sensor modules: (i) information for assessment of worker's safety and well being (e.g. stress levels), (ii) information for mapping the territory (e.g. temperature, noise, air quality), (iii) information for logging the work (e.g. location of operations, number of persons rescued).

Finally some data (e.g. air quality, location) can be easily quantified and collected with automatic methods. Workers might however provide critical data that cannot be quantitatively measured but should be self-reported, for example the perceived level of panic in an area. Information captured by multiple sensors, quantitative and qualitative, might help to build a more complete perspective. Yet, capturing qualitative or self-reported data need the practitioners to interact with computer interfaces whose design space is constrained by rescue protocols. For example, the user interface to the capturing tool should be designed to leave both hands free (e.g. to carry someone on a stretcher) and to be as little disruptive as possible for the work.

8   Conclusions and Future Work

In this paper we investigated the use of sensor data collected in the field to promote reflection after a training event. This investigation has been performed by developing and evaluating an application for collecting data and two applications to support two scenarios of crisis training. The results are encouraging and demonstrate that sensor data, though presenting some limitations, can be used to enrich and complement current training. The paper is addressing two very different scenarios. They have been chosen to show how the approach can apply to a wide range of scenarios. However, this makes it difficult a detailed comparison of the two scenarios. Further empirical investigation is needed.

As part of our current work, we are developing a toolkit for making WATCHiT fully modular, so that it is possible to easily assemble a device that supports the needs for data collection of different scenarios.

In our work we have focused on debriefing after training events. As part of future work we plan to investigate the use of similar tools also for debriefing on real crisis events. Our hypothesis is that the overall approach is applicable. However, it is important to understand what additional requirements are emerging, e.g. in terms of robustness of the device and non-intrusiveness of the interaction.

Acknowledgments. This work is co-funded by EU-ICT 7FP MIRROR project (http://www.mirror-project.eu). We thank Mr. Gianni della Valle for sharing his insight into crisis work and helping with the organization of the evaluation; Marco Parigi from Regola for his support throughout the development of the prototypes; Dr. Birgit Krogstie for many discussion on reflection; the students who helped with the development of the prototypes and the volunteers who evaluated the prototypes.

References

1. Keramitsoglou, I., Kiranoudis, C.T., Sarimvels, H., Sifakis, N.: A Multidisciplinary Decision Support System for Forest Fire Crisis Management. Environmental Management 33, 212–225 (2004)
2. Vivacqua, A.S., Borges, M.R.S.: Taking advantage of collective knowledge in emergency response systems. Journal of Network and Computer Applications 35, 189–198 (2012)

3. Frassl, M., Lichtenstern, M., Khider, M., Angermann, M.: Developing a system for information management in disaster relief-methodology and requirements. In: Proc. of the 7th International ISCRAM Conference (2010)
4. Boin, A., Hart, P.T.: The crisis approach. In: Handbook of Disaster Research, pp. 42–54 (2007)
5. Boud, D., Keogh, R., Walker, D.: Reflection: turning experience into learning. Routledge (1985)
6. Schön, D.A.: The reflective practitioner: how professionals think in action. Basic Boo (1983)
7. Krogstie, B.R., Divitini, M.: Supporting reflection in software development with everyday working tools. Presented at the Proceedings of the 9th International Conference on the Design of Cooperative Systems, COOP 2010 (2010)
8. Krogstie, B.R., Prilla, M., Pammer, V.: Understanding and supporting reflective learning processes in the workplace: The CSRL model. In: Hernández-Leo, D., Ley, T., Klamma, R., Harrer, A. (eds.) EC-TEL 2013. LNCS, vol. 8095, pp. 151–164. Springer, Heidelberg (2013)
9. Prilla, M., Pammer, V., Krogstie, B.: Fostering Collaborative Redesign of Work Practice: Challenges for Tools Supporting Reflection at Work. Presented at the Proceedings of the European Conference on Computer Supported Cooperative Work, ECSCW 2013 (2013)
10. Mora, S., Boron, A., Divitini, M.: CroMAR: Mobile Augmented Reality for Supporting Reflection on Crowd Management. International Journal of Mobile Human Computer Interaction (IJMHCI), 88–101 (2012)
11. Stefanovic, D.: Supporting reflection on crisis work with WATCHiT Procedure Trainer. Norwegian University of Science and Technology Master Thesis
12. Kristiansen, A., Storlien, A., Mora, S., Krogstie, B.R., Divitini, M.: Mobile and Collaborative Timelines for Reflection. In: IADIS International Conference Mobile Learning, pp. 1–9 (2012)
13. Grudin, J.: Why CSCW Applications Fail: Problems in the Design and Evaluationof Organizational Interfaces. Presented at the Proceedings of the 1988 ACM Conference on Computer-supported Cooperative Work, New York, NY, USA (1988)

Citizen Participation and Social Technologies: Exploring the Perspective of Emergency Organizations

Paloma Díaz, Ignacio Aedo, and Sergio Herranz

Interactive Systems –DEILab
Computer Science Department
Universidad Carlos III de Madrid
{pdp,sherranz}@inf.uc3m.es,
aedo@ia.uc3m.es

Abstract. Current technological advances on ubiquitous computing and web 2.0 open up new possibilities to promote an active participation of citizens in different domains including emergency management. Such a kind of participative model requires not a proactive attitude from citizens but also of the implication of emergency management organizations that have the responsibility of managing the situation. Emergency management is a highly professional domain characterized by the stress that emergency workers experience when facing unpredictable events that have a social and economic impact in society. Citizens could contribute in this process as far as they do not interfere with the protocols and activities of professional workers who will not accept any change that could compromise their efficacy. Many research works focus on how citizens utilize social technologies during emergency situations for self-organizing or for citizen journalism, however, the perspective of emergency management organization has been less explored. In this paper, we present a study that goes deeper into how organizations envision the use of technologies to increase citizen participation in their procedures. This study aims at being a step further to understand how a more active and effective citizen role could be reached and how technologies could contribute to this end.

Keywords: Web 2.0 and social technologies, citizen participation, citizen empowerment.

1 Introduction

Disasters occur first at the local level, the place where the event takes place. For this reason, citizens from the local and surrounding areas are always the first responders in case of a crisis situation since they are there and the natural reaction is to try to minimize the effects of the event or to escape from the area [1]. Government policies are increasingly recognizing the importance of citizen participation [2] and consequently are leading emergency management (EM henceforth) from a traditional model based on a rigid and command and control approaches where all the process is controlled by authorities to a more social and participative one that pushes citizens to

C. Hanachi, F. Bénaben, and F. Charoy (Eds.): ISCRAM-med 2014, LNBIP 196, pp. 85–97, 2014.
© Springer International Publishing Switzerland 2014

play a proactive role. Successfully implementing this new social and participative EM model requires not only an active involvement and engagement of citizens but also of the alignment of EM organizations that are responsible to manage the situations. They should be aware of the value of citizen participation and integrate it into their work practices. However, emergency management is a professional domain in which emergency workers must cope with critical and unexpected situations. Under these conditions, citizen participation will only be incorporated to the EM process when organizations feel that this participation neither interfere with their protocols nor compromise their efficacy.

Although the potential of citizen participation has been recognized [3], advances on social technologies such as social networks or blogs are expanding and making more visible this phenomenon during crisis situations [1]. This kind of technologies offers new possibilities to disseminate information in a viral way, giving citizens a voice during disasters. Similarly, EM organizations can take advantage of these technologies by keeping in touch with citizens and obtaining timely information from them that cannot be otherwise easily obtained.

Many research works have studied the use of social technologies by citizens during crisis situations such as the 2005 Hurricane Katrina [4], the 2007 Southern California fires [5], or the 2011 Japan earthquake [6]. These works have shown how social technologies have been widely adopted by citizens for journalism or self-organizing, allowing them to collectively produce relevant information sometimes in advance of official communications [5]. However, EM organizations have more recently realized of the potential of these technologies [7]. Maybe motivated by this, the perspective of EM organizations and agencies has been much less explored than the citizen perspective. This paper presents a study that involves emergency organizations from Canada, USA and Spain to explore both the current and the future of integrating citizen participation in the EM process as well as the role that technology should play.

The remaining of the paper is organized as follows. The second section provides an overview of the potential role of social technology for supporting citizen participation in EM. The next section details the design and results of the study with EM practitioners. Despite the general recognition of the benefits of citizen participation and the fundamental role of social technologies, this study shows how citizen participation remains still challenging. Efficiently processing the citizen-generated information, guaranteeing reliability of sources, and supporting citizen participation from different roles are some of these challenges discussed in the study. As a step further to design technologies adapted to the capabilities and needs of the agencies and citizens, a potential ecology of participants in EM is explained in the fourth section as a resource that might help to envision technological applications. Finally, conclusions are drawn in the last section.

2   The Role of Social Technologies in EM

Social technologies are defined as any type of "*computing application that serves as an intermediary or a focus for a social relationship*" [8], such as online social networks sites (e.g. Facebook or Twitter), wikis, blogs, instant messaging applications, or forums.

This kind of technologies offers citizens new opportunities to collaborate with autorithies and be more actively involved in an emergency.

Reuter et al [9] discuss these new opportunities and characterize the communication of citizens through social technologies in a two-by-two matrix shown in Figure 1. The quadrant A represents the communication from citizens to organizations in order to integrate and aggregate citizen-generated content with the agency information. Some of the advantages of social technologies are the possibility to obtain timely information about warnings and promote the involvement of citizens [10]. An example of this usage could be the Social Media Disaster Response Center launched by the American Red Cross [11]. In quadrant B organizations broadcast information to alert, notify or communicate with citizens. The main benefit of this usage lies in the easy and immediate dissemination of information in a viral way during emergency situations [12]. However this option has to be considered as an additional mechanism complementing other traditional communication media in order to avoid a communication break with less technological citizens. Quadrant C characterizes peer-to-peer communication between citizens, which derives in self-help communities of interest that emerge during crisis situations. Finally, the quadrant D represents information exchange between EM organizations for crisis management purposes.

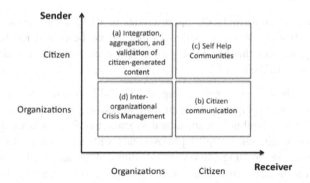

Fig. 1. Communication Matrix from Reuter et al [9]

However, the use of social technologies in such a complex domain as EM has also some concerns that need to be addressed properly from the point of view of the EM agencies as wells as from the perspective of citizens. In terms of citizen-generated information, validating the credibility of the information sources is one of the most important problems that organizations face to take advantage of social technologies [13]. Another important problem is the large quantity of information that the active participation of citizens generates. As an example, during the 2011 earthquake of Japan there were more than 1,200 tweets per minute and 4.5 millions of status updates that mentioned the words "Japan" and "earthquake" [14]. This could result in an information overload and provoke difficulties to efficiently process the data [12]. Regarding to the dissemination of information from EM organizations, most important problems are related to security and privacy issues [15] such as message manipulation or identity theft.

3   Citizen Participation: A Study to Explore the Perception of EM Organizations

Citizens are a valuable resource that can be mobilized in disasters or crisis. Their participation can take a variety of forms such as tracking alerts, collaborating in first response activities, or acting as sensors providing timely information on the ground. Latest technological advances on social computing have contributed to enhance and make more visible citizen participation in emergency situations. In this sense, there is an extensive research focused on analyzing how citizens utilize social technologies during disasters [4, 5, 6]. However, in order to fully take advantage of the potential of citizen participation it is necessary not only to understand the role of citizens but also to explore how governmental agencies value this participation and how they consider that it could be effectively integrated in their daily practice. Since, as far as we know, the perspective of EM organizations has been much less explored, we carried out a two-stage study focused on exploring how EM organizations envision successful citizen participation and how they perceive that social technologies could contribute to that end.

3.1   First Study: Social Media and EM

With the purpose of confirming the opportunities of using social media in the EM domain and identifying the main challenges that should be considered to achieve a successful integration of these technologies in EM organizations, a study with EM practitioners was carried out.

Study Details. This study was run in August 23rd 2012, in a face-to-face workshop that counted with the participation of 36 practitioners from 18 different agencies from the areas of British Columbia in Canada and Washington State in USA. Participants conformed a heterogeneous group of professionals with expertise in different areas and real experience in handling emergency situations. After an introduction on social media and its use in EM, participants were required to fill out a questionnaire that aimed at exploring the possible benefits and potential problems of using social media in their daily EM activities. At the end of the study, a discussion was opened to go deeper into the issues raised in the questionnaire.

The questionnaire was divided intro two sets of questions according to the two quadrants (A) and (B) of Reuter's matrix [9] (see Figure 1). The first one was related to the possible use of social media to disseminate information and communicate with citizens, and the second group of questions was about their perception as receivers of citizen information through social media. In each of these sections, we posed a set of benefits and problems to be answered using a 5-point Likert scale. Mean and variance were utilized as central tendency measurements.

Results. The results of the first section reveal that participants positively valued that EM organizations use social media to communicate with citizens though with a high variance ($\mu=4,28$; $\sigma=1,76$). The main benefits highlighted by participants were related to the potential of social media as communication channels that enable spreading information very quickly (μ=4,5; σ=0,6) and reaching more people (μ=4,44; σ=0,45). However, participants valued lower the utility to promote the creation of self-help communities (μ=3,94; σ=0.9) and crowd intelligence processes (μ=3,56; σ=1). Despite the highlighted benefits, participants also showed significant concerns about this usage (see Table 1). In particular, the most important ones were those related to necessity to be constantly active in social media (μ=4,19; σ=0,6) and guarantee integrity of information (μ=3,41; σ=2,6). The high level of variation obtained in the perception of practitioners about these concerns (see table 1) might be due to the variety of sizes of the organizations as well as the approach they all assumed that social media is a complementary channel to communicate with users.

Table 1. Causes that might deter official agencies from using social media to send information to citizens. (values range from 1-is not important to 5-is very important).

	μ	σ
You might be not reaching all the people you think	2,91	2,86
Messages can be manipulated	3,41	2,6
You need to be constantly active in the social media	4,19	0,8
Messages have to be specially designed to be effective (short informative texts, use of multimedia...)	3,31	1,58
You need to build a reputation in the social network before using it as a communication channel	3,16	2,5
There is a duplication of effort in information dissemination that might be difficult to manage at the organizational level	3,09	1,6

Answers in the second section showed a more homogenous tendency about the need of integrating social media as a source of information in EM organizations (μ=4,16; σ=0.6). The main benefits of this integration according to the participans would be to get a better idea of how people perceive the situation (μ=4,34; σ=0.5) and to understand its evolution (μ=4,00; σ=0.8). Regarding to the main concerns of participants (see Table 2), the two highest rated were the difficulty to guarantee reliability (μ=4,41; σ=0.8) and the complexity of efficiently processing large volumes of information (μ=4,19; σ=0.7). Emergencies situations are critical events in which an immediate response is required. Maybe for that reason, participants are especially concerned about how to analyse large amounts of data, not all of them trusted, to provide an efficient and adequate response.

In general, results of this study confirm the positive perception of organizations about the use of social media to establish a fluid communication with citizens during emergency situations. In spite of this positive perception, participants identified several troubles that seem to be hindering the application of this kind of technologies in their domain.

Table 2. Causes that might deter official agencies from using social media to receive information from citizens. (values range from 1-is not important to 5-is very important).

	μ	σ
You cannot guarantee the source of the information is reliable	4,41	0,8
There is too much information to be processed efficiently	4,19	0,7
There are many different social media applications to be checked	3,84	1,1
Other media (TV, radio, public screens, messages to community leaders...) are more effective	2,53	1,9

3.2   Second Study: Analysing Current and Future Citizen Participation

In the spring of 2013 we conducted a new study since the use of social technologies is becoming to be almost pervasive in most crisis situations, but there was still a need to explore how citizen participation could be more efficiently integrated within EM organizations. In this case we run a longer-term study to explore the view that EM practitioners have about citizen participation in emergency management and how this participation could be improved using technologies.

Study Details. The study was based on a web questionnaire that was open from April to May 2013. During this period of time, several Spanish emergency organizations were invited to access and complete it. Particularly, participants were 29 emergency practitioners (professional paid workers) who belonged to 7 different organizations in charge of cities or regions that in total involved more than 3,5M people. The first contact with the selected organizations was through their coordinators who were in charge of motivating participation. Once we obtained the approval of coordinators to perform the study, we sent all the practitioners who worked in these organizations an email with a link to the questionnaire. Responses of participants were automatically processed and stored in an online spreadsheet. Prior to running the study, a pilot test of the questionnaire was performed with three emergency practitioners. They completed the questionnaire using a think-aloud protocol [16], which helped to identify some minor terminology inaccuracies.

The questionnaire was divided intro three sections: the introduction to characterize the professional profile of participants; the second section to analyse how is current citizen participation in EM; and the last section to explore how participants envision the future of citizen participation in this domain and how technologies could contribute to improve this future. For most questions, a 4-point Likert scale was employed from 1 (lowest level) to 4 (highest level). Mean and variance were utilized to measure central tendency.

Results. Based on the results, participants can be characterized as professional paid workers who have more than five years of experience as emergency practitioners, attend an important variety of emergencies (traffic accidents, fires, domestic accidents, serious weather situation, etc.) and whose labour is mainly focused on intervention, coordination, and management tasks.

One of the first insights obtained from the study was that EM practitioners considered citizen participation a useful source of information ($\mu=2,94$; $\sigma=0,4$). However, as shown Table 3, current level of citizen participation in general terms (independently of the channel) was assessed mostly low ($\mu=1,55$; $\sigma=0,38$), especially for specific demographic groups such as disabled people ($\mu=1,34$; $\sigma=0,36$) or the elderly ($\mu=1,45$; $\sigma=0,45$). The exception was the participation of emergency services volunteers, which was assessed slightly higher ($\mu=2,89$; $\sigma=0,98$). These results confirm the relevant role that trusted people like volunteers can play. As an example, the groups of volunteers organized to use and monitor social media during emergencies, the so-called Virtual Operations Support Teams (VOST, vosg.us), are gaining importance and presence in the EM landscape.

Table 3. Current level of participation. (values range from 1-is very low to 4-is very high).

Groups	μ	σ	Groups within citizens	μ	σ
Citizens	1,55	0,38	Adults	2,2	0,92
			Disabled people	1,34	0,36
			Elderly	1,45	0,45
			Immigrants	1,52	0,46
Emergency Services Volunteers	2,89	0,98			
Communities of Interest	1,69	0,76			

According to participants, the communication channels currently utilized by citizens to keep in touch with authorities in an emergency situation can vary from traditional ones such as telephone calls (82,76%) and face-to-face reports (34,48%) to later ones like social network sites (37,93%). The usage of these new channels of participation is generally correlated with the citizen's age. As a participant specified, "*social network sites are mostly used by young people*". The main problems identified in current participation of citizens were basically the same that appeared in the first study: the difficulty to trust the information provided by the citizens ($\mu=3$; $\sigma=0,27$), and the lack of resources to handle the large streams of information provided by the citizens in real situations ($\mu=2,76$; $\sigma=0,87$).

Last section aimed at exploring how organizations envision future citizen participation. The first part of this section was about identifying potential roles and activities in which user participation could be increased from the point of view of the organizations. Thus, to characterise potential roles three options were assessed: citizens as mere informants (called *sensors*), citizens informing and reacting to an event following the instructions of authorities (called *reactive sensors*) and citizens taking the lead in EM activities (called *proactive sensors*). Surprisingly, the preferred role was *reactive sensors* (see Figure 2), that is, citizens with an involvement that goes further of just providing information. Indeed, the main barrier to move to proactive sensors in the words of one of the participants was that "*you need to invest in preparation and training before trusting them*". Therefore, organizations would like more engaged citizens that are actively involved in emergency situations.

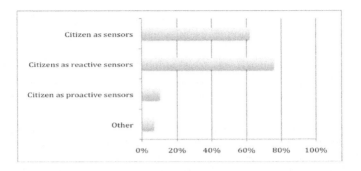

Fig. 2. Assessment of the different citizen roles

Still exploring the vision of participants about the future, we asked about what aspects could be improved in citizen participation. As summarised in Table 4, the highest values (framed in blue) were obtained for transforming citizens into well-prepared emergency actors who understand how professionals work, getting ready to react to an emergency and being better informed.

Table 4. Aspects that could be improved in citizen participation. (values range from 1-strongly disagree to 4-strongly agree).

	μ	σ
The communication channels between citizens and professionals should be improved	3,45	0,33
The participation of formal groups of volunteers should be fostered	3,27	0,20
Citizens should be more aware of how professionals respond to an emergency	3,58	0,25
Citizens should know that they have to be prepared and know how to react	3,62	0,24
The dissemination of information amongst citizens should be more effective	3,48	0,33
It would be necessary to guarantee the trustworthiness of the information provided	3,34	0,38
Citizens should take a more active part in following the alerts	3,07	0,57
Citizens should take a more active part in the recovery process	3,03	0,46
Citizens should take a more active part in the response process	3,03	0,25
We should be able to process the information provided by citizens in a more efficient way	3,27	0,28

3.3   Discussion

In spite that EM organizations recognize the benefits and potential of citizen participation, the study shows that it is still below what is expected and desired. This low level of citizen participation can be attributed to different causes such as a governmental legislation and policies that are not conducive to citizen participation

[17], the idea that citizens cannot be qualified enough to make meaningful contributions [17], or the challenges associated to existing social technologies to efficiently integrate citizen participation in EM organizations [1]. In this sense, the study confirms the key role of social technologies for establishing fluid communications between EM organizations and citizens during emergency situations. However, the use of these technologies to assist the creation of self-help communities or crowd intelligence processes is not as recognized by participants. It seems that they underestimate the potential of social technologies, limiting their utility to a one-way communication channel that transforms citizens into human sensors that contribute to quickly understand the evolution of a situation. Furthermore, participants of both studies coincide in drawing attention to the particular need of addressing two concerns regarding to the application of these technologies for such purpose. The first one is related to the problem of efficiently processing the incontrollable amount information that can be generated by citizens through these channels. This problem can produce information overload in a domain in which a rapid and efficient decision-making is vital to provide an adequate response [13]. The second remarkable concern for participants was the difficulty to guarantee the credibility of the information sources, which is highly consistent with the literature [1, 13]. EM is a critical domain in which invalid information can lead authorities to give an incorrect response, which can result in loss of human lives. Reputation systems [19], client location services [1], or network analysis methods to infer influence and replication [18] are some of the techniques that are beginning to be utilized to address validity of sources and data.

One of the most relevant findings of the study was to identify that EM practitioners value the role of citizens not only as information providers but also as reactive sensors that take part in the situation by following the instructions of EM workers. Many research works have shown the immense potential of citizens as information providers [20]. The results of this study not only confirm the validity of this potential from the perspective of EM organizations but also, and surprisingly, show how they value a more active and direct participation. This is coherent with the idea that real citizen participation is achieved when citizens work as partners and take part in the situations that affect their communities [21]. According to the opinion of participants, more active and engaged roles need of more prepared and informed citizens. Actively participating in such a professional domain as EM requires knowledge and skills that not all citizens could have [17]. For this reason, moving citizens toward these active roles involves training and preparation efforts that transform them into a more reliable and prepared emergency actors. Maybe for this reason, participation of well-prepared and trained citizens such as volunteers was assessed higher by participants. An adequate preparation is also a key factor to successfully employ social technologies in EM. Citizen should be educated to take caution when receiving information through social technologies and think carefully about the quality and reliability of the information they disseminate [22].

4 Identifying Ecologies of Participants in EM

This study reveals that EM agencies value different forms of citizen participation; from citizens as information providers to more active roles in which citizens act as reactive sensors directed by authorities. According to the study, these active and reliable roles must be adopted by those citizens who have demonstrated an adequate level of preparation and capabilities. As an example, well-prepared citizens such as retired EM workers, volunteers, or trained citizens could provide an additional support in case of emergency beyond of providing information. For this reason, the heterogeneous profiles that compose the crowd of citizens need to be characterized and conceptualized before designing social technologies for improving citizen participation in EM.

Motivated by this, we created a model of ecology of participants [23] that conceptualizes citizen participants in five different roles (see Figure 3): *citizen*, *sensor*, *trusted sensor*, *node*, and *agent*. The ecology was validated in a focus group with professionals and policy makers from Madrid 112, the operation centre where the different corps and agencies in charge of Madrid Community collaborate to respond to emergencies. Six participants took part in the focus group, representing the police, firemen, forest services and ambulances services, and the operational centre. All of them had more than 5 years of experience in managing EM services for the whole Community of Madrid that has a population of more than 3.2 million of residents.

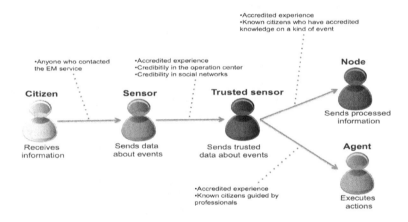

Fig. 3. Ecology of participants in EM

As shown in Figure 3, this conceptualization includes the migration paths between roles and the conditions to move from one role to the other. *Citizens* become *Sensors* as soon as they contact with an EM service. *Sensors* can send data to the EM services and they become *trusted sensor* when authorities trust them so their data about events can be directly processed in the operation center. *Sensors* might be known citizens or people who have a central position and a reputation in social networks, so they are not expected to intentionally distribute hoaxes and false information. As an example, a formal volunteer with expertise in EM or a citizen who has positively contributed during past emergency situations could accredit this experience and credibility, therefore being considered a *trusted sensor*. *Nodes* can not only send data but also process them and generate more elaborated information, like aid requests or evaluation of impact reports. To be a *node*, a citizen needs to have an accredited technical knowledge that enables her to understand the data in a proper and useful way for the operation center. Finally, *agents* can perform actions on themselves or guided by professionals for which they need to have specific skills and capabilities. In terms of the impact for designing technologies, proving experience and credibility could require reputation mechanisms or rich individual profiles. Furthermore, while information provided by *trusted sensors* can be directly presented to decisions makers since it is considered valid and, therefore, it can be directly taken intro account for the response process, the information provided by *sensors* would need additional mining and filtering processes such as collective rating or reflection, propagation-based analysis, or location-based services. In any case, all these information and data have to be integrated with other sources of information at the operation center so that to support rational decision taking proper visualizations will be required.

This ecology represents a step further to understand how social technologies should be designed to successfully integrate citizen participation in EM activities. It is important to keep in mind that citizens are not a homogenous group of people and that each citizen can be valuable in a specific way. Technologies have to be designed in order to take profit of that specific value in a way that is also useful for the professionals that are in charge of EM. The ecology can be used to identify the different profiles of an heterogeneous crowd of citizens to envision how they can use social technologies to support the EM process, not only in the response phase but also in the preparation, recovery or mitigation phases. As an example this ecology has inspired a number of different mobile applications to support citizen participation in emergency response within the emergenSys project [24]. In this case, the conceptualization of roles helped to identify the capabilities each profile can contribute with during the response phase using mobile applications that improved the communication with the operation center. Further work on social technologies can also take advantage of this conceptualization to ideate ways to transform the crowd capabilities into social capital and to align the potential capability of the crowd with the agencies needs and expectations.

5   Conclusions

Taking advantage of citizen participation in EM needs the implication not only of citizens but also of EM agencies that should integrate this participation in their work practices. Since the perception of citizen has been extensively studied, this paper presents a study aimed at exploring the other side: the perspective of EM organizations about integrating citizen participation and the usage of social technologies for such purpose.

EM organizations seem to positively perceive the application of a participatory approach in the EM context, considering citizen participation as a necessary instrument to make more informed decisions and provide an adequate response to the complex crisis situations associated to modern societies. In addition, the study reveals how they recognize the potential of social technologies as a key element to empower citizen participation. In spite of this, results indicate that it is necessary to make significant efforts to design social technologies adapted to the specific needs of such a complex domain as EM. Particularly, according to participants, processing efficiently citizen-generated content and guaranteeing the reliability of information sources remain still challenging. EM is a critical domain in which agencies will not support the integration of these technologies if they do not totally rely on them. In addition, our approach is that it is necessary to understand the heterogeneous crowd of citizens before designing social technologies and do not consider solutions that apply the "one size fit all" approach, since neither the citizens nor the agencies can be treated as homogeneous groups. Results of our studies seem to indicate that the role played by a citizen in an emergency situation should be determined according to her capabilities and skills. Keeping with the perspective of EM organizations, the more prepared citizens the more active role they could play. Therefore it is required to understand the capabilities and needs of these roles to design technologies that bring out the best of each of them and align the need of the agencies with the potential underlying the crowd of citizens.

Acknowledgments. This work is supported by the project emerCien grant funded by the Spanish Ministry of Economy and Competitivity (TIN2012-09687). We'd like to thank Richard Arias for this help in organizing the first study reported in this paper and the emerCien project members for their comments on the questionnaire of the second study. Of course, we also have to thank all the participants in Canada, USA and Spain who were so generous as to share with us their opinions and concerns.

References

1. Palen, L., Anderson, K.M., Mark, G., Martin, J., Sicker, D., Palmer, M., Grunwald, D.: A vision for technology-mediated support for public participation and assistance in mass emergencies and disasters. In: Proceedings of the 2010 ACM-BCS Visions of Computer Science Conference (ACM-BCS 2010), British Computer Society, Swinton (2010)
2. Taylor, M.: Community Participation in the Real World: Opportunities and Pitfalls in New Governance Spaces. Urban Studies 44(2), 297–317 (2007)
3. Arnstein, S.R.: A Ladder of Citizen Participation. JAIP 35(4), 216–224 (1969)
4. Shklovski, I., Burke, M., Kiesler, S., Kraut, R.: Use of Communication Technologies in Hurricane Katrina Aftermath. Position paper for the HCI for Emergencies Workshop at SIGCHI 2008 (2008)
5. Sutton, J., Palen, L., Shklovski, I.: Backchannels on the front lines: Emergent uses of social media in the 2007 southern California wildfires. In: Proc. Information Systems for Crisis Response and Management Conference, ISCRAM (May 2008)
6. Miyabe, M., Miura, A., Aramaki, E.: Use trend analysis of twitter after the great east Japan earthquake. In: Proc. ACM Conference on Computer Supported Cooperative Work Companion (February 2012)
7. Yates, D., Wagner, C., Majchrzak, A.: Factors affecting shapers of organizational wikis. Journal of the American Society for Information Science and Technology 61(3), 543–554 (2010)
8. Schuler, D.: Social computing. Communications of the ACM (1994)

9. Reuter, C., Marx, A., Pipek, V.: Social Software as an Infrastructure for Crisis Management: A case study about current practice and potential usage. In: 8th international conference on Information Systems for Crisis Response and Management (ISCRAM 2011), Lisbon, Portugal (May 2011)
10. White, C.M.: Social Media, Crisis, Communication, and Emergency Management: Leveraging Web 2.0 Technologies. CRC Press (2007)
11. Fox, Z.: Red Cross launches social media disaster response center. Mashable, `http://mashable.com/2012/03/07/red-cross-digital-operations-center/` (accessed May 10, 2014)
12. White, C., Plotnick, L., Kushma, J., Hiltz, S.R., Turoff, M.: An Online Social Network for Emergency Management. In: Proc. Information Systems for Crisis Response and Management Conference, ISCRAM (May 2009)
13. Hagar, C.: Crisis Informatics: Perspectives of Trust–Is Social Media a Mixed Blessing? SLIS Student Research Journal 2, 2 (2013)
14. Crowe, A.: Disasters 2.0: The application of social media systems for modern emergency management. CRC Press (2012)
15. Oxley, A.: Security Risks in Social Media Technologies: Safe practices in public service applications. Elsevier (2013)
16. Ericsson, K.A., Simon, H.A.: Protocol analysis. MIT press (1985)
17. Oulahen, G.S.: Citizen participation in post-disaster flood hazard mitigation planning: Exploring strategic choices in Peterborough, Ontario (2008)
18. Cheong, F., Cheong, C.: Social Media Data Mining: A Social Network Analysis Of Tweets During The 2010-2011 Australian Floods. In: PACIS (2011)
19. Caverlee, J., Liu, L., Webb, S.: Socialtrust: tamper-resilient trust establishment in online communities. In: Proceedings of the 8th ACM/IEEE-CS Joint Conference on Digital Libraries, pp. 104–114. ACM (2008)
20. Goodchild, M.F.: Citizens as sensors: the world of volunteered geography. GeoJournal 69(4), 211–221 (2007)
21. Florin, P., Wandersman, A.: An introduction to citizen participation, voluntary organizations, and community development: Insights for empowerment through research. American Journal of Community Psychology 18(1), 41–54 (1990)
22. Kongthon, A., Haruechaiyasak, C., Pailai, J., Kongyoung, S.: The role of Twitter during a natural disaster: Case study of 2011 Thai Flood. In: 2012 Proceedings of PICMET 2012 Technology Management for Emerging Technologies (PICMET), pp. 2227–2232. IEEE (2012)
23. Fischer, G., Piccino, A., Ye, Y.: The ecology of participants in co-evolving socio-technical environments. Engineering Interactive Systems, pp. 279–286. Springer, Heidelberg (2008)
24. Díaz, P., Aedo, I., Romano, M., Onorati, T.: Supporting Citizens 2.0 in Disasters Response. In: Proceeding of: MeTTeG 2013: Conference on Methodologies, Technologies and Tools enabling e-Government (2013)

Access Control Privileges Management for Risk Areas

Mariagrazia Fugini and Mahsa Teimourikia

Department of Electronics, Information and Bioengineering
Politecnico di Milano
Milan, Italy
{mariagrazia.fugini,mahsa.teimourikia}@polimi.it

Abstract. This paper presents adaptive access control for areas where risks require modifying authorizations dynamically at run time to enlarge and/or restrict privileges for risk rescue teams. Resources, which have a spatial description, as well as data elements of the areas to be protected, are considered. Based on a risk scenario, principles of access control based on the ABAC (Attribute Based Access Control) model for Subjects and Objects are given. Adaptivity of access control rules apply to subjects who intervene in the risk area and who require enlarged privileges to access to resources. The Access Control Domain concept models the policies of adaptive changes to Subject/Object attributes to face the crisis events. Events have a spatial description to enable managing the crisis according to where the event has occurred, since the same event can have different impacts on the environment depending on where it happens.

Keywords: environment risk, adaptive access control, access control domain, attribute-based access control, space-dependent events.

1 Introduction

Security and safety of smart environments [1] where a crisis, due to a risk or an emergency occurs, needs proper models, methods and tools in order to intervene in face of a crisis, to react to dangerous events in the monitored areas and to locate people at risk. However, even in the case of disasters, one wants to preserve data and resource confidentiality and privacy, while allowing for dynamic adaptation of access control rules to face risks.

Access control on data and resources (*Objects*), including people who need protection, depends on what happens in the environment, and has various purposes depending on the *Subjects* and their organizational roles, such as rescue teams in charge of intervention. There is a need for adaptivity of the access control rules in order to be able to manage risks and disasters in time, and to perform necessary actions to control the situation while minimizing the damages for confidentiality, privacy and safety of resources and people.

In recent years, due to the tremendous advances in Information and Communication Technologies (ICT), several infrastructures, technologies and methods have been introduced for risk and disaster management [2].

C. Hanachi, F. Bénaben, and F. Charoy (Eds.): ISCRAM-med 2014, LNBIP 196, pp. 98–111, 2014.
© Springer International Publishing Switzerland 2014

The damages caused by risks in an environment, such as fire, explosion, and etc. along with the damages to life or property caused by natural disasters like earthquakes and tornados can be greatly reduced by preparedness to manage such cases [3]. In the meanwhile, considerable attention has been paid to cybersecurity, in particular to *access control* to data and resources and to *privacy* of people in such cases, showing that significant access control requirements exist for civilian government and corporations to meet their operational, control, and strategic goals. Civilian governments are concerned with confidentiality of data and privacy of people, namely with the protection of individuals' data, policies and intervention plans in economy, social, healthcare and other sectors of organizations.

Adaptivity of access control models is a currently popular topic in various areas of information systems [4]. In this paper, we address adaptation of access control rules to risks detected in the environment and to natural disasters, which are communicated through disaster management services [2]. We use *Subjects* to model entities that take actions in the environment, and *Objects* to model: i) physical resources (e.g., areas, tools, sensors, video cameras), and people to be protected; ii) informative entities (e.g., data, maps, and sensor data) whose sensitivity needs be ensured even during a crisis.

The access control model dynamically changes the authorizations of Subjects to access Objects based on the *risk level* and *risk type*, and on Subject/Object access requirements. Meaning that Subjects can receive new access privileges, temporarily to handle the risk, and then return to the "normal" situation having these emergency privileges revoked. The access control principles regard aggregating intelligence from masses of data acquired from an area via sensors, GPS, monitoring devices, and so on, to observe risks and emergencies signaled in a given area. The model is based on Attribute-Based Access Control (ABAC) [5] where attributes describe Subjects, Objects and the Environment, including geo-referenced information for positioning people, resources, events, which signal a risk and which have to be located to understand the dangerousness of the situation, and risk areas.

Under the need-to-know access control policy, we define *flexible access control rules*, which are activated/deactivated to adapt access of Subjects to Objects according to risks. Adaptivity is modeled by introducing *Access Control Domains* (*ACDs*) for Subjects on Objects linked to each other by temporary privileges: *ACDs* are security policies which delimit the set of access control rules to be activated in case of risk and deactivated upon the conclusion of risk. For handling the conflicts between the access control rules due to run-time activation and deactivation, we adopt the XACML policy language [6] that includes many combining algorithms to avoid conflicts; we extend it to include the adaptivity to risks using *ACDs* to establish which rules apply in which context.

The novelty of our approach lies in the use of the ABAC paradigm and extending the architecture model of XACML for risk management. For risk and disaster recognition, we rely on the proposed solutions in [7] and [2].

The paper is organized as follows. Section 2 reviews related works. Section 3 introduces the concepts of risks and access control, and reviews the basics of our Risk Management System. Section 4 explains the adaptive access control model and its components. Section 5 concludes the paper and discusses future work.

2   Related Work

In recent years the data of natural disaster prediction and detections are available to public, and can be integrated with the infrastructures in smart buildings. It is also possible to access them in time to prevent some of the damages caused by the crisis [1]. In particular, European projects such as OSIRIS [8] and projects in the US like IPAWS-OPEN [9], have made tools and standards available for interoperability of multi-domain sensor networks, and for processing and employing data (which currently emerge as themes of Big Data) provided by sensors for managing disasters and risks.

There are common alert message standards that have been widely used and are available to public through online services namely, Common Alert Protocol (CAP) [10] which is an alert message standard. Using these standards, it is possible to access emergency alerts and take actions to manage them using the infrastructures provided in "smart environments" [1].

Coming to access control models, recently, there has been considerable interest in Attribute Based Access Control (ABAC) [5] due to the limitations of the dominant and mostly used models such as Mandatory Access Control (MAC), Discretionary Access Control (DAC), and Role-Based Access Control (RBAC) [5]. ABAC successfully encompasses the benefits of before-mentioned classical access control models while surpassing their issues. The characteristics of ABAC that facilitate the dynamic changes in attributes of its components, such as the time of the day or geo-referenced attributes, make this model adequate for our risk-aware access control. Furthermore, the XACML policy language [6] is adopted here, since it facilitates the avoidance of conflicts between policies and rules. By exploiting the expressive power of XACML, it will be used in the service-oriented implementation of our approach.

Our model aims at allowing activation/deactivation of access control rules through the use of *Access Control Domains* (*ACD*), which are need-to-know policies ruling out which access control rules apply during a given risk or emergency situation.

Recently, adaptive access control models have attracted many researchers. Many different constraints are considered to affect the adaptivity of the access control. However, few papers consider the access control to physical environments and the adaptation to the environmental risk. Authors in [11], present the Criticality Aware Access Control (CAAC) for emergency management in smart environments based on RBAC. By Criticality they refer to the occurrence of the health problem for a person like falling, or pressure in the chest and the access control system dynamically and proactively makes changes in the individual privileges to let them have the necessary access to sensitive data. Yet, in our work, we imagine a more general case in which a risk like fire, or explosion is happening in the environment and different strategies need to take place to manage the situation, hence needing an adaptation in the access control rules.   To set some other examples, authors in [12] consider a location aware access control by extending RBAC, in which the location of the Subject with respect to the Resource that needs to be accessed affects the access control decision. In our paper, by adopting the ABAC paradigm, such adaptations are possible by considering geo-attributes for Subjects, Resources and the Environment that include the location in which the risk is happening. In another work [13], authors elaborate on risk-based adaptive access control (RAdAC) to semi-automatically adjust access control risk to provide access to resources accounting for operational needs, risk factors, and situational factors. In this work they consider a dynamic balance between the need to access information and the risk and cost of the information compromise. While, in this work, we consider the happening of environmental risks, emergencies and crisis as the dynamic factor that can affect the access control decision. However, RAdAC can exist in parallel with our model to evaluate the cost of the temporary relaxation of access control decision for management of the risk situation to avoid compromising highly sensitive data.

3   Risk and Access Control: Concepts

We assume we are in the discretionary-based access control policy (privileges can change for Subjects on Objects) and in the ABAC paradigm [5]. We define the Subject as an entity taking actions in the system. We define the Object (a resource and in general a geo-referenced element) as an entity to be protected from unauthorized use, such as data, devices, services, physical objects, areas, and persons. An access control or authorization policy is the set of rules allowing taking a decision to permit or deny access from a Subject to a set of Objects.   From now on, the terms authorization and access control will be used synonymously throughout this paper. In particular, access control is equaled to confidentiality while integrity and other access control properties are not dealt with.

Privileges represent the "authorized behavior of a Subject"; they are defined by an authority. In our case, they represent both the right to perform elementary actions (e.g., "read" privilege on environment Objects, which will map into "view", "read", "zoom in/out" privileges, depending on the technology used for monitoring the environment, and the set of privileges defined therein) and the right to perform activities (e.g., process the images from a camera or rescue a person).

We consider the Environment as a set of monitored factors used at decision time to influence an access control decision. Risks and Emergencies are recognized using a *Risk Management System* (*RMS*), which monitors the Environment. Also, external crisis management systems can notify the *RMS* about the occurrence of natural disasters. In this paper, however, we do not deal with risk and disaster *recognition*. We assume that sensors and devices are in place for this purpose, and also assume recognition methods have a suitable level of accuracy, while deepening these issues will be object of our short-term research steps. We rely on works in detection such as [7] and [2], and assume an accurate notification of risks, ignoring errors for sake of simplicity.   The *RMS* will introduce a strategy to manage a recognized risk by proposing a set of *risk actions*. These actions, like turning on an alarm, or opening an emergency door, can sometimes need to be undertaken by modifying the access control privileges that normally hold between Subjects and Objects. These modifications require adaptive access control to face a risk on a temporary basis. Access control rules are changed for example by granting more privileges to some Subjects on some Objects and therefore bypassing the existing access control, which is then rolled back to the previous access control privileges once the risk has been managed.

We consider the ECA (Event-Condition-Action) paradigm [14] to model adaptive access control policies: given an event (e.g. risk), we consider the conditions to dynamically activate the Access Control Domain (*ACD*) and hence access control rules. Also, Subject and Object attributes might change due to an event that can affect the authorization decisions later on. ECA allows us to express environment policies that affect security policies, which in turn are expressed by *ACDs*. In fact, an *ACD* is a policy that establishes how the access rules are allowed to change depending on what happens in the environment areas, namely which rules apply, in a given situation and at a given time, to a set of Subject Attributes over a given set of Object Attributes using which Privileges. This means that some *ACDs* are activated (e.g., the *Fire ACD* applies when the *fire* risk is detected), while others are deactivated (e.g., the *CheckPoint ACD* is deactivated upon the fire risk) in order to dynamically adjust the set of access control rules applied for the time necessary to handle the risky situation.

Finally, we use the term "access clearance" or "sensitivity" referring to a threshold or a range of admitted values for confidentiality or other access control elements in a discretionary style (no mandatory policies are obviously considered in our approach).

3.1   Risks and Access Control: Monitored Environment

Our access control scenarios deal with what we call an Environment, where various technologies and models are in place for surveillance e.g., in urban areas, transportation, buildings, crowded environments and so on. In particular, in the Environment, some events can occur creating potential risks for people and assets, which need to be managed.

In our considered Environment, risks are signaled by alarms, rose by sensors and various surveillance instruments, and must be reacted upon by putting in place actions to face the risk. In particular, risks must be managed by authorized people only, in order to mitigate risks for people, objects, and areas.

We assume the Environment is a set of areas, forming the Environment in a composition relationship. An area is a space defined according to its scopes and functionality, has a topology, can be located in its position, and contains a set of known risk sources. Risk sources are all the elements (electric plugs, gas/fire emission points, water sins), which potentially create risk events. We do not consider unexpected risks in this paper.

In a sample scenario, the monitored Environment can be a space (e.g. an airport or a hospital) having parking areas, stairs, buildings, main/emergency exits, evacuation paths, and so on. The Environment is exposed to various types of risks (e.g., depending on whether we consider open-air or closed areas, which have different risks and different surveillance technologies). The Environment is a geo-referenced Object that has a blueprint of its areas, has surveillance sensors, conveys its surveillance data to area servers in form of sensor data, and has localization devices for detection.

In such a scenario, considering Subjects and Objects of the ABAC model, the Security Staff is a sample Subject in charge of monitoring the Environment and planning/executing interventions in case of risk. Moving Subjects and Objects, including people, are monitored using sensor networks, localization systems, and GIS. The Security Personnel Subjects need to be cleared to access services (Objects) that locate a risk event, or people's data including their positions (Objects) that exposed to risk. Security Personnel has different access clearances that limit their access to sensitive resources. For instance, the Security Manager (Subject) has the highest access clearance and can access Objects with virtually no limitations during a risk; the Security Staff (Subject) has a lower clearance and can execute only some actions (e.g., launch an alarm) on a limited set of Objects; the Environment Surveillance Staff (Subject) can intervene only for minor problems or first-aid alarms. Subjects can receive an upgrade in their access control level if a risk occurs. For instance, the Surveillance Staff can gain privileges related to the positioning of people at risk (which they usually do not hold for privacy reasons), and later have this privilege revoked when the risk ceases. The control on misuse of privileges that might happen during this upgrade of access is out of the scope of this paper. Still, we consider the minimum sensitivity and maximum access levels that can be set for any Object and Subject according to access policies, so avoiding compromising the confidentiality of resources.

*ACD*s establish which *Subjects* can execute which *operations* on which *Object*. So they determine the set of active access rules. A sample set of *ACD*s in our example is composed of the *Fire ACD* that represents the situation of risk of fire, as detected by the *RMS*; the *Evacuation ACD* (the environment is being evacuated in case of an emergency), and the *Earthquake ACD* (an earthquake occurrence is reported by the external crisis management system). By monitoring the dynamic changes in Environment factors (e.g., the position of personnel or resources, internal or external sensor data, or time), the *RMS* might detect risks, which can activate and/or deactivate *ACD*s allowing the dynamic changes in access control rules. The detected risks might also lead to some changes in the Subject and Object attributes, for example to increase the access control clearance attribute of the security staff Subject, to allow this Subject to intervene to handle a risky event.

3.2   Fundamentals of a Risk Management System (*RMS*)

Starting from a simple example motivating the need for enhanced solutions to prevent risks and to change the *ACD*s, we briefly summarize the basics of an *RMS*, which monitors and helps planning interventions during a risk scenario.

For example, the *loss of gas* is a risk that may lead to an explosion, if not timely revealed. The causes of the loss of gas may be deterioration of the gas conducts in time, the interaction of persons which produces an indirect and undesired effect on the gas transportation pipe lines, or an external event that can damage the gas pipes, e.g. in the occurrence of the earthquake, tornado, and etc. The *RMS* must collect data from sensors revealing the presence of gas and must determine if we are in a soft situation (risk) or in a dramatic situation (emergency).

A gas loss can be easily identified through gas sensors, which create an event of type "gas loss". Depending on the risk level, there may be various solutions for this risk management, including: close the gas provisioning, or turn electricity off.

Moreover, it is possible to receive data about occurrence of natural disasters some seconds before they happen. This can help adopting preventive strategies before they happen and be prepared to manage them while and after they have occurred [7].

The *RMS* exploits the Monitoring, Analyzing, Planning, and Executing (MAPE) loop [15] typical of control systems used in engineering of self-adaptive and self-managing systems. This loop observes the environment, detects the anomalies by analyzing data collected through monitoring devices, decides if a risk occurred and if intervention/change is needed and of what type, and puts in place (executes) the planned modifications in the environment. Preventive actions are put in place when the risk is between the Risk Threshold and the Emergency Threshold.

When a parameter exceeds a threshold, the *RMS* implements a strategy (Preventive actions) to restore the optimal parameter values before the risk evolves further. Beyond the Emergency Threshold, we have an emergency and move to a deterministic approach, using off the shelf, real-time corrective actions that patch the situation immediately. A corrective action can consist in lighting out an escape path to evacuation of people out of an area or sending emergency alarms and teams' interventions. Below the Risk Threshold, the systems operate in normal mode; namely, all the parameters are in their defined range of normality.

4   Adaptive Access Control: Considering Risks and Disasters

When the *RMS* detects risks, there might be a need to make changes in the access control rules and/or Subject/Object attributes to be able to manage the risk situation. In the following, the components of the Dynamic Access Control Model is detailed and defined formally.

4.1   Dynamic Access Control Model

Coming to access control modeling, under need-to-know access clearances, we adapt the ABAC paradigm and XACML policy language to meet our needs for adaptive access control according to events in the environment. We discussed the architecture of access control mechanism in [16] that extends the XACML policy language to accommodate the adaptations of ABAC to risk management scenarios. Here, we first introduce the components of the access control model and then briefly explain the different components in the dynamic access control mechanism, whose architecture is shown in Fig. 1. The components of the access control model are modeled in Fig. 2.

The model components are defined as follows.

Environment e: We consider a composed Environment *e*, including open and closed areas. Each area has at least one access point used as an entrance, an exit, and/or as an emergency exit. In the Environment there are several factors that might cause risks and should be monitored, e.g. water and gas pipes, electrical wires and so on.

RMS and Monitoring Devices d: These elements model the technological elements needed for the environment surveillance. The *RMS* is a dashboard where environmental data collected by devices (*d*) are conveyed, so that persons are notified about the current risks in the various areas. In our model, *d* are the various monitoring devices such as sensors for the temperature, light, smoke levels, smart phones and wearable devices that can be used for getting data about people's positions and health status like heartbeat. These *d* elements notify risks to the *RMS*, which selects the

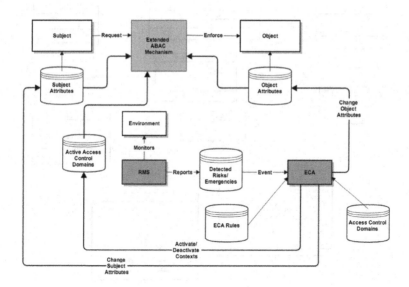

Fig. 1. Architecture of Risk Management System and Dynamic Access Control

strategies to be followed in a risky situation. The details about the specific kinds of sensors used, their costs, and the accuracy of the data given by the sensors are out of the scope of this paper. And for the sake of simplicity we assume that the risks are reported based on accurate data. We also assume that the *RMS* can both deploy automatic actions (e.g., lock the doors, turn the electricity off, and so on) and suggest actions to humans who have to intervene or to decide what actions to undertake for risk.

Object o: This abstracts resources that a *Subject* can access or act on. *Objects* in our definition are any resource to be protected. *Objects* hold three groups of attributes (*OA*): 1) *General Attributes* can be *Object* specific and differ depending on the type of the object. 2) *Geo Attributes*, including geo referenced coordinates (latitude, longitude), and levels of granularity (they exist at various zooming levels) available in the repository, and the objects in the vicinity, 3) *Security Attributes* define restrictions on information in terms of privacy, owner, level of sensitivity, time restrictions, age/location restrictions, and groups:

Object o: {{GeneralAttributes: ID, ObjType, ...}

{GeoAttributes: [Latitude, Longitude], ZoomingLevel, {VicinityObjs}, ...}

{SecurityAttributes: Privacy, Owner, SensitivityLevel, {TimeRestriction}, {AgeRestriction}, {LocationRestriction}, {Groups}}}

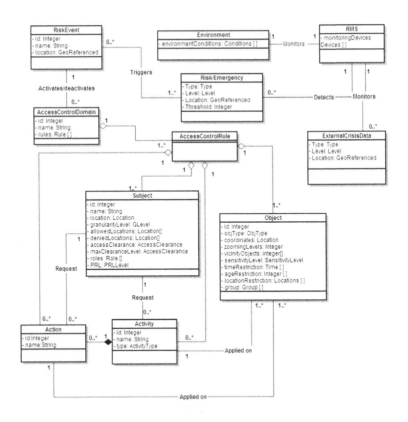

Fig. 2. Modeling the Risk and Access Control Model Components

Subject s: This abstracts a *Subject*, an application or a process wanting to perform an action on a resource/object. A Subject can hold many attributes (*SA*). We consider the following three groups of *SA*: 1) *General Attributes*: define the general characteristics of a subject, such as its identity, name, and etc. 2) *Geo Attributes*: define geo properties of a subject, such as location, reachable positions, etc. Geo attributes can be given at various levels of granularity, i.e., for privacy reasons, the exact location of the *Subject* might be hidden while the subject's logical position, usual location, and the places that the Subject is allowed to have access to are visible; 3) *Access control Attributes*: define the access control-related properties of the subject, such as access clearances, highest-possible access clearance roles which can be active at a given instant, and so on. Moreover, each Subject has been associated with a *Personal Risk Level (PRL)* [7]. To adopt the *PRL* introduced in [7] in our model, we make some modifications to apply it in a general situation (in [7] we were treating work areas and their specific risks). The used *PRL* depends on the Physical location, expressing the presence of risk sources and persons in the environment, Role of the Subject, and the Objects that they need to access.

Formally,

$$PRL = f(s.Position, s.Role, \{o.ID\}).$$

The Subject Role and accessed Objects (that are recognized by their IDs) are evaluated using an evaluation function, while the location is evaluated using the environmental risk map [7]; f is an opportune evaluation function. A possible choice is given by the following function (where eval stands for evaluation):

$$PRL = \sum (eval(s.Location), eval(s.Role), eval(\{o.ID\}))$$

To summarize, a Subject is defined as follows:

Subject s: {{GeneralAttributes: ID, Name, ...}

{GeoAttributes: [Latitude, Longitude], GranularityLevel, {AllowedLocations}, {DeniedLocations}, ...}

{SecurityAttributes: ClearanceLevel, MaxClearanceLevel, {roles}, PRL}}

In our model, *Subject Attributes* (*SA*) and *Object Attributes* (*OA*) are assigned by an authoritative subject, or by a group of subjects, that collaborate and balance one another's decision/control.

Actions and Activities a: These are operations (i.e. privileges) that can be executed by subjects on objects in a given *ACD* (where the *ACD* is defined hereafter). We consider two types of operations: *simple operations* (*actions*), such as read, write, update, execute, zoom-in/out; and *complex operations*, called *activities*, which combine simple actions to model a task, a process, an application, or even a physical action. Examples of activities in an environment are "View persons localization data", or "Turn on the fire alarm protocol", "Guide an ambulance towards the crisis area center". Actions and activities are assigned with a unique id to be able to differentiate them. Activities can consist of different actions, and, for the purpose of Separation of Duties, each component action can be executed by a different Subject. However, for the sake of simplicity, we define actions and activities in the same way and assume that they can be performed by the same Subject. If a request for performing an activity is authorized, it means that all the sub actions that are included in that activity are also authorized to ensure that the activity can be completed.

Access Control Rule r, and ACD c: The *ACD* component of our model indicates a set of access control rules, which are valid in a certain situation, based on dynamic changes in the environment, in particular the occurrence of risks. In other words, *ACD*s are access control domains, in which rules are defined that are the operations allowed to Subjects on specific Objects in an environment under certain circumstances. We assume that the access control rules in each *ACD* are defined by the function *DefineRule(a, outcome)* where '*a*' and '*outcome*' are the operation and the authorization result, respectively. As an example, for the *EmergencyACD*, we can define the rule specifying that the subjects with the role of Security Manager and access clearance higher than L3 are permitted to turn on (activity) the alarms (Object o) whose sensitivity level is less than S4. Note that the clearance and sensitivity are shown with indexes and higher indexes are correlated to more clearance or higher sensitivity, respectively. Thus, we can state:

R_1: DefineRule(turnon, EmergencyACD) →

   (s.Role =" SecurityManager") and (s.AccessClearance > "L_3") and (o.Group = "alarm") and (o.SensitivityLevel < "S_4").

These rules can be addressed with the definition of <Rule> entity in XACML. The ACD then maps into the definition of the <Policy> entity. The <Policy> is constructed out of <Rule> entities following the specified rule combining algorithms (defined in XACML) to avoid overlaps for the rules belonging to an ACD.

For receiving a permission to execute an operation, a request should be submitted to the access control system as depicted in Fig. 1. This request is specified by three elements: the requesting *Subject* (access subject), the operation to be permitted, and the *Object* to be accessed as in the standard XACML [6]. Considering S, O, and A as a set of *Subjects*, *Objects*, and *Actions/Activities* respectively, a request will be defined as follows:

Request(s:S, o:O, a:A).

Considering the *operation*, attributes related to the *Subject*, *Object* and the rules in the active ACDs, *Request* returns Y, N, or NA, meaning that access is allowed, denied, or not applicable, respectively, based on the standard XACML.

Risk r / Emergency em: Some factors that change dynamically and are monitored by the *RMS* can signal the occurrence of a risk situation, which can be recognized [7] based on parameters such as: type, level, and location of the risk factors. It is then possible to decide how to adapt the access control rules when the risk r has to be handled. The *RMS* is able to recognize the risks that can happen in the environment. When a risk is recognized, the *RMS* identifies the root cause of the risk, its location and the persons at risk (according to their *PRL*), and tries to propose the optimal strategy to manage the risk. On the other hand, an emergency occurs when a risk exceeds a given threshold or when a parameter exceeds a threshold (e.g., if the environment temperature exceeds 70°C).

Risk Event ev: Identifications of risks in the environment can trigger *risk events*, as shown in Fig. 1. Risk events, which can be localized due to their geo reference attribute, activate/deactivate ACDs. Events may also cause the modification of the attributes of *Subjects* and *Objects* within the ACD, according to the strategies suggested by the *RMS*. The details of how we handle the impact of risk events on ACDs and Object and Subject attributes are discussed in the next section of this paper; risk events play a key role in dynamic adaptation of access control in response to changes in the environment.

Knowing the components of the access control model, and having the risks and emergencies that can cause risk events, we can specify our approach of adaptive access control in the following subsection.

4.2   Adaptive Access Control

Risk events are triggered due to environment factors out of range, which are identified as risks, as shown in Fig. 1. Therefore, assignment of access control rules should be carried out dynamically as soon as the incident is identified to adapt the access control rules to the risky situation.

The *RMS* proposes a strategy to manage risks and emergencies that can take place to handle the risky situation. The *location, type* and *intensity* of the risk can affect the strategies suggested and/or deployed directly by the *RMS*.

For example, if smoke is detected as an out-of-range parameter, which means a possible *fire event*, the *RMS* evaluates where the source of the risk is. If the event occurs near gas pipes, it is potentially very dangerous and hence needs fast corrective strategies (evacuation, fire brigades, locking of doors and so on) since it is an emergency. Instead, if the same factor (presence of smoke) occurs in locations where no special danger is present, this is a risk, which can be handled through preventive actions, such as smooth interventions to check what the origin of the smoke is, while evacuation is not needed.

In the first case, to give an example, the *RMS* is notified that a medium intensity fire risk exists near the gas pipes, and hence triggers a fire risk event. A sample strategy in this case would be: activating alarms, closing the gas pipes, notifying that evacuation is needed, and notifying the risk manager. This is specified as follows:

If (r.Type: "fire") and (r.Level: "medium") and (r.Location: "closeToGasPipes") :

TriggerRiskEvent(r),

Strategy = { Activate ({alarms}), Close(gasPipes), Notify (Evacuation),
Notify(s.RiskManager) }

The authorization to execute these actions might need a change in the access control rules. Therefore, access control rules should also get adapted according to the risk event by activating/deactivating necessary *ACDs* and changing Subject/Object attributes. Activation/deactivation is ruled out by ECA rules.

There can be multiple rules per *ACD* and different *ACDs* can share the same rules. Each *ACD* activation should enable the corresponding access control rules. Since we adopt XACML as the policy language, such conflicts can be avoided using the policy combining rules defined in XACML. As we mapped our *ACDs* into the definition of <Policy> entity in XACML, the set of activated *ACDs* are relevant to the <PolicySet> entity, and therefore, the policy combination algorithms can be applied to avoid conflicts between the activated *ACDs*.

We introduced the concepts of adaptivity using ECA paradigm in [17]. An ECA rule indicates that in case of an *event*, if the *condition* holds, then (a) certain action(s) should take place, where "action" denotes the *activation/deactivation* of *ACD*(s) or/and modifications in the attributes of Subjects/Objects by the function *ChangeAttr(attribute, condition, new-value)*. The event in the ECA paradigm is the risk event triggered by the risks identified in the environment and notified by the *RMS* as shown in Fig. 1.

To clarify, let us set some examples. Suppose we have the following ECA statement:

RiskEvent : *(em.Type: 'Explosion')*
Conditions : *(em.Level: 'high')*
Actions: *Activate(EvacuationACD) and Deactive(CheckPointACD)*

In this example, the conditions indicate the case of an occurrence of an explosion risk, with *high* level of danger. Therefore, the *Evacuation ACD* should be activated. And the *CheckPoint ACD* is deactivated to allow persons to evacuate the area quickly without the need to pass through security checkpoints.

The *Evacuation ACD* can include rules that facilitate the evacuation, like low sensitivity level for doors that need an access card to allow everyone to pass. Or letting the rescue teams to view the location data of the people at risk:

EvacuationACD.Rule$_1$: s.Role = SecurityStaff, p=read, o.Group = Location, effect= Permit
EvacuationACD.Rule$_2$: s.Role = ANY, p= open, o.Group = doors, effect= Permit

Another example is the following:

RiskEvent : *(r.Type: ANY)*

Conditions : *(e.locateSubjects(r.Position) != 0)*

Actions: *ChangeAttr(s.GranularityLevel, s.Position: r.Position, 'Exact')*

This specifies that, in case of occurrence of any type of risk, if there are persons in the risk area, their exact location should be available to the rescue teams, meaning that the subjects *GranularityLevel* at which the observations can be made on the risky area should be equal to the exact location that is available.

One further example can be as follows:

RiskEvent : *(r.Type: ANY)*

Conditions : *s.PRL > Threshold*

Actions: *ChangeAttr(o.SensitivityLevel, ((o. ObjType: "HealthData") and (o.Owner: s.ID)) , 'L$_2$')*

Where the sensitivity level of health data (*o*) of a person with Personal Risk Level (*PRL*), higher than a threshold, is reduced, so this data can be available for emergency doctors.

5   Conclusions and Future Works

This paper presented dynamic access control for environmental risks. We consider environments where some factors (e.g. temperature, images captured by cameras, presence of people) are monitored by sensors and devices. Risks are recognized and managed by a *Risk Management System* (*RMS*) based on data acquired from the environment, and on information possibly available from crisis and natural disasters detection systems. Based on ABAC and XACML, we have discussed an access control model, which is adaptive to risks in that access control rules are modified dynamically for subjects and objects so that the risk can be managed. To enact adaptivity, we introduced the notion of *ACD* as policies, which dynamically authorize subjects to access resources. We are working towards inclusion of the access control model in the Risk Management Tool described in [**7**], based on a Matlab-based simulator and on a web application.

References

1. Liao, W., Ou, Y., Chu, E., Shih, C., Liu, J.: Ubiquitous Smart Devices and Applications for Disaster Preparedness. In: 9th International Conference on Autonomic & Trusted Computing, UIC/ATC (2012)
2. Liu, J., Shih, C., Chu, E.: Cyberphysical Elements of Disaster-Prepared Smart Environments. IEEE Computer 46(2), 69–75 (2013)
3. Liu, S., Shaw, D., Brewster, C.: Ontologies for Crisis Management: A Review of State of the Art in Ontology Design and Usability. In: The Information Systems for Crisis Response and Management conference ISCRAM (2013)
4. Mayrhofer, R., Schmidtke, H., Sigg, S.: Security and trust in context-aware applications. Personal and Ubiquitous Computing 1(2) (2014)
5. Hu, V., Ferraiolo, D., Kuhn, R., Schnitzer, A., Sandlin, K., Miller, R., Scarfone, K.: Guide to Attribute Based Access Control (ABAC) (2014)
6. Rissanen, E.: eXtensible access control markup language (XACML) version 3.0., OASIS standard (2012)
7. In: OSIRIS - Open architecture for Smart and Interoperable networks in Risk management based on In-situ Sensors http://www.osiris-fp6.eu/ (accessed June 2014)
8. Fugini, M., Raibulet, C., Ubezio, L.: Risk assessment in work environments: modeling and simulation. Concurrency and Computation: Practice and Experience 24(18), 2381–2403 (2012)
9. FEMA. In: Integrated Public Alert and Warning System (IPAWS) http://www.fema.gov/emergency/ipaws/about.shtm (accessed June 2014)
10. CAP: Common Alert Protocol, V1.2, http://docs.oasis-open.org/emergency/cap/v1.2/CAP-v1.2-os.html (accessed June 2014)
11. Venkatasubramanian, K., Mukherjee, T., Gupta, S.: CAAC: An Adaptive and Proactive Access Control Approach for Emergencies in Smart Infrastructures. ACM Transactions on Autonomous and Adaptive Systems (TAAS) 8(4), 20 (2014)
12. Kirkpatrick, M., Bertino, E.: Enforcing spatial constraints for mobile RBAC systems. In: The 15th ACM symposium on Access control models and technologies, pp. 99–108 (2010)
13. Kandala, S., Sandhu, R., Bhamidipati, V.: An attribute based framework for risk-adaptive access control models. In: Sixth International Conference on Availability, Reliability and Security (ARES), pp. 236–241. IEEE (2011)
14. Wu, M., Ke, C., Liu, J.: Active Role-based Access Control Model with Event-Condition-Action Rule and Case-Based Reasoning. Journal of Convergence Information Technology 6(4) (2011)
15. Cheng, B.H.C., et al.: Software Engineering for Self-Adaptive Systems: A research roadmap. In: Cheng, B.H.C., de Lemos, R., Giese, H., Inverardi, P., Magee, J. (eds.) Software Engineering for Self-Adaptive Systems. LNCS, vol. 5525, pp. 1–26. Springer, Heidelberg (2009)
16. Fugini, M., Hadjichristofi, G., Teimourikia, M.: Adaptive Security for Risk Management Using Spatial Data. In: 25th International Conference on Database and Expert Systems Applications, DEXA (2014)
17. Fugini, M., Hadjichristofi, G., Teimourikia, M.: Dynamic Security Modelling in Risk Management Using Environmental Knowledge. In: 23th IEEE Conference on Enabling Technologies: Infrastructure for Collaborative Enterprises, WETICE (2014)

A Formal Modeling Approach for Emergency Crisis Response in Health during Catastrophic Situation[*]

Mohammed Ouzzif[1], Marouane Hamdani[2], Hassan Mountassir[3], and Mohammed Erradi[4]

[1] ESTC, Hassan II Ain Chock University, Casablanca, Morocco
ouzzif@est-uh2c.ac.ma
[2] SAMU, Ibn Sina Hospital School, Rabat, Morocco
dochamdani@gmail.com
[3] Femto, Franche-Comté University, Besançon, France
hmountas@femto-st.fr
[4] ENSIAS, Mohammed V Souissi University, Rabat, Morocco
mohamed.erradi@gmail.com

Abstract. The EMS (Emergency Medical Services: *"SAMU"*), which is affiliated to the Moroccan Ministry of Health, is normally dedicated to coordinate, regulate and carry the sick and road casualty to the most suitable hospital facilities. In times of crisis, the EMS (SAMU) collaborates and coordinates with other stakeholders namely Civil Protection and Military health services by setting up advanced Medical positions (PMA). In this work we will focus mainly on the collaborative work between doctors and the EMS (SAMU) in order to provide a remote diagnosis during emergency situations. One objective of this paper is to formally specify the behavior of different components of a collaborative system architecture in telemedicine. The objective of these formal specifications is to increase the confidence in the collaborative architecture and to verify the consistency of the components assembly. This is important towards building a robust system free from specification errors and inconsistencies.

Keywords: Emergency specifications, Collaborative systems, remote diagnosis, telemedicine.

1   Introduction

To decrease the effect of a crisis or a disaster, managerial measures are required upstream, on time and downstream, according to a predefined organizational approach which should be tested and simulated in times of "peace". The advent of the ORSEC plan (Rescue organization) as a tool and methods for crisis management is essential.

This is because it provides the best answers to rescue requests. In Morocco, the management of this kind of situation is governed by the 1957 decree establishing it

---

[*] This work was supported by the CSPT Research Grant (SeCoM).

C. Hanachi, F. Bénaben, and F. Charoy (Eds.): ISCRAM-med 2014, LNBIP 196, pp. 112–119, 2014.
© Springer International Publishing Switzerland 2014

among the missions of the Ministry of Interior. The 1955 law on civil protection and the 78-00 law on communal charter highlight the role of each department of the government involving multiple stakeholders such as Governors, as regional or provincial coordinators, with other departmental representatives.

The Ministry of Health, through the SAMU (Emergency Medical Services), will normally coordinate, regulate and carry the sick and road casualty to the most suitable hospital facilities. In times of crisis, the SAMU collaborates and coordinates with other stakeholders namely Civil Protection and Military health services by setting up advanced Medical positions (PMA), which play the role of a sorting and filtering center while treating mild cases and describing the situation near the scene of the disaster. This will facilitate the orientation of patients and victims towards the most appropriate hospital facilities and under best time conditions.

The SAMU develops and collaborate with other hospital services a called White Plan, in order to review the internal organization of each hospital to facilitate victims' access to the best cares. The SAMU is also equipped with means of transport, experienced human resources, and also the means of communication that we would like to strengthen using telemedicine facilities according to a cross-sectional schema. Such Schema concerns the coordination, the regulation with available health structures as a tool to ease Medical decision making in a very short term as well as long-term. Another aspect concerns a vertical schema in order to inform decision makers in real time about the events.

In this work we will focus mainly on the collaborative work between doctors and the SAMU in order to provide a remote diagnosis during emergency situations. One objective of this paper is to formally specify the behavior of different components of a collaborative system architecture in telemedicine. These formal specifications are based on automata to describe the dynamic behavior of the actors collaborating towards a patient' diagnosis. We start with an architecture specified as interacting components which offer services to determine the different states of these components and the exchanged messages between them. These specifications describe remote collaborations among doctor teams and specialists to provide a remote diagnosis. The objective of these formal specifications is to increase confidence in the collaborative architecture and to verify the consistency of the components assembly.

2   Related Work

The medical information technology research community has recently been facing the challenge of dealing with emergency cases derived from accidents or catastrophes. Therefore, many researches came up with medical information systems to help quick intervention of different stakeholders: doctors, nurses, clinicians, emergencies etc. Most of the proposed systems focus mainly on sharing, communicating and storing medical records. [1] describes emergency management business process based on Qinzhou government's emergency management work. It also designs a city integrated emergency response system (CIERS) according to this business process and the actual situations of the city's emergency are also considered.

[2] presents the design, implementation, and evaluation of a community-based virtual database, which maximally utilizes all of the available information and network resources of a community to better manage natural and man-made disasters. [3] focuses on the design of decision support systems for emergency managers in charge of planning, coordinating and controlling the actions carried out to respond to a critical situation. A novel knowledge-centered design methodology is proposed and demonstrated through the application in a concrete case study in the field of pandemic flu emergency management.

[4] proposes a model of a web-aided decision support system to assess the extent to which public facilities can be used as evacuation centers for the victims of an earthquake and/or tsunami. Attebury et al. in [5] took into consideration the distributed aspect of their system, and they proposed HDFS (Hadoop Distributed File System) which is a file system that stores large file across multiple machines. In order to facilitate the search of data during the quick intervention of doctors, Vienna-Ferreira et al [6] proposed a system called Digoogle. This system is considered as a research engine to facilitate the quick research of huge files such as medical records and scans.

However the previous work did not address the formalization of their suggested approaches. Therefore such formalization will increase the confidence in such systems in terms of consistency and robustness. Furthermore, they don't take in consideration the aspect of collaboration between different actors during the transfer or the sharing of information. In our work, we suggest a formal specification of the architecture of a system based on collaboration between different entities (PAM, SAMU, Clinical Hospital etc).

3   Architecture

The suggested architecture consists of several components: hospitals, SAMU and PAM, and ambulances. An abstract view of the suggested system, as shown in figure 1, considered it as set of components interacting thought their interfaces. These components could be primitive or composite. The initial architecture is composed mainly of the PMA component, the SAMU component, the CHU component, the BD component, the CS (Collaborative Session) component and the ambulance component.

When a victim arrives to the PMA and according to its situation, the PMA entity will take one of these three decisions: treat locally the victim, request the remote support and collaboration of a CHU, or transfer the victim to an appropriate CHU via an ambulance. In the case of a remote collaboration with a CHU, the PMA initiates a collaborative session in which the SAMU is invited first. This component seeks the available doctors "specialists in most cases" within a collaborative CHU entity and invites them to join the collaborative session. Following the collaboration among the different components (PMA, CHU and SAMU), the SAMU component enriches the medical record by the results of the diagnosis and records them in the BD (Data Base) component.

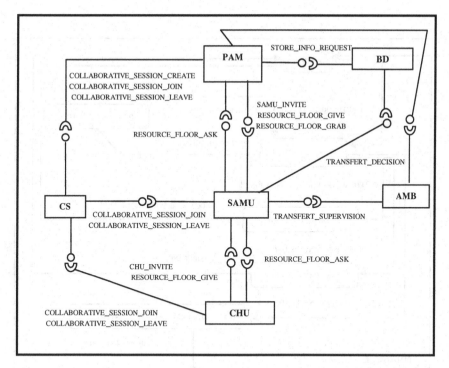

Fig. 1. Component based architecture of the emergency collaborative system

4   Component Behaviors

Due to space constraints we give only a description of PAM behavior (Figure 2). This behavior is initiated by the ready state. Once a disaster or emergency victim is received, the medical information is collected and stored. After, a decision can be made by the PAM entity which can occur in one of the three following cases: local treatment, victim transfer via ambulance to the CHU or the solicitation of remote assistance of the CHU.

The third case requires the creation of a collaboration session which leads to the remote diagnosis state. Once the session creation acknowlgement is returned by the collaboration session entity, the PAM invites the SAMU entity and will be engaged in the collaboration session. It can request and release some resources of the collaborative session which will be granted under the control and the coordination of the SAMU entity. The SAMU entity may also grab some resource access to the PAM if another priority entity such as the CHU entity, requests this resource.

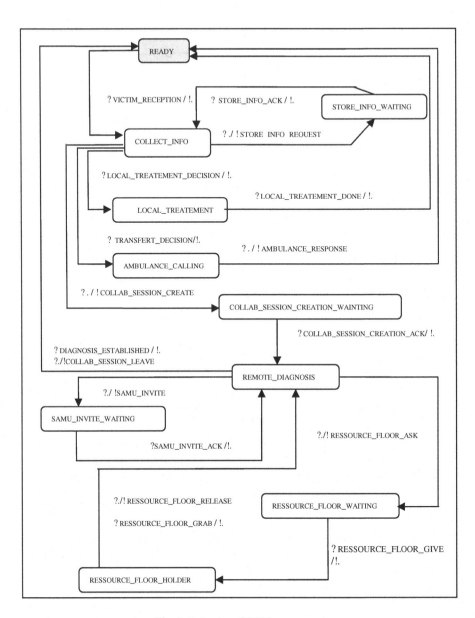

Fig. 2. Behavior of PAM component

5   Properties

In this section, we define a set of properties to be satisfied by our system. Then, a formal description of these properties is given using LTL (Linear Temporal Logic) notation.

5.1   Informal Description

-    Property 1: The SAMU must join a collaborative session after the reception of the PAM invitation.
-    Property 2: A join solicitation by a SAMU or CHU actor must be immediately accomplished by the Collaborative session entity.
-    Property 3: When a disaster victim is received, an urgent decision among the following must be taken: a local treatment, a victim transfer to hospital or a treatment with remote assistance.
-    Property 4: In the case of remote diagnosis, a collaborative session must be initiated by the Collaborative Session actor.
-    Property 5: The CHU must join a collaborative session after the reception of the SAMU invitation.
-    Property 6: A participant must be informed that he has been granted the floor of some resource.
-    Property 7: The SAMU can grab the floor related to some resource to the PAM actor if it is solicited by the CHU
-    Property 8: The floor related to a resource must be granted in a mutual exclusion and coordinated by the SAMU actor.

5.2   LTL Description

The properties mentioned above are described according to the states of automata presented in the previous section. For each property, we give the propositions and temporal operators used in linear logic. Afterwards, we use the notations for the LTL as described in [7] : the operator "always" symbolized by $\wedge$ and the operator fatality by $\Diamond$. The propositions uses classical logic operator: $\neg$, $\wedge$, $\vee$ and $\rightarrow$. The properties fluently used are expressed by $\wedge$ (p $\rightarrow$q) or $\wedge$ (p $\rightarrow\Diamond$ q), where p and q are propositions. The first case expresses, the fact that at every time a state of system verifies p, it should verify q. The second case express, that at every time, the system verifies p, in all the future executions, it should verify q. For space constraints, we give the LTL description of the third property.

$\wedge$ (PAM_INVITE_RECEIVED $\rightarrow$ $\Diamond$ SAMU_INVITE_PROCESS)
where :
- PAM_INVITE_RECEIVED: represents   that   the   SAMU   entity   is   in   the
  INVITE_PROCESS state.
- SAMU_INVITE_PROCESS: represents   that   the   SAMU   entity   is   in   the
  COLLAB_SESSION_JOIN_WAINTING state.

6   Properties Verification

We start the validation of our Promela Model by checking that there are no deadlocks, no dead code [8]. This means that all the transitions are executed. We also check that there are neither livelocks nor end_state unless for terminal states that belong to the specification of whole processes. The verification is done using Spin from Bell Labs. It consists of translating the LTL properties to Buchi automaton that are afterwards translated into Promela. The verification uses the model-checking technique based on the accessible states and consists of confronting this model to the property that has to be checked. The obtained diagnosis is the result of synchronous product of both automata.

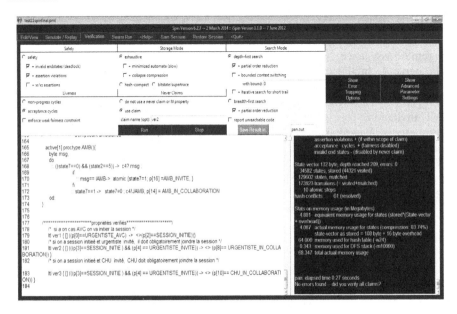

Fig. 3. Properties verification

Practically, for each property, we start by writing down the propositions used by the property. This is done by using the macro-instruction #define in the symbols definition part. Thereafter, we introduce the property in question, and we generate the automata related to the property (with the Never Claim generator) before launching the verification process. Figure 3 depicts the verification of the properties 3 and 4 (given in the section 5.1).

7   Conclusion

In this work we have shown how to formally specify the components of the architecture of a distributed collaborative application and the dynamic behavior of these components. The provided specification is based on automata to describe the interfaces of the system component and allows the verification of the specified system. The formal specification of the main components was shown. Also a set of formal temporal properties specified in LTL (linear temporal logic) was presented. We have used spin/promela tool to validate those properties of the specified collaborative system. The verification uses the model-checking technique based on the accessible states and consists in comparing this model to the property that has to be checked. The obtained results have shown that the described temporal properties hold for the formal description of the distributed collaborative system dedicated to remote diagnosis during emergency situations.

Another important issue for this kind of application is related to security issues. This concerns the importance of the exchanged data and its protection. As a future work we are extending this work to specify security policies in the context of a cloud environment. Some preliminary results have been presented in a recently published work [9].

References

[1] Wang D.Y.A., Pan L.W.B., Lu L.A., Zhu J.P.A., Liao G.X.A.: Integrated Emergency Response System Structure Design for a City in China. In: International Conference on Performance-based Fire and Fire Protection Engineering (2012)

[2] Li, J., Li, Q., Liu, C., Khan, S.U., Ghani, N.: Community-based collaborativeinformation system for emergency management. Original Research Article Computers & Operations Research 42, 116–124 (2014)

[3] Hadiguna, R.A., Kamil, I., Delati, A., Reed, R.: Implementing a web-based decision support system for disaster logistics: A case study of an evacuation location assessment for Indonesia. Original Research Article International Journal of Disaster Risk Reduction 9, 38–47 (2014)

[4] Attebury, G., Baranovski, A., Bloom, K., Bockelman, B.: Hadoop distributed file system for the Grid. In: 2009 IEEE Nuclear Science Symposium Conference Record (NSS/MIC), Orlando, FL. Univ. of Nebraska Lincoln, Lincoln (2009)

[5] Viana-Ferreira, C., Costa, C., Oliveira, J.: Dicoogle Relay – a Cloud Communications Bridge for Medical Imaging. In: chez 25th International Symposium on Computer-Based Medical Systems (CBMS), Rome (2012)

[6] Manna, Z., Pnuelli, A.: The Temporal Logic of Reactive and Concurrent Systems: Specification. Spinger (1992) ISBN 0-387-97664-7

[7] Holzmann, G.: The model checker Spin. IEEE Transactions on Software Enginnering 23(15) (1996)

[8] Krombi, W., Erradi, M., Khoumsi, A.: Automata-Based Approach to Design and Analyze Security Policies. In: IEEE 12th Int. Conf. on Privacy Security and Trust, Toronto (July 2014)

Collaborative Re-orderings in Humanitarian Aid Networks

Simeon Vidolov

LaSalle – Ramon Llull University, Barcelona, Spain
simeonv@salleurl.edu

Abstract. This paper explores the processes underlying the ongoing endeavours to establish collaborative relationships between traditional, formal humanitarian and the non-traditional volunteer networks (VTC). In contrast with the 'informational' and 'connectivist' concerns, which dominate the crisis response literature, this paper synthesizes a perspective on multi-network/actor collaboration that is informed by STS and Practice theory studies. Thus, network-wide continuous efforts to establish ways of working between these two very different types of actors are conceptualized as complex collaborative re-orderings constituted of the inter-related practices of 'reconfiguring' and 'fusing'. This perspective offers valuable insights into the dynamic processes of network transformations and changes, triggered by the co-emerging and coalescing endeavours of traditional and volunteer organisations.

Keywords: collaborative re-ordering, humanitarian networks, volunteer and technical communities, reconfiguring and fusing, STS studies.

1 Introduction

The area of humanitarian affairs has been undergoing profound changes [1, 2]. One of the precursors for these changes is the use of ICTs such as social media that have afforded new ways for communication in disaster situations. In particular, affected communities can communicate with friends and family and seek information and help or provide it to others [3-5].

Related to this change is the emergence of new form of "digital volunteerism". Grassroots volunteer and technical communities are engaging people around the world to tackle problems of common interest using these new tools and approaches [6]. The potential of these efforts has received some attention in disaster management and humanitarian aid [4, 7]. For instance, the VTCs have played a crucial role in Haiti in 2010, where the massive scale of the earthquake disaster made opened wide gaps in the coordination and information sharing. In particular, these distributed 'digitally savvy' global citizens, informally organized, began to interact directly with the affected population via ICTs and were relaying actionable information to the traditional humanitarian aid actors [2:p. 11]. While, the benefits related to the participation of the VTCs have been unquestionable, the establishment of a sustainable, long-term

C. Hanachi, F. Bénaben, and F. Charoy (Eds.): ISCRAM-med 2014, LNBIP 196, pp. 120–134, 2014.
© Springer International Publishing Switzerland 2014

collaboration with the traditional humanitarian network has not been without its problems [2, 6, 8, 9]. In addition, this phenomenon has remained relatively under-explored and under-theorized.

On the other hand, the process of collaboration in the humanitarian area has been widely perceived in narrow 'informational' and 'technologist' terms. For instance, issues related to information overload, number of communication channels, and filtering and processing of information are frequently pointed out as central to the success of crisis response situations [10, 11]. Studies in the area of humanitarian affairs have emphasized the importance of information flows and relevant impediments as central to collaborative processes [12, 13]. Researchers have identified numerous information management related problems, including the quality and timeliness of information [14, 15], unpredictability of required information [16], unwillingness to share [17], and mismatch in location, information overload, misinterpretation of information [18]. Relatively less attention has been paid to the way collaboration is established, including pertinent issues such as trust, relational infrastructure and commitment [19]. The difficulties and challenges of developing collaborative relationships between formal traditional and VTCs, and the complexity and dynamics of their interactions have received little research attention. These processes are considered crucial for the future of humanitarian response processes and have been interrogated by both practitioners and researchers [2, 6, 8, 9].

Consequently, this paper attempts to synthesize a perspective on collaboration, informed by relational and performative ontology, with a view to offer insights into the complexity and dynamics of collaboration between VTCs and formal humanitarian organisations. More specifically, this perspective suggests that collaboration is more than just 'connecting' or 'transmitting of information', but is a process of developing new set of relationships, inter-dependences and styles of working together that re-shape the extant network through practices of reconfiguring and fusing. As a result this perspective offers insights into the complex, heterogeneous, multi-network interactions and attempts to account for the oftentimes-neglected issues of trust, credibility, commitment and power.

The paper is structured as follows. First, the paper offers a more detailed review of the relevant crisis response literature. Then the broader literature on distributed collaboration is also briefly reviewed and some of its shortcomings highlighted. The paper then presents a perspective, informed by STS and Practice theory studies, which then are drawn upon as a sensitizing device to scrutinize inter-network collaborative interactions and endeavours between VTCs and formal humanitarian actors. The paper then ends with outlining its contributions and future research directions.

2   Literature Positioning

2.1   Collaboration and Disaster Response Literature

Crisis situations are complex and dynamic events that require a timely, coordinated and informed intervention by the relevant crisis response agencies [20]. Central to these activities are the management and coordination of the information flows. The lack of information that is up-do-date and that reflects the dynamic circumstances and parameters of the crisis might further exacerbate the crisis [21, 22]. In particular, it is argued that such complex and dynamic situations require continuous re-interpretation and updating of information by creating new or modifying existing communication and information channels and re-adjusting of various stakeholders' involvement [23]. Among the key challenges highlighted in the literature are ensuring the timeliness of information delivery from multiple sources; the avoidance of information overload and the establishment of accountability with fragmented information [24]. Other authors highlight the issues of information overload; the availability of fewer communication channels; and the omitting, delaying, and filtering of information, and processing of incorrect information [10-12]. For instance, Bharosa and Janssen [13] identify seven major impediments to the flow of information across a crisis response actors: data inaccessibility, data inconsistency, inadequate stream of information, low information priority, source identification difficulty, storage media misalignment, and unreliability. These difficulties are deteriorating the process of information sharing, whose effectiveness is captured by the term 'information quality' (IQ) [13].

The technological advances known as Web 2.0 or social media enable citizens to take part in crisis response and to collaborate by exchanging information, comments and photos [25]. While, these processes seem to be also viewed in information sharing terms, it is also argued that the communication with victims and the public has been underexplored [20], it is even less so with the volunteer and technical communities (VTCs) that are mediating these processes. For instance, the contributions of the VTCs are sometimes equated with information overload [2].

Fewer studies see collaboration between disaster response actors to encompass issues of trust and establishing productive relationships [26, 27]. Such studies also highlight the difficulties related to the participation of heterogeneous actors with diverse educational background, expertise and technological mediation [28, 29]. While, technologist and informational perspectives seem to dominate the understanding of collaboration in the literature on disaster response, in the next section, we offer insights into some of the subtler perspectives on collaboration in the information systems and organisation studies literature.

2.2   Collaboration and Information Systems and Organisation Studies Literature

The literature on distributed collaboration has problematized the model of collaboration based on the "message transmitting model" of the conduit conception of communication [30, 31]. This perspective assumes that communication is an unproblematic exchange of well-packaged items among communicating parties through a conduit. More specifically, this perspective has been critiqued for neglecting the importance of 'social factors' and 'context' [31, 32].

The alternative approaches that see collaboration as a complex process that requires developing mutual understanding are broadly called 'constructivist' [33]. Following this tradition Majchrzak, More and Faraj [34] outline two dominant positions on how collaboration works: traversing and transcending. The former is about transforming the local understanding into shared meanings and common knowledge so that a co-constructed interpretation of the situation can be reached. This involves appreciation of the difference in the knowledge composition that can mobilize collective action by traversing the boundaries through deep knowledge dialogue i.e. sensemaking emerges in relation to sense-giving of the 'other' [35]. Hence, this deep knowledge dialogue can help distributed parties to exchange and verify contextual information and develop mutual understandings [36] despite the differences in cultural and demographic attributes and individual backgrounds [37]. The latter approach to collaboration (transcending) also involves dialogic interactions that are instead focused on creating of common collaborative landscape that allows for team members to transform their expertise into collective knowledge without clarifying and resolving underlying differences [25]. The process of coordinating collective action relies on shared knowledge such as words, phrases and images that, however, do not determine the production of meaning [38]. Instead it is argued that collaboration is a product of situated practices that emerge of the need of reacting to circumstances and correcting errors "on the fly" [39].

Whereas, these studies offer valuable insights into the practices through which collaborative processes can be developed and sustained, they are less sensitive to the broader relational dynamics, and the commitment and engagement of distributed actors. Moreover, these perspectives seem to be less pertinent to a context of loosely coupled, disparate, heterogeneous multi-agent/networks interactions that attempt to co-adapt and re-order their practices.

3 STS and Practice Theory Studies

The sociomaterial turn [40-42] emerges as a response to the neglect of technology in management literature. On one hand it is positioned against an understanding of technology and organizations as discrete and independent entities related by causal linkages. On the other hand, it is critical towards studies that adopt an 'ensemble or web ontology' [41] according to which actors and things are inter-related through interactions to become mutually dependent ensembles. Hence, this group of studies is not focused on the effects produced by organizations and technologies as independent or dependent variables but rather adopt a processual logic and views the outcomes as a result of complex interactions. These authors claim that technology is considered part of organizational analysis only at certain times of IT-induced re-organization. Hence, it is argued that by introducing an alternative theorization of the relationship between technology and organizations as ontologically inseparable, one will be able to see 'materiality' as intrinsic part of organizing at all times (ibid.). In particular, Orlikowski and Scott [41] contend that the turn to 'sociomateriality' needs to go beyond seeing the relationship between technology and organizations as 'mutual interaction' but as "inextricably fused" [41: 463] or "constitutively entangled" [40: 1437].

These conceptual insights are related to a diverse body of existing literature such as ANT [43, 44], Suchman's ethnographic studies of work practices [45], Barad's agential realism [46], and practice theory approaches [47, 48]. A common trait of these literatures is that they are premised on a 'relational ontology' that presumes that the social and material are inherently inseparable. A distinctive aspect of this theorization is that material and human agencies are mutually and emergently productive of each other [44]. Hence, humans or technologies acquire form, attributes and capabilities only through inter-penetration [40, 41]. The conceptual commonalities of these studies can be identified in two major principles 'irreducibility' and 'performativity' (ibid.).

The principle of irreducibility suggests that all things (of all kinds human and non-human) in the world are being relational effects, inter-connected in webs and irreducible to a single dimension [44, 49]. This intellectual tradition treats everything in the natural and social worlds as a continuously generated effect of the webs of relations within which they are located. The principle of ontological performativity points out that all entities are performed in, by, and through the relationships in which they are involved: stability is the result of an effort, not an intrinsic quality of things [50]. The order and "nature" of things is therefore always a reversible and uncertain outcome, an effect of operations, maneuvers and processes that keep things in place. Heterogeneous arrangements are then effects of performances irrespective of how stable certain effect may appear to be at certain point in time. Therefore, ANT explains how arrangements between disparate actors (both human and nonhuman) are achieved, how facts become such, how order is performed, how things are put in place and stay that way, and how change comes about (ibid.).

It can be argued that actor-networks do not merely 'connect' through technologies, but form 'sociomaterial entanglements' of 'inextricably fused' participants whose roles and meanings are not determined before their enactment. Instead, Barad [46] contends that such 'collectives' co-emerge and intra-act as a result of certain practices. Consequently, the inter-related practices of reconfiguring and fusing are constitutive of the process of collaboration that entails the enactment of new relationships, inter-dependences, roles and identities.

These conceptual sensibilities offer space for exploring the processes underlying the emergence and evolution of such heterogeneous, geographically distributed arrangements. In addition, this tradition offers subtler and non-deterministic perspective to understanding the dynamics and complexity that surround and shape such sociomaterial inter-organisational formations and their continuous re-ordering. The following section will illuminate how these conceptual insights can help us make sense the on-going, transformational processes in the Humanitarian aid arena.

4   Methods

The objective of this study is to explore the ordering practices related to the integration of the VTCs and the traditional humanitarian networks. The exploratory nature of the study leads to adoption of a qualitative case study approach that aims to generate novel insights from the data in an inductive and grounded manner [51, 52].

This study continued over five months and entailed a detailed exploration of various data sources that can be divided into four main groups. Firstly, websites, blogs, discussion groups that offered insights into the actual practices of both formal and non-traditional networks. Secondly, documents, reports, VTCs meetings and conferences and media interviews with key actors. Thirdly, research or industry reports and analyses, founded on in-depth primary data collection through interviews and personal correspondence. Fourthly, a database with 14 transcribed interviews with major representatives from both traditional humanitarian organisations and

VTCs. These interviews were not conducted by the author, but were conducted for the purpose of a similar study that was aimed to explore the collaboration between the VTCs and the traditional humanitarian actors [i.e. 6].

The collection and analysis of data was exploratory, expecting to generate insights into the practices constitute the network innovation. The examination of the data and its collection continued over the period in a non-linear manner. The analytical strategy borrowed heavily from a grounded theory research perspective [51, 52]. Although the author decided against explicitly coding the data, his concern was to identify key themes therein and develop them with reference to extant theoretical literatures [53]. The process of data collection and analysis was iterative allowing new themes to emerge. The analysis consisted of multiple readings of the various materials. The raw data was further analyzed in different smaller documents with regard to other similar in-depth accounts and conceptual perspectives that ultimately facilitated the identification of important practices and relations that were involved in the process of network innovation.

5   Collaborative Re-orderings in Humanitarian Networks: Reconfiguring and Fusing

This section explores the collaborative endeavours and challenges in the humanitarian aid arena, and delineates two major practices of re-configuring and fusing that offer rich insights into the transformations taking place.

5.1   Humanitarian Aid Networks Facing Opportunities and Challenges

The volunteer and technical communities (VTCs) are heterogeneous and evolving networks of distributed technical savvy individuals who may or may not be solely dedicated to disaster response. They draw their ideology and working methods from the following elements: open-source ideology; flexible structure and hierarchy; collaborative workflow; altruistic nature; desire to cultivate and disseminate technical skills; and enthusiasm for partnership [6: 7]. The VTCs are able to provide disaster responders with a range of tools and services including (but not limited to) translation, geospatial mapping, social media listening, incident tracking, and data aggregation. VTCs aim to harness this massive influx of data by applying volunteer communities to assist disaster responders in managing this information and as a result, make more informed decisions. For example, during Hurricane Sandy, "6,717 volunteers analyzed more than 35,535 photographs of the US eastern seaboard... completing more than half of that work in the first 48 hours" which allowed FEMA to begin targeted response faster than ever before [54].

The collaboration of these non-traditional actors with the traditional humanitarian network is not without challenges. On one hand, the traditional humanitarian actors form a conservative system that is relatively hierarchical and inflexible. On the other hand, the VTCs demonstrate flattened and decentralized organizational structure that has been inspired by "online communities like Wikipedia and open source software development projects (and allow for VTCs to move) faster than larger players in nearly all circumstances" [55: 3]. Besides these differences and the respective challenges for collaboration between these two camps (of formal and volunteer organisations), it is believed that developing of collaborative inter-facing would be beneficial:

"For all the exciting possibilities that exist for VTCs to accelerate the tempo of humanitarian response and disaster risk management, they face important challenges that will shape their ability to define a new paradigm. It is an open moment for the traditional operators to ensure that we make best use of this rich resource...There is great potential to include these communities and technologies within the preparation stage." [55: 17].

Importantly, it is also deemed that such collaboration would contribute to the core humanitarian values and ends such as 'saving lives':

"Disaster Relief 2.0... has the potential to save many lives, mobilize international interest and resources, and improve the effective allocation of limited resources" [56: 9].

Importantly, however, humanitarian actors seem to suggest that such integration is not a straightforward process of 'connecting' that can be easily enabled by technologies. Instead, the development of such collaborative interface is associated with many difficulties such as lack of credibility, legitimacy and trust between the new volunteer formations and the old traditional organisations. Moreover, it is oftentimes suggested that the integration of the VTCs as a long-term partner in the current traditional humanitarian network would result into repercussions for the whole network, and will lead to changes that will require a re-definition of their identities, structures and processes:

"It has become clear over time that in order for the work of V&TCs to meet its true potential, they will have to meet formal organizations halfway" [2: 45-6].

"One cannot for certain say how these models will evolve and morph." (Sanjana Hattotuwa, ICT For Peace Foundation)

Drawing on the sensibilities of the relational/performative ontology, we explore and attempt to understand the process of co-emergence of these networks by delineating two types of practices i.e. practices of reconfiguring and practices of fusing. The former type of practice points to the transformational processes that are taking place in both traditional and volunteer organisations that would enable their fusing and co-emergence. The latter practice points to the related process of fusing that relate to the co-constructing of the new network with redefined identities, roles and practices. In the following section we will illustrate how these insights can help us make sense of the changes and transformations undergoing the area of Humanitarian aid.

5.2   Reconfiguring the Traditional Humanitarian Networks

The humanitarian network comprised of the traditional, formal organisations can be characterized as dominated by bureaucracy and formalization especially when compared to the volunteer formations:

"Bureaucratic delays and impediments, old thinking, senior management that is excited by the prospect of working with V&TCs yet don't sign off on the institutional resources - financial and human - necessary to foster such collaboration, information overload and a sense of hopelessness driven by the inability to analyze this flood" (Sanjana Hattotuwa, ICT For Peace Foundation)

"A humanitarian event is fast moving and these (traditional and formal organisations) are slow moving by the book organizations." (Charles Conley, iMMAP)

The predictions for a common future that suggests that both camps traditional and non-traditional have to inevitably develop ways to work together is putting pressure on the formal organisations to become more open and embrace the opportunities offered by the VTCs. Moreover, it can be argued that the contrasting organisational practices and cultures are making the formal organisations, which are still "firmly rooted in a paradigm of documents and databases passed through hierarchies" [2: 34], to drift away from their established way of working and adopting more flexible approaches:

"V&TCs can generate an environment of innovation and growth for humanitarian organizations, giving them the chance to experiment with new ways of collecting, analyzing and managing information" [6]

Hence, it is believed that the VTCs can augment the existing efforts that OCHA was making to improve information management and coordination and look for ways that open its structures to better interface with non-traditional actors [8: 41]. Although remaining invisible to public gaze decentralization, flattening and openness are among the undergoing OCHA's structural changes (ibid.). More specifically, for instance, UNOCHA have initiated processes of flattening and introducing more flexibility into their operations [8].

These reconfigurations in the traditional humanitarian actors would potentially help these organisations become more susceptible to working with the VTCS. Currently this collaboration is considered problematic:

"Federal agencies have a much easier time working with corporations that engage in collective intelligence than with the communities that emerge from grassroots processes." [54: 16].

Importantly, many of the challenges to introducing this change are due to the fact that the traditional networks have developed internal mechanisms and structures, formalized in response to 'best practices' and 'lessons learnt' sometimes in response to the needs of donors and demands of managing that make them too conservative and unsusceptible to change [9: 13].

5.3   Reconfiguring the VTC Networks

Contrasted with the traditional humanitarian actors, the VTCs can be characterized as flexible, flat, fast and innovative:

"VTCs moved far faster than larger players in nearly all circumstances - and perhaps faster than established protocols will allow. It is here - in the politics and tempo of this new volunteer capability - that the bottom-up, grassroots structures need protocols to work with the top-down systems within large organisations" [55: 3].

The multiple commentaries suggest that in order to avoid the collaboration problems with the traditional network, the VTCs must become sustainable, better funded, reliable and professionalized in their activities. The rhetoric emphasizes the benefits as mechanisms for incentivizing and seducing. In particular, increasing the impact of the VTCs in the humanitarian aid field is claimed to be major motivation:

"Collaborating with humanitarian organizations increases the local and global impact of VTCs and organizations…Working with these organizations can potentially provide more awareness of how the skills and the passions of your volunteers can most directly meet the needs of the affected population" [55-16].

It's been suggested that in order for the VTCs to become a well-established partner in the humanitarian field they have to re-configure their operations by moving towards the traditional organisations that have to recognize them as a reliable, credible and legitimate partner. Moreover, it is argued that by introducing formalization and professionalization into its organization, the VTCs will be able to overcome the lack of reliability and trust:

"[VTCs] need to be seen as predictable and reliable. In essence, we need to know—whether I'm dealing with Central African Republic in a conflict or I'm dealing with a mega disaster—I'm going to get the same level of support. Because we need to structure; the response system has to be predictable. If you want to play the game you need to be stepping up each and every time as a predictable partner, because people will rely on you." (Brendan McDonald, OCHA)

Such re-configuration processes have to be fine-tuned to avoid clashing with the existing ideological motivations of volunteers, but to also introduce changes that can be amenable to the coalescing of the two networks:

"Governance and organization models in order to prevent against the negative aspects of informal hierarchy, elitism, and hyper-politicization that occur within naturally evolving networks. This is entirely possible to do while retaining a flat organizational structure and distributed decision making as we have seen in the Wikipedia case example" [9].

Importantly the VTCs have developed a pervasive rhetoric about the introduction of such re-configurations that would bring benefits of improved visibility, credibility and impact for the different volunteer groups and communities:

"…Additionally, the formal organizations can provide a sense of legitimacy to the work of the VTCs in the eyes of sometimes skeptical regional and national governments. In essence, the humanitarian organization's reputation of reliability and accountability is shared with its VTC partner during collaboration, providing greater credibility and thus opportunities to their volunteers" [55: 15-6]

5.4   Fusing Practices and Mechanisms

Both the reconfiguring and fusing practices are important for the co-emergence of the new collaborative ordering that will form a new humanitarian network. While, it can be argued that the fusing practices trigger the move towards re-configuration, it is also important to acknowledge that only by introducing certain re-configurations, fusing can be established in the long run. The fusing practices span a range of activities from increasing the awareness and improving the familiarity between the traditional and non-traditional actors to developing personal relationships and the role of people who can span network boundaries:

"Some individuals had a sense of what that [the V&TC's] capability is, just as a volunteer workforce, not to mention the technical capabilities. But I think most of straight up crew in info management with the traditional ways of doing things did not feel frustration, because they did not even realize what had been missed..." Nigel Snoad, UNDAC

Importantly, we can differentiate between two different approaches of fusing/ engaging – that is, bottom-up and local, on one hand; and top-bottom and centralized forms of fusing, on the other hand. Whereas, these two approaches appear to be significantly different and even polar, they can co-exist and complement each other. The generic, local and transcending approach would not obstruct the more centralized, mediated and traversing dialogue. Both approaches introduce forms of enrollment by providing different itineraries of engagement. These approaches attempt to increase the awareness and willingness for collaboration:

"Maximizing the benefit and effectiveness of VTC engagements with traditional humanitarian entities is only possible if both sides remain ready and willing to work and learn together"[6: 11].

Bottom-Up and Decentralized Approach to Fusing and Engaging. This bottom-up approach concerns the emergence of local collaborations between various traditional and non-traditional actors that are developing a collaborative ordering through 'learning-by-doing'. An instrumental role in making such relationships emerge and work played different mediators and focal points that provided the needed local relational infrastructure upon which these collaborations emerged:

"Every organization is made up of people. It's about knowing a lot of people, and caring about what they do" (Brugh Willow, Geeks Without Bounds).

Some individuals have become boundary spanners or translators [57] and have opened a space for the emergence of informal interfacing between representatives from both networks:

"Andrej is the quintessential champion within more traditional organizations. When you have these people within more traditional entities, and you have them pushing their colleagues to get more engaged, this is a really great thing. It works the other way around too" (Natalie Chang, Internews).

This approach can be also seen as co-emergence of the traditional and non-traditional actors into a new hybrid collaborative orderings that emerge both peripherally and locally. Whereas, such collaborative, traversing inter-facing is while being local and peripheral, it slowly and steadily permeates the broader network, in which reputation and power easily inter-link. In contrast, some of the centralized, top-down mechanisms inevitably also influence the emergence of the bottom-up and local processes.

Top-Down and Centralized Approach to Fusing and Engaging. This top-bottom, structured and centralized approach is about co-participation in a dialogue with a view of establishing "a formal channel for these groups to engage in a dialogue about the underlying problems of information management" (Harvard Humanitarian Initiative 2011: 13). There have been different suggestions for the precise format of these arrangements: "intermediary,' 'interface,' or 'board,' to act as a connection between the two sides" [8]. Such a dialogue would aim to facilitate the processes of supporting, mediating, encouraging the interactions and integrating the two networks (ibid). According to the Harvard Humanitarian Institute [2: 9] the development of different initiatives such as 'neutral forum' 'innovation space', 'research and training' consortium would provide a space and mediate the discussions about common problems, experimenting, sharing tools and practices. Importantly, such a dialogue would lead to a 'clear operational interface' (ibid) that outlines agreed upon communication practices, standards, protocols, roles and priorities. This approach resembles the 'traversing' form of collaboration that aims to establish common contextual awareness and commonalities performed by dialogic collaborative practices.

In addition, this approach has been centrally orchestrated by providing documents that offer guidelines how the traditional humanitarian and VTCs can collaborate with each other [6, 9]. These documents capture the experience of some of the successful collaborations in the area and enhance the awareness between the two networks. These documents set out a route for developing successful collaboration that can help the emergence of the network not through centrally concerted activities of negotiation but through developing local relationships of trust and predictability. This approach carries the characteristics of the 'transcending' approach [25] of collaboration that is about developing a common landscape on basis of which in situ collaborative practices and relationships can spur. These might then offer a sustainable basis for the emergence of a generic network that would essentially merge the existing formal and VTC networks.

Furthermore, various inscriptions, reports, memoranda, documents, survey results, scientific papers, materials and money, or more generally physical and social displacements have spanned easier some of the network boundaries and served to 'amplify the voices' [58] for integrating and aligning the two networks. Meetings and conferences also played a pivotal role in promoting the dialogue for central coordinating of collective efforts to develop awareness and engagement:

"The majority of collaborative relationships grow out of face-to-face environments, where collaborative partners have an opportunity to put a face to a name. Trust and reliability are critical elements of the humanitarian system, so establish collaborative relationships in person and within a trusted community setting to solidify the relationship" (Natalie Chang, Internews).

Finally, a group of VTCs established the Digital Humanitarian Network (DHNetwork) to act as a unified face for the networks to the formal humanitarian organizations. It is considered that this entity has the potential to become a major vehicle for enrolling the VTC actor-networks:

"We want to inform other humanitarian organizations that VTCs like the Digital Humanitarian Network have established formal and predictable procedures for engagement and activation" (Meier, Patrick, iRevolution).

The DHNetwork attempts become the 'obligatory point of passage' [58, 59] for those organisations who seek legitimacy and credibility, and who are ready to accept certain standards around ethics code, communication and activation protocols and procedures:

"The bureaucracy, the larger governance and lack of interest in embracing VTC models and frameworks. Seems like some organizations don't even know how and if we fit in and who we are. I hope that the new initiative, DHNetwork, would alleviate the latter problem" (Shoreh Elhami, GISCorps).

6   Discussion and Conclusion

This paper identified two major practices of reconfiguring and fusing that shape the endeavours of establishing a collaborative ordering between the traditional and volunteer humanitarian organisations. These two sets of practices are inter-related and co-exist in the process of coalescing and co-emerging of a new humanitarian network. More specifically, the practices of reconfiguring point to the reorganizing processes towards flattening, decentralization and flexibility in the traditional organisations, and the move towards moderate formalization and professionalization that mark the evolution of the VTCs. These re-configurings are both motivated and are motivating the practices of engaging and fusing that bring these two types of actors together by both centrally orchestrated, top-down approach, and peripherally and locally spurred endeavours. Importantly, these practices reveal a process of complex collaborative re-ordering that leads to the co-emergence of new humanitarian network with re-defined identities, inter-dependences and roles.

This paper attempts to contribute to the crisis response literature that is dominated by 'informational' and 'technologist' perspectives on collaboration. Instead, the paper develops a perspective on collaboration informed by relational/ performative ontologies that account for issues of trust, legitimacy, relational context and power, which are oftentimes neglected by more mainstream studies conceptualizing the process of collaboration. While, 'connectivist' perspectives on collaboration oftentimes offer overly simplified descriptions of mechanistic linking between disparate actors, this work opens a space for a more nuanced understanding of the complexity and dynamics of the network-wide interactions and changes. More specifically, it is suggested that establishing of a new collaborative ordering in the Humanitarian network entails more profound changes that re-configure the actors who are shaped by bundles of practices and identities that become instantiated only in relation to other network actors, and by being inextricably linked they form a network with a new characteristics.

The findings of this paper can also have implications for the broader organisational literature on distributed collaboration which despite offering a very sophisticated theorization of the way distributed communities collaborate with each other, seems to neglect the issues related to engagement, lack of commitment and power and relational dynamics. More specifically, this paper shows that the dialogic processes of meaning production ('transcending' and 'traversing') [25] are contingent on a relational (network) context that has to afford certain relational engagement, trust/ credibility production and alignment of interests. Moreover, this perspective is particularly suited for exploring complex, sociomaterial multi-level interactions between disparate and heterogeneous actors and networks.

Future research can continue exploring how the humanitarian aid network continues to change as a result of the maturation of the practices of re-configuring and fusing. Furthermore, the perspective synthesized here can be further developed and extended by focusing on the local collaboration between a particular VTC and a traditional humanitarian representative, so that it can offer richer and more granular insights into the in situ processes of re-configuring and fusing.

References

1. United Nations: OCHA in 2012 & 2013, Plan and Budget (2012),
   `https://ochanet.unocha.org/p/Documents/OCHA_in_2012_13.pdf`
2. Harvard Humanitarian Initiative: Disaster Relief 2.0: The Future of Information Sharing in Humanitarian Emergencies (2011), `http://www.unfoundation.org/assets/pdf/disaster-relief-20-report.pdf`
3. Hughes, A., Palen, L., Sutton, J., Liu, S., Vieweg, S.: Site- Seeing in Disaster: An Examination of On-Line Social Convergence. In: Proc. of Information Systems for Crisis Response and Management Conference, ISCRAM (2008)
4. Palen, L., Liu, S.: Citizen Communications in Crisis: Anticipating a Future of ICT-Supported Participation. In: Proc. of CHI, pp. 727–736 (2007)
5. Palen, L., Starbird, K.: Voluntweeters: Self-Organizing by Digital Volunteers in Times of Crisis. In: Proc. of CHI (2011)
6. Capelo, L., Chang, N., Verity, A.: Guidance for Collaborating with Volunteer & Technical Communities (2013), `http://www.digitalhumanitarians.com`
7. Goodchild, M., Glennon, J.: Crowdsourcing geographic information for disaster response: A research frontier. International Journal of Digital Earth 3, 231–241 (2010)
8. Milner, M., Verity, A.: Collaborative Innovation in Humanitarian Affairs: Organization and Governance in the Era of Digital Humanitarianism (2013), `http://blog.veritythink.com`
9. Waldman, A., Andrej, V., Shadrock, R.: Digital Humanitarian Network: Guidance for Collaborating with Volunteer & Technical Communities (2013), `https://app.box.com/s/qpuu11mwadxfllcd7xwu`
10. Nunamaker Jr., J., Weber, S., Chen, M.: Organizational crisis management systems: planning for intelligent action. Journal of Management Information Systems 5, 7–32 (1989)
11. Sniezek, J., Wilkins, D., Wadlington, P., Baumann, M.: Training for crisis decision-making: psychological issues and computer-based solutions. Journal of Management Information Systems 18, 147–168 (2002)
12. Day, J., Junglas, I., Silva, L.I.: Information flow impediments in disaster relief supply chains. Journal of the Association for Information Systems 10, 637–660 (2009)
13. Bharosa, N., Janssen, M., Tan, Y.-H.: A research agenda for information quality assurance in public safety networks: information orchestration as the middle ground between hierarchical and netcentric approaches. Cognition, Technology & Work 13, 203–216 (2011)
14. De Bruijn, H.: One Fight, One Team: The 9/11 Commision Report on Intelligence, Fragmentation and Information. Public Administration 84(2), 267–287 (2006)
15. Fisher, C.W., Kingma, D.R.: Criticality of Data Quality as exemplified in two disasters. Information & Management 39, 109–116 (2001)
16. Longstaff, P.H.: Security, Resilience, and Communication in Unpredictable Environments Such as Terrorism, Natural Disasters, and Complex Technology (2005), `http://pirp.harvard.edu/pubs_pdf/longsta/longsta-p05-3.pdf`
17. Ngamassi, L., Maldonado, E., Zhao, K., Robinson, H., Maitland, C., Tapia, A.: Exploring Barriers to Coordination between Humanitarian NGOs: A Comparative Case Study of Two NGO"s Information Technology Coordination Bodies. International Journal of Information Systems and Social Change, special issue on IS/IT in Nonprofits (2010)

18. Saab, D., Maldonado, E., Orendovici, R., Ngamassi, L., Gorp, A., Zhao, K., Maitland, C., Tapia, A.: Building global bridges: Coordination bodies for improved information sharing among humanitarian relief agencies. In: Proceedings of the 5th International ISCRAM Conference, Washington, DC, USA (2008)

19. Tapia, A., Moore, K., Johnson, N.: Beyond the Trustworthy Tweet: A Deeper Understanding of Microblogged Data Use by Disaster Response and Humanitarian Relief Organizations. In: 10th International ISCRAM Conference, Baden-Baden, Germany (2013)

20. Leidner, D., Pan, G., Pan, S.: The role of IT in crisis response: lessons from the SARS and Asian Tsunami disasters. The Journal of Strategic Information Systems 18, 80–99 (2009)

21. Hale, J.: A layered communication architecture for the support of crisis response. Journal of Management Information Systems 14, 235–255 (1997)

22. Majchrzak, A., Jarvenpaa, S., Hollingshead, A.: Coordinating expertise among emergent groups responding to disasters. Organization Science 18, 147–161 (2007)

23. National Research Council. Summary of a Workshop on using Information Technology to Enhance Disaster Management, USA (2005)

24. Turoff, M., Chumer, M., Van de Walle, B., Yao, X.: The design of a dynamic emergency response management information systems (DERMIS). Journal of Information Technology Theory and Application 5, 1–35 (2004)

25. Majchrzak, A., More, P.H.B., Faraj, S.: Transcending Knowledge Differences in Cross-Functional Teams. Organization Science, 1–20 (2011)

26. Odlund, A.: Pulling the Same Way? A Multi-Perspectivist Study of Crisis Cooperation in Government. Journal of Contingencies and Crisis Management 18(2), 96–107 (2010)

27. Pan, G., Pan, S., Leidner, D.: Crisis Response Information Networks. The Journal of Strategic Information Systems 13, 31–56 (2011)

28. Comfort, L.K.: Crisis Management in Hindsight: Cognition, Communication, Coordination, and Control. Public Administration Review 67, 189–197 (2007)

29. Schraagen, J.M., van de Ven, J.: Human factors aspects of ICT for crisis management. Cognition, Technology & Work 13, 175–187 (2011)

30. Boland, R.: Why shared meanings have no place in structuration theory: A reply to Scapens and Macintosh. Accounting, Organizations and Society 21, 691–698 (1996)

31. Ngwenyama, O.K., Lee, A.S.: Communication Richness in Electronic Mail: Critical Social Theory and the Contextuality of Meaning. MIS Quarterly 21, 145–167 (1997)

32. Carlson, J.R., Zmud, R.W.: Channel expansion theory and the experiential nature of media richness perceptions. Academy of Management Journal 42, 153–170 (1999)

33. Hinds, P., Weisband, S.: Knowledge sharing and shared understanding in virtual teams. In: Gibson, C., Cohen, S. (eds.) Creating conditions for effective virtual teams, pp. 21-36. Jossey-Bass, San Francisco (2003)

34. Majchrzak, A., More, P.H.B., Faraj, S.: Transcending Knowledge Differences in Cross-Functional Teams. Organization Science 1526-5455 (2011)

35. Merleau-Ponty, M.: Phenomenology of Perception. Routledge, London (1962)

36. Vlaar, P.W., van Fenema, P., Tiwari, V.: Cocreating Understanding and Value in Distributed Work: How Members of Onsite and Offshore ISD Vendor Teams Give, Make, Demand and Break Sense. MIS Quarterly (2008)

37. Cramton, C.D., Hinds, P.L.: Subgroup Dynamics in Internationally Distributed Teams: Ethnocentrism or Cross National Learning? Research in Organizational Behaviour 26, 231–263 (2005)

38. Giddens, A.: The Constitution of Society. Polity Press, Cambridge (1984)

39. Boland, R.: Perspective Making and Perspective Taking in Communities of Knowing. Organisation Science 6, 350–372 (1995)
40. Orlikowski, W.: Sociomaterial Practices: Exploring Technology at Work. Organization Studies 28, 1435 (2007)
41. Orlikowski, W., Scott, S.: Sociomateriality: Challenging the Separation of Technology, Work and Organisation. The Academy of Management Annals 2, 433–474 (2008)
42. Wagner, E., Newell, S., Piccoli, G.: Understanding Project Survival in an ES Environment: A Sociomaterial Practice Perspective. JAIS 11, 276–297 (2010)
43. Law, J.: Organizing Modernity. Blackwell Publishers (1994)
44. Latour, B.: Reassmbling the Social: An Introduction to Actor Network Theory (Clarendon Lectures in Management Studies). Oxford University Press (2005)
45. Suchman, L.: Organising alignment: a case of bridgebuilding. Organization 7, 311–327 (2000)
46. Barad, K.: Meeting the Universe Halfway: quantum physics and the entanglement of matter and meaning. Duke University Press, London (2007)
47. Reckwitz, A.: Toward a Theory of Social Practices: A Development in Culturalist Theorizing. European Journal of Social Theory 5, 243–263 (2002a)
48. Schatzki, T., Knorr Cetina, K., von Savigny, E. (eds.): The Practice Turn in Contemporary Theory. Routledge, London (2001)
49. Latour, B.: We Have Never Been Modern. Harvester Wheatsheaf, London (1993)
50. Law, J.: Actor Network Theory and Material Semiotics (2007), http://www.heterogeneities.net/publications/Law-ANTandMaterialSemiotics.pdf
51. Strauss, A.L., Corbin, J.: Basics of Qualitative Research. Sage Publications (1990)
52. Strauss, A.L., Corbin, J.: Grounded Theory in Practice. Sage Publications (1997)
53. Walsham, G.: Interpretive studies in IS research: nature and method. European Journal of Information Systems 4, 74–81 (1995)
54. Crowley, J.: Connecting Grassroots and Government for Disaster Response. Wilson Centre & Commons Lab (2013), http://www.wilsoncenter.org/sites/default/files/crowleyupdated2.pdf
55. GFDRR: Volunteer Technology Communities: Open Development (2011), http://www.gfdrr.org/sites/gfdrr.org/files/publication/VolunteerTechnologyCommunities-OpenDevelopment.pdf
56. Villaveces, J.: Disaster Response 2.0. Forced Migration Review (2013), http://www.fmreview.org/technology/villaveces.html
57. Star, S.L., Griesemer, J.R.: Institutional ecology, "translations" and boundary objects: Amateurs and professionals in Berkeley's Museum of Vertebrate Zoology. Social Study of Science 19(3), 1907–1939 (1989)
58. Callon, M.: Some Elements of a Sociology of Translation: Domestication of the Scallops and the Fishermen of St Brieuc Bay. In: Law, J. (ed.) Power, Action & Belief. A New Sociology of Knowledge? pp. 196–229. Routledge & Kegan Paul, London
59. Callon, M.: The Sociology of an Actor-Network: The Case of the Electric Vehicle: Mapping the Dynamics of Science and Technology, pp. 19–34. Macmillan Press, London (1986a)

Towards Better Coordination of Rescue Teams in Crisis Situations: A Promising ACO Algorithm

Jason Mahdjoub[1], Francis Rousseaux[1], and Eddie Soulier[2]

[1] CReSTIC, University of Reims Champagne-Ardenne, France
{jason.mahdjoub,francis.rousseaux}@univ-reims.fr
[2] Tech-CICO, University of Technology of Troyes, France
eddie.soulier@utt.fr

Abstract. Crisis management challenges decision support systems designers. One problem in the decision making is developing systems able to help the coordination of the different involved teams. Another challenge is to make the system work with a degraded communication infrastructure. Each workstation or embedded application must be designed assuming that potential decisions made by other workstations are treated as eventualities. We propose in this article a multi-agent model, based on an ant colony optimization algorithm, and designed to manage the inherent complexity in the deployment of resources used to solve a crisis. This model manages data uncertainty. Its global goal is to optimize in a stable way fitness functions, like saving lives. Moreover, thanks to a reflexive process, the model manages the effects of its decisions into the environment to take more appropriate decisions. Thanks to our transactional model, the system takes into account a large data amount and finds global optimums without exploring all potential solutions. Users will have to define a rule database using an adapted graphical interface. Then, if the nature of the crisis is deeply unchanged, users should be able to change the rule databases.

1 Introduction

Today, crisis management is an important domain throughout the world. Crisis can be earthquakes, industrial accidents, nuclear crises, etc [1]. Moreover, crises can appear as a result of several emergencies, which can produce more complex crises. One issue is to manage and minimize the effects of this complexity. Our work is centered on tasks planning and resources deployment, through an embedded application distributed into an asynchronous network.

This study refers to the project AidCrisis, financed by the French Region Champagne-Ardenne and the European Regional Development Fund. The project aims to produce solutions for the decision making, in order to prevent mainly from nuclear, radiological, bacteriologic and chemical risks. Three kinds of aspects have been discriminated [2]. The first one consists of preparing or anticipating potential crises, through classification of circumstances, identification

C. Hanachi, F. Bénaben, and F. Charoy (Eds.): ISCRAM-med 2014, LNBIP 196, pp. 135–142, 2014.
© Springer International Publishing Switzerland 2014

of critical sites, training, scripting events [3], simulation, etc. The second aspect consists of treating an ongoing crisis, by identifying it, deploying resources and managing the logistic, dealing with localized events, and exposing results. The third aspect consists of analyzing the crisis after its progression, in order to learn lessons.

During the treatment step, several groups, such as first aid agents, police, doctors, government delegates, among others, must collaborate in the working site. Each group has to follow its own organization, and its own goals, according to a categorized event. Three kinds of groups have been segmented [1], which are the management centers, the hospital centers, and the agents working on the accident area.

This paper presents a model that enables the constitution of a strategy to be applied considering a crisis scenario and the deployment optimization of the human and material resources.

In section 2, we relate the different algorithms of optimization and we justify our choice. According to a particular data structure articulating events, goals, tasks, and resources, we propose an adaptation of the chosen algorithm in section 3. This model is adapted for large scale applications, manages uncertainty, and by a reflexive process, adapts its decision process according to the effect of its decisions over the time. We end with a conclusion and perspectives in section 4.

2   Related Work

2.1   Criticisms on Statistical Approaches

Statistical approaches can provide good predictions (in average). On the other hand, they can seriously induce the human and computer deliberation to severe faults. For example, Parunak et al. [4] have demonstrated how a colony of agents, typically a prey/predator ecosystem, can prove wrong a statistical approach. Others objections have been done about more complex statistical approaches, for example in the finance domain [5,6]. [6] proposes to prefer more stable laws like those of Pareto to deal with random variables which does not follow a normal distribution.

The interpretation of a model is often developed according to the model itself, and the only way to develop the criticism and to avoid a kind of fatalism would be to construct new models. By opposition or competition with statistical based models, our way is to develop a simulation based model designed for coordination and assignment of human and material resources. Simulation based model have the advantage to make appear empirically unlikely phenomena, where statistical approaches can consider some potentially important events as insignificant. However, both simulation and statistical based model can accumulate approximations, which should make the system producing incoherent data, then incoherent decisions. To avoid, or at least to limit this phenomenon, we suppose that the introduction of data uncertainty should force the system to have a stable reaction.

Simulation, optimizations, and finally decision making are done according to several goals which can be independent or correlated. The following section describes the related approaches that deal with multi-goal optimization.

2.2   Combinatorial Optimization

A problem of combinatorial optimization can be defined as follows: considering a set of combinations S and a fitness function $f : S \to IR$, the combinatorial optimization consists of find the combination $s \in S$ minimizing f such as: $f(s) \leq f(s_i), \forall s_i \in S$.

According the related work exposed in [7], two main types of optimization algorithms exist: complete approaches and heuristic approaches.

Complete approaches, like branch and bound solutions, or dynamic programming solutions, have to explore every combination contained into S. They do not permit to resolve problems whose complexity class is NP.

Heuristic approaches can be decomposed into two kinds of approaches: local search approaches and constructive approaches.

Local search approaches [8] consist of making solutions progressing into their neighborhood. The main difficulty of these approaches is to avoid local optimum. Simulated annealing method [9] was inspired from annealing in metallurgy. It is a statistical method which consists of virtually controlling the temperature of the material, i.e. the set of solutions. If the temperature is hot (or cold), particles are free (or not) and then solutions are free to move from one to another (or not). Then, the method consists of progressively decreasing the temperature, to make the system converging to the better optimums. Inspired from observations of the nature, genetic approaches [10] consist of generating competition between individuals of a population, thanks to reproducing, genetic mutations, and fitness functions. Several strategies have been developed in the genetic algorithms domain, to avoid local optimums, but global optimums cannot be insured. Particle swarm optimization [11] is also an evolutionary approach, but based on a stochastic approach. The method is inspired from the observation of the movement of organisms in a bird flock or fish school. Particles adapt their speed and their directions according to the current optimal solutions, to discover new potential solutions.

Constructive approaches start with empty solutions, and construct them progressively. With greedy algorithms, the choice of each element can be made randomly, or according to a heuristic, called gradient criterion. The performance of theses approaches depend highly on the gradient criterion. So it is not adapted for all applications. Estimation of distribution algorithms [12] are evolutionary models based on the progressive construction of probabilities defining the quality of each choice. Initially proposed in [13], optimizations by ant colony consist of taking advantage in the use of intelligence emerging from a collective work of an ant colony. The ant colony optimization (ACO) consists of ants in finding the shortest path between the anthill and the nearest located food.

Ant colony algorithms are well adapted for problems whose complexity class is NP. We will see how this algorithm is mathematically formalized for multi-goal optimization problems.

In most time, our application should coordinate local resources to manage a crisis. Moreover, every combination of task and every strategy do not have to use all human and material resources. But sometimes, in a severe crisis context, the system could take into account a large set of resources. For example, in a forest fire context, the system could have to call firemen which come from other regions, and sometimes from other countries. Taking account of every resource of every region could become a very complex problem. However the ant colony algorithm shows that ants do not really explore their entire environment and stay near to their anthill. Moreover it is possible to limit the exploration of the ants according to the best current obtained path. Then, even if a workstation does not have the entire data of the entire regions, the ants can move from a workstation to another to look for their goal. And because, they don't have to explore all their environment, the system can resolve a goal without making all workstations contributing to the problem. For this reason, ant colony algorithm appears for us well adapted.

3   The Proposed Approach

3.1   Goals

Thanks to a rule database defined by competent actors, the system has to generate both an action and a deployment plan of the different resources, in order to manage the ongoing crisis, its uncertainty, and its dynamical reaction to human intervention. Another challenge is to work with different workstations represented by actors located on different regions. The reason for this distribution is justified by the necessity to, 1) enable the system working with a deteriorated network, and 2) involve actors coming from other regions in some cases. We present an optimization algorithm which does not explore all the space of solutions.

3.2   Data Structure

Structurally, the input data is organized as follows. Different actors of the management center can enter into the system different kinds of possible events. This is defined using a graphical interface before the crisis detection. These events correspond to possible real events like fire, health problem, aggression, etc. Each of these events/problems can be specialized into sub-events. For example, fire can be specified as a house fire, a public building fire or a nuclear power station fire. Moreover, a set of events can be a superposed state. Moreover, each event can trigger other events according specific functions, which can depend from time and more generally from the evolution of the parent event parameters. For each event, the system has to solve a goal. A goal can have several fitness functions to minimize. To reach this goal, the user has to enter a graph of possible tasks to apply. For each task, a list of resources can be used. Moreover, each task can be localized or not. If it is the case, the system generates tasks of transportation of resources.

3.3 Ant Colony Optimization (ACO) for Multi-goal Optimization Problems

Our system must be able to solve problems which are formalized according to several goals, i.e. several fitness functions. [14] discussed several ACO approaches adapted to multi-goal problems. Experimentations have been done in [7] and it appears that the best of these approaches (m-ACO_6) is also a Pareto based approach. m-ACO_6 appears also better than several evolutionary algorithms [7]. We have adapted this model according the algorithm described in the next subsection.

3.4 Algorithm

The first step of our method is to decompose according to a discrete grid, events which have superposed time positions and superposed space positions, into superposed events which have unique positions.

Then the system deduces the list of goals it has to solve. For each goal, the system will have to plan the allocation of resources according to time and space, and without conflict with other goals. One solution to solve these goals is to consider them as a global multi-goal optimization problem. However, this solution will force the system to process a global optimization centralized into one server, and making the entire network dependent from this server. Instead of this solution, we propose a transactional model. Our solution consists of optimizing each individual goal as bubble of realities. Then, if two bubbles have conflicts of resources, a parent bubble will be generated to solve these conflicts by generating sets of constraints adapted for each possible alternative solution. Thanks to this transactional model, resources data which can be located only into other servers, workstations, or smart-phones, are explored during the goal optimization step only when no close free resource has been detected. As for the transactional memory programming [15], this method should give in most cases, better performances. The figure 1 shows how node bubbles are optimized. When all bubbles have been optimized, and when all bubbles have no conflict with any bubbles, than the system goes to the dynamical projection step.

When a task is applied into the environment, the state of the system is likely of changing. With our data structure, the application of a task, or the application of another task will change the evolution of the events, and those of the triggered events. So deliberation of the system can alter the variables responsible of this deliberation, and then alter this deliberation. Since we do not consider global exploration, we have developed the next strategy. When all bubbles have been optimized, the system projects for each bubble their related decisions over time, and deduces new future events. These last are merged with equivalent events which have been deduced in the previous loops. The fusion process consists of

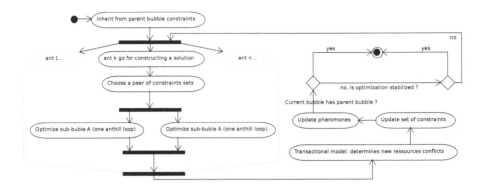

Fig. 1. Node bubble optimization process (diagram of activities)

considering a same deduced event as an event which has superposed states. From this set of deduced events, it is deduced a new set of bubbles. If changes have been detected, the system goes back to the bubble optimization step. Otherwise, it proposes its plan of resources deployment and its plan of tasks to apply.

3.5   Example Scenario

We give here an simple example of scenario which concerns an accident of bus in a highway.

1. witnesses declare the accident into our application;
2. the system propagates information toward every workstation or embedded systems;
3. the system superposes contradictory information given by witnesses;
4. teams belonging to the police, firefighers, and medical services, which are free and near the accident are guest to locate this last;
5. teams confirm they accept their new mission;
6. the system elaborates strategics paths for each teams in order to locate the accident as quickly as possible, considering that the highway can be spaned;
7. the chief responsible of the crisis management makes a balance sheet of the context. Moreover he labels every victim and enters all data into our application;
8. the system improves its strategy of tasks planification and of ressources deployment :
   - considering that the weather is good, the nearest free hellicopter is called because a victim has a neurological problem;
   - the nearest free $N-2$ ambulances are called, which N being the number of victims;

- the police has to reroute the traffic;
- civilians receive a notification into their smartphone telling them to avoid the accident;

9. for each ambulance, the system elaborates a path with the nearest hospital, and considers the gravity of the victims, the availability of the hospital ressources, and the availability of the hospital specialities.

At every step, decision centers can control the stategy of the system. If these decision centers are overloaded, the system continue to work autonomously, in a decentralized way. If the network is degraded, deconnected workstations can work locally with their sub-networks. Moreover each workstation considers all eventuallities related to each deconnected workstations, according to statistics given by the experience the system have got during past crises.

4 Conclusion and Perspectives

We have proposed a model able to plan a set of tasks and able to deploy a set of resources according to declared events during a crisis, but also according to a set of simulated events over the future. The system processes a reflexive deliberation by applying a projection of its decisions over time, and by deducing related issues to deal with. Moreover, it manages data uncertainty, according to a formalism based on the Pareto law that produces stable results, in the context of a stochastic environment. Finally, the model produces a global optimum by exploring solutions locally in a first step, and globally if necessary. This solution is then adapted to large scale systems, that should be a huge distributed network of workstations. This work can then be introduced into a more global project, i.e. the conception of an asynchronous and distributed embedded application able to manage the deployment of human and material resources in the context of a crisis.

Future works should be centered into: the introduction of a user avatar taking into account the preferences of the user; the management of uncertainty related to avatars when workstations are disconnected from the network; the simplification of data managed by users through a participative solution and through an ergonomic interface [16,17]; the process of experimentations and evaluations.

References

1. Traore, M., Sayed-Mouchaweh, M., Billaudel, P.: Learning Diagnoser and Supervision Pattern in Discrete Event System: Application to Crisis Management. In: Annual Conference of the Prognostics and Health Management Society (2013)
2. Sediri, M., Matta, N., Loriette, S., Hugerot, A.: Vers une représentation de situations de crise gérées par le SAMU. In: IC 2012 Paris (2012)
3. El Mawas, N., Cahier, J.-P.: Towards a knowledge-intensive serious game for training emergency medical services.. In: Proceedings of the 10th International Conference on Information Systems for Crisis Response and Management (ISCRAM), Baden-Baden, Germany (2013)

4. Van Dyke Parunak, H., Brueckner, S.A., Sauter, J.A., Matthews, R.: Global convergence of local agent behaviors. In: AAMAS 2005: Proceedings of the Fourth International Joint Conference on Autonomous Agents and multiagent Systems, pp. 305–312. ACM, New York (2005)
5. Mandelbrot, B., Hudson, R.L.: The Misbehavior of Markets: A Fractal View of Financial Turbulence. Basic Books (2006)
6. Taleb, N.N.: The Black Swan: Second Edition: The Impact of the Highly Improbable. Random House Trade Paperbacks (2010)
7. Alaya, I.: Optimisation multi-objectif par colonies de fourmis. Cas des problèmes de sac à dos. PhD thesis, Unveristé de la Manouba et Université Claude Bernard Lyon 1 (2009)
8. Glover, F.: Future paths for integer programming and links to artificial intelligence. Computers & Operations Research 13(5), 533–549 (1986)
9. Kirkpatrick, S., Gelatt, C.D., Vecchi, M.P.: Optimization by simulated annealing. Science 220(4598), 671–680 (1983)
10. Holland, J.H.: Adaptation in Natural and Artificial Systems: An Introductory Analysis with Applications to Biology, Control and Artificial Intelligence. MIT Press (May 1992)
11. Kennedy, J., Eberhart, R.: Particle swarm optimization. In: Proceedings of ICNN 1995 - International Conference on Neural Networks, vol. 4, pp. 1942–1948. IEEE (1995)
12. Larraaga, P., Lozano, J.: Estimation of Distribution Algorithms. A New Tool for Evolutionary Computation. Kluwer Academic Publisher (2001)
13. Dorigo, M.: Optimization, Learning and Natural Algorithms (1992) (in Italian)
14. Iredi, S., Merkle, D., Middendorf, M.: Bi-criterion optimization with multi colony ant algorithms. In: Zitzler, E., Deb, K., Thiele, L., Coello Coello, C.A., Corne, D.W. (eds.) EMO 2001. LNCS, vol. 1993, pp. 359–372. Springer, Heidelberg (2001)
15. Larus, J.R., Rajwar, R.: Transactional Memory. Synthesis Lectures on Computer Architecture 1(1), 1–226 (2006)
16. Ma, X., Cahier, J.-P.: Semantically Structured VDL-Based Iconic Tags System. In: Yamamoto, S. (ed.) HCI 2013, Part I. LNCS, vol. 8016, pp. 465–474. Springer, Heidelberg (2013)
17. Rousseaux, F., Petit, J.: Towards an Anthropological-Based Knowledge Management. In: 10th International Conference on Intellectual Capital Knowledge Management & Organisational Learning, Washington (2013)

A Multi-agent Organizational Model for a Snow Storm Crisis Management

Inès Thabet, Mohamed Chaawa, and Lamjed Ben Said

Stratégie d'Optimisation et Informatique IntelligentE,
ISG Tunis, 41 Rue de la Liberté, Cité Bouchoucha 2000 Le Bardo, Tunis-Tunisie
{Ines.Thabetk,Mohamed.chaawa}@gmail.com,
BenSaid_Lamjed@yahoo.com

Abstract. This paper introduces an organizational multi-agent model for crisis management. The considered crisis is a heavy snow storm, occurred at a north Tunisian delegation. The studied crisis caused severe infrastructure damages and endangered people's lives. Crisis systems are generally made of several heterogeneous and autonomous organizations. Each organization is given tasks and their tasks are strongly correlated. Organizations have to interact frequently and cooperate at a high level to deal with the crisis. In this context, thinking the crisis management at a macro level with an organizational view as well as structuring organizations' communications and their functioning is a crucial requirement. Following this view, the main purpose of our work is to propose a multi-agent system organization that manages resources efficiently, structure the communication among all the actors involved in the crisis management and orchestrate their work. More precisely, we provide an environment model that identifies all concepts and entities involved in the snow storm crisis. We specify, using GAIA methodology, a multi-agent organizational model that defines the roles involved in the system and the interaction protocols to realize organizational objectives. Finally, a simulator has been implemented to demonstrate the feasibility of our approach.

Keywords: Crisis Management, Multi-Agent System, Organization.

1 Introduction

Disasters, both natural (tsunami, earthquake, wildfire…) and man-made (Chemical or nuclear warfare, cyber attacks, …) are more and more frequent. They are extremely harmful since they threaten people's lives (deaths, injuries, diseases…) and heavily affect the economy.

Crisis management is the process by which an organization deals with a major unpredictable event that threatens an organization or the whole society [1, 2]. Dealing with a crisis requires quick intervention in order to reduce damages.

During a crisis, the environment is always dynamic and evolves in an unpredictable way. Crisis conditions may change and taken decisions can no longer be appropriate.

C. Hanachi, F. Bénaben, and F. Charoy (Eds.): ISCRAM-med 2014, LNBIP 196, pp. 143–156, 2014.
© Springer International Publishing Switzerland 2014

Crisis management involves many people from various organizations under the auspice of different authorities (police, medics, army, etc.) including voluntary organizations. Each organization is given tasks and their tasks needs to be coordinated since they are strongly correlated. The more the crisis increases, the more the number of involved organizations increases as well. Participants are also not fixed and evolve as people join or leave organizations.

As a consequence, crises are complex systems due to the dynamicity of the environment and the complexity of the interactions among different parts. The complexity of the interactions is due to the fact that most crisis treatment systems are made of several heterogeneous and autonomous organizations that may have not worked together previously. These organizations have to interact frequently and cooperate at a high level to deal with the crisis. As a result, the efficiency of the crisis management system depends on the communication among organizations. Structuring organizations communications and their functioning is therefore a crucial requirement. Without regulation, interactions among the involved organizations can become numerous, costly and unpredictable and thus lead to a chaotic collective behavior.

In this context, agents [3, 4] are known to be an appropriate paradigm for modelling complex, open and distributed systems. Indeed, agents provide high level abstraction to build autonomous, reactive and proactive software components with social abilities enabling communication with sophisticated languages and protocols. Agents also provide high level organizational concepts (groups, roles, commitments, interaction protocols) allowing to abstract a system at a high level with macro and social concepts (roles, interaction protocols, groups). Flexible management of changing organizational structures can be naturally achieved using these concepts. As a results, multi-agent systems (MAS) are widely recognized to be suitable for developing complex applications that can be naturally modeled as societies of autonomous interacting entities and therefore for crisis management [5, 6, 7]. In this context, agent-based simulation systems, such as the Robocup Rescue [8], the STORMI [9], the Rescue [10] projects have been proposed and used in order to test and optimize crisis management processes. In fact, MAS have been recognized as a powerful tool that allows designing and running controlled experiments with different scenarios that help deciders to assess, test and optimize their response strategies. Other agent-based systems have also been proposed [11, 12] in order to observe people behaviors during crisis and their effect on the crisis management process. Communications among involved organizations as well as heterogeneous information mediation and collaborative process in crisis treatment systems have also been investigated in the literature [13, 14]. Further, agent-based systems have been used for real time decision support [15, 16, 17] during crisis. For example, they can support the decision makers during a forest fire by simulating its propagation and supporting their decisions regarding the optimal way to pick up, the distribution of fireman in accordance with the fire propagation, etc.

Unfortunately, these systems do not consider the organizational aspect of the crisis management system. However, as the crisis environment is always dynamic, thinking the crisis management at a macro level with an organizational view [18, 19], as in the systems [1, 20, 21], is also important. The objective is to reflect the environment change and the dynamic behavior of its components (change of involved parties' number, change of the roles played by actors, communication change, etc.). The importance of organizing MAS and the impact of organizational structures on the efficiency of the crisis treatment system have been proven in [20]. More precisely, the authors show, using graph theory measures [22], that the structural aspect and the organization topology (hierarchical, decentralized, etc.) highly impact the crisis management system's efficiency.

Following this view, this paper adopts an agent-based organizational perspective to design and simulate a crisis management system. The organizational perspective constitutes a design support since it makes it possible to apprehend and to structure a multi-agent system (MAS) through various roles and their interactions. Moreover, the crisis management system operates through the cooperation of many interacting subsystems. The organizational perspective structures the MAS execution since it defines, through the attribution of roles to the agents, behavioral and interaction rules to which the agents must conform.

The contribution of this paper is the definition of an agent based organizational model for crisis management. More precisely, our contributions consist of:

— Firstly, we define *a conceptual modelling of the crisis environment* that identifies the concepts, their properties, and their relations. More precisely, our model is intended to a heavy snow storm crisis that happened in Ain Draham, a delegation located in the north west of Tunisia.
— Secondly, we propose *a specification of a multi-agent organizational model for the snow storm crisis management* that identifies the roles involved in our system, the links that exist among them and the protocols that rule their cooperation.
— Finally, we implement *a multi-agent organizational snow storm management simulator* to demonstrate the feasibility of our approach.

The remainder of this paper is organized as follows. In section 2, we firstly introduce our case study: a snow storm crisis. Secondly, we specify a multi-agent organizational model for a snow storm crisis management: the environment, the roles and the interaction protocols. Our multi-agent organizational snow storm management simulator is described in section 3. Finally, we summarize and lay out our future work.

2   A Multi-agent Organizational Model for Snow Storm Crisis Management

In this section we firstly introduce our case study: a snow storm crisis. We also give an overview on organizations involved in the crisis management process and the activities they were responsible on. Then, we describe our organizational multi-agent model (OM for short) for the snow storm crisis management. We have applied the widely used "GAIA" [24] methodology to design our OM. GAIA offers a conceptual tool including notations and models to guide the analysis and the design of multi-agent system with an organizational perspective. As a result, we have followed the separation of concerns principles and modeled our OM as several interacting models: the *environment*, the *role* and the *interactions models*. Each model is coping with a well-defined function and is used to describe the structure and the functioning of our OM. This representation facilitates the reusability and the maintainability of each model.

2.1   Case Study: Heavy Snow Storm Crisis

Our paper deals with a crisis happened in "Aïn Draham", a delegation of the city of Jendouba located in the north west of Tunisia. The considered crisis caused major losses in the infrastructure and the local population lives.

In fact, in February 2012, Ain Draham was hard hit by the most intensive snowfall ever known since the seventies. Snow depth reached 1.7 meter so that all this mountainous area became inaccessible making difficult all evacuation and rescue operations. Some buildings also collapsed under snow weight causing severe injured and homeless people. The interruption of essential services such as water, electricity and transportation networks endangered the humanitarian situation. To make matters worse, the snow melts few weeks later causing flooding and landslides. The nearby dams overflowed and many surrounding areas were left under water. The flood even reached the suburbs of the capital Tunis.

Moreover, it is important to notice that Tunisia is known for its moderate climate and infrastructures are not adapted to such extreme conditions. The Tunisian government used to deal only with common crisis such as severe drought, flooding, forest fire, etc. As a result, the government rescue services were not prepared to such natural catastrophe and took four days to react efficiently.

The snow storm crisis has been managed by local, regional and national authorities namely: the National Guard, the Army, the Medical Staff, the Civil Protection and the Civic Organization.

— *National Guard (NG)*. It is a paramilitary unit from the interior ministry. National Guards (NG) are organized by delegation. The NG agents of Ain Draham are the first actors dealing with the crisis. They act as crisis manager. They are in charge of exploring the region and reporting information on field and streets status. More precisely, they notice blocked and unsecure ways and ask the operational units to clear, secure and restore them.

— *Army (AR)*. The Tunisian government provided a human assistance and necessary equipment from the closest army barrack to help the local parties to deal with the crisis. The army is responsible for securing and clearing streets using adequate equipment such as bulldozers, securing unsafe building and evacuating people to refugee's centers.

— *Civil protection (CP)*. It gives assistance to the victims. More precisely, it provides the first aids and rescues victims. It also evacuates people from the stricken areas to refugee's centers.

— *Medical staff (MS)*. Is a unit of doctors and nurses that treats victims depending on their specialties. Severe injured are generally treated in other regional hospitals (Jendouba, Tunis, Beja, etc.).

— *Civic organization (CO)*. Several autonomous civic organizations, composed of volunteers, joined Ain Draham delegation in order to help the local population. They provide disaster victims with necessary aid and reliefs (food, clothes, etc.).

The involved organizations were not trained or structured for the complex tasks of inter organizational coordination. However, collaboration is needed when facing such critical situation.

2.2   Conceptual Modeling of the Environment

The environmental model in GAIA is an abstract representation of the environment in which evolves the agent that may be the physical world, a user via a graphical user interface, a collection of other agents and a combination of these objects. In our case, our environment is a representation of the concepts involved in the snow storm crisis and their relations. More precisely, our domain defines the goods that can be damaged by the crisis and their related geographical information and the used resources to manage the crisis with their connections, their availabilities and their location. The identified concepts and properties mentioned were selected following a deep investigation of the domain [13] as well as press reviews, public meetings and interviews with the involved parties concerning the crisis. Our domain is represented using UML (Unified Modelling Language) notation.

The final model is depicted in figure 1. The environment is considered according to two aspects. The first one concerns the damaged goods and infrastructures. In our case, during the crisis, all ways leading to the delegation of Ain Draham were cut, some buildings were unsecure or collapsed under snow weight, electricity and water distribution were interrupted and related authorities were unable to restore them until roads are cleared. The second aspect is related to resources used to manage the crisis, more precisely, all the assets allowing organizations to restore damaged infrastructures, to transport people to refugee's centers and to treat victims. The identified entities are referenced geographically by mark points. Information about the region, the delegation and the city where they are situated are also recorded.

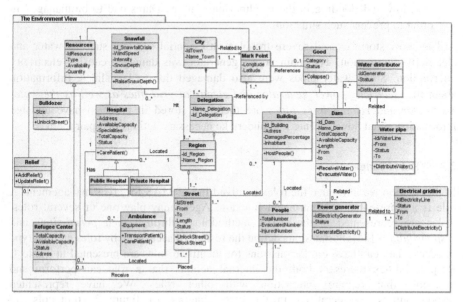

Fig. 1. Conceptual modeling of the snow storm crisis

The most important concepts of this model are:

— *Snowfall*. This entity records information about the crisis such as the measurement of the snow depth, the intensity...These properties are used to define the crisis severity and therefore the nature of needed interventions.
— *Resource*. Resources are required to deal with the snow storm crisis. The resource can be a *bulldozer* used to clear streets, an *ambulance* for first aid and victim's transportation, a *hospital* where victims receive treatment thanks to specialized staff and equipment, a *refugee's centre* that hosts people temporarily, keeps them in safe conditions and provides them with basic *reliefs*. Resources can be endowed with some capabilities and has both static and dynamic characteristics. Static characteristics are about the type, the quantity, the resources size, etc. Dynamic characteristics concern information that can evolve over time such as the as the capacity of a hospital or a refugee's center, the equipments availabilities, the number of available bulldozer, ambulance, etc.
— *Street*. Represents the region's streets. During the crisis, the National Guard reports field's information and asks the operational units to clear, secure and restore blocked ways.
— *Building*. Represents the region's buildings. They are described by their address and are referenced geographically. The objective is to locate unsecure building and evacuate their people to refugee's centers.
— *People*. Concerns all persons affected or injured during the crisis.
— *Dam*. The delegation of Ain Draham holds the national rainfall record. The rainfall is retained in dams in order to prevent water flow. Information about dam, such as its capacity and its available capacity is recorded. This information is of paramount importance as the snow melts after the crisis causing dams overflow and flooding in the neighboring regions. Dams had to be managed in order to prevent such situation.

The snow storm caused severe troubles on essential services such as water and electricity distribution. The main power generator was damaged causing electricity interruption. Some water pipes were also damaged due to landslides. Information about the *electricity power generator and electrical grid lines as well as the water distributor* and *related lines pipes* are therefore stored in order to have updated information about downed lines and undertake necessary actions to repair them.

2.3   Role Model

In this section we introduce the roles involved in our MAS for crisis management. A role is a representation of an agent function. Agent may play one or several roles. Roles are represented in the GAIA methodology through their *permissions* and *responsibilities* [24]. Permissions define the resources accessible by roles and the type of access they can have on. Permissions for identified roles are presented in Table 1. Responsibilities represent both the internal actions that a role can perform and protocols that require interaction with other roles. We have represented responsibilities as operations in the class diagram of figure 2 (protocols are underlined). The interaction protocols will be detailed in the next section.

Our work focus on organizing the executing system functioning. More precisely, the executing system is responsible for clearing ways, securing unsafe streets and buildings, evacuating people from sinister areas to refuge's centers, giving medical treatment to injured and providing reliefs to people. These specific use cases assume the intervention of the actors introduced in the section 2.1. The list of involved actors serves as a basis for the agent's roles identification during the functional analysis.

Let us introduce the defined roles:

— *National Guard Commander (NGC).* The National Guard (NG) units are organized by delegation. Each unit is composed of a NG commander and officers. The NGC is responsible for managing NG officers belonging to the same delegation. It plans the exploration tasks and decides how many agents will be dedicated to this task. The NGC asks officers to explore the delegation areas and/ or subcontracts the exploration of some specified areas to NG commander acquaintances from surrounding cities using the Contract Net (CN) Protocol [25]. The exploration is subcontracted when the number of local NG officers is not sufficient to rapidly explore all impacted regions. Once the exploration task is achieved by NG officers, the NG commander reports streets status to the army commanders and asks them to undertake necessary actions.

— *National Guard Officer (NGO).* Is in charge of exploring the region and reporting field's information as well as streets status to its NG commander.

— *Army Commander (ARC).* Receives field information from the NG commander. The army commander is then responsible for allocating tasks to its soldiers unit according to received information (areas to clear, street location, etc.) and resources availabilities (number of bulldozers, number of soldiers, etc.). In case of lack of resources, the ARC can ask for reinforcements from its acquaintances (ARC from neighborhoods barracks). The army commander is also responsible for coordinating its soldiers' works. Once, the streets are cleared and secured, the army commander asks the civic organization to evacuate people from stricken areas to refugee's centers.

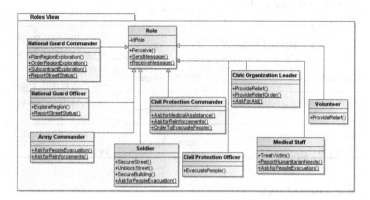

Fig. 2. The roles model

— *Soldier.* Clears blocked ways, checks streets and buildings security status and finally secures those who risk to collapse. Once tasks are accomplished, the soldier reports updated field information to its commander.
— *Civil Protection Commander (CPC).* Civil protection units are organized by delegation. The CPC receives information about civilians located in damaged or unsecure area from the army commander. Based on these information (victims' location, street status, etc.) and resources information (refugee's center location, available capacity, etc.), the civil protection commander asks its workers to evacuate people and/ or ask for human assistance from its peers from neighboring cities using the contract net protocol. Human assistance is needed when the number of workers is insufficient to rapidly rescue victims. The civil protection commander receives information about critical patients from its workers. In this case, the CPC broadcasts the information to the medical staff in the different regions of the delegation of Ain Draham and negotiates the possibility of victim's transportation to the nearest available hospital using an available ambulance. Once people are evacuated to refugee's centers, the civil protection commander asks the civic organization leader to provide them with the necessary relief.
— *Civil Protection Worker (CPW).* Checks civilians' health status, provides the first aid and evacuates them to secure refugee's centers. CPW also reports information about realized tasks to its commander.
— *Medical Staff (MS).* Treats the victims depending on their specialties. It can also ask civic organization commander to provide victims with reliefs.
— *Civic Organization Leader (COL).* Plans the volunteers' works and dispatches them on refugee's centers. It can also ask its acquaintances from other civic organizations for more relief and human assistance using the CN protocol.
— *Volunteer.* Provides disaster victims with necessary aid and reliefs (food, water, clothes, etc.) and reports information on the needed relief to its leader.

Table 1. Roles and permissions

Role	Permission	Resources
National guard commander and officer	Reads, changes	Snowfall, street
Army commander and soldier	Reads, changes	Street, building, people, refugee's center, bulldozer
Medical Staff	Reads, changes	Street, ambulance, building, people, hospital
Civil protection commander/ worker	Reads, changes	Street, building, people, refugee's center
Civic organization leader/ volunteer	Reads, changes	Refugee's center, relief, people

2.4   Interaction Model

The interaction model describes the relationship among roles through protocols. These protocols are described by the following attributes: name, initiator role, partner (responding role), input (information used by initiator) and output (information provided by partner). Interaction protocols among defined roles are shown in Table 2.

Interactions among agents playing the same roles are based on the Contract Net (CN) protocol [25]. More precisely, the SubcontractExploaration, AskforMedicalAssistance, AskforAid and AskforReinforcement are abstracted from the CN. The use of the CN is justified since it is one of the most flexible and efficient negotiation mechanisms and it eases tasks allocation.

In our case, the agents involved in the contract net protocol are partitioned based on a geographical neighborhood relationship. The objective is to reduce the number of exchanged messages and therefore enhance the crisis treatment time. In fact, in such emergency situation, the time to arrive to destination is critical to rapidly deal with the crisis. To this end, we create communication spaces composed of agents playing the same role based on neighborhood relationship. Communication between two independent groups is made through agents that belong to both. For instance, the CN initiator broadcasts a call for proposal to its acquaintances in the same group specifying its requirements. The agents receiving the call for proposal can either propose if the initiator requirements can be satisfied or broadcast in their turn a call for proposal to their neighbors. The process is repeated until the requirements are satisfied or cancelled by the initiator.

Table 2. Interaction model

Protocol name	Initiator	Partner	Input	Output
OrderRegionExploration	NGC	NGO	Region's map	-
SubcontractExploaration	NGC	NGC (acquaintance)	Number of NGO	Message to NGC
ReportStreetStatus	NGO	NGC	Street assessment	Intervention plan
ReportStreetStatus	NGC	ARC	Street assessment	Message to ARC
AskforPeopleEvacuation	Soldier	ARC	Information about people	Evacuation request
AskforReinforcements	ARC	ARC (acquaintance)	Number of needed soldiers	Message to ARC
AskforPeopleEvacuation	ARC	CPC	Information about people	Message to ARC
OrderToEvacuatePeople	CPC	CPO	Information about people	-
AskforReinforcements	CPC	CPC (acquaintance)	Number of needed CPW	Message to CPC
AskforMedicalAssistance	CPC	MS	Information about victims	Message to CPC
ReportHumanitarianNeeds	MS	COL	Humanitarian needs	Message to MS
ReportHumanitarianNeeds	CPC	COL	Humanitarian needs	Message to COL
ProvideReliefOrder	COL	Volunteer	Needed aid	Message to volunteer
AskforAid	COL	COL	Needed aid	Message to volunteer

For example, the National Guard commander (NGC) requests proposals from its NGC acquaintance in the same neighborhood group to subcontract specific areas exploration under certain conditions. Conditions include requirements such as the number of needed NG officers, maximum time to arrive, etc. The NGC can propose, refuse or broadcast a call for proposal to its neighbors. The NGC initiator receives several proposals from its acquaintances then chooses the best one. An acceptance message is sent to the chosen agent and a refuse message is sent to the others.

3   A Multi-agent Organizational Snow Storm Management Simulator

We implemented an agent-based organizational snow storm management simulator in order to validate the feasibility of our approach. The previously defined model is implemented using GAMA platform [26]. GAMA is an open-source generic agent-based modelling and simulation platform. It provides modelers, experts and scientists with a complete modelling and simulation development environment for building complex multi-agent models and simulations. This platform provides an intuitive modelling language with high-level primitives to define a huge number of agents with various architectures and their environment. In addition, GAMA holds powerful features in terms of Geographical Information Systems (GIS) integration. As a result, GAMA has been successfully used to develop various large-scale applications with strong interactions among agents and their environment such as the MAELIA platform for water management problems simulation [27], the AMEL model for earthquake evacuation simulation [11], etc.

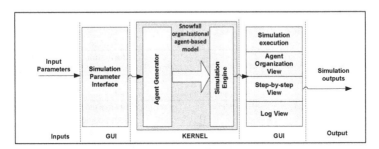

Fig. 3. Organizational multi-agent based snow storm simulator

Our simulator offers the following services:
— It allows users to enter simulations parameters,
— It simulates agent's functioning, organization and interaction for crisis managing step by step,
— It finally outputs performance metrics on a log file. Performance metrics concern the evaluation of the crisis management time, the evacuated people number, the snow depth evolution and the number of exchanged messages.

The structure of our simulator is illustrated in figure 3. It includes an *input GUI*, a *kernel* and an *output GUI*.

Figure 4 shows a screenshot of our GUI. We distinguish between two types of GUIs: the *input parameter GUI* (right side Fig.4) and the *simulation area GUI* (left side Fig.4).

— The *input parameter GUI* allows the user to enter simulation parameters such as the number of agents (National Guard, medical staff, civic organization…), the population number, the snow depth, etc. The simulation GUI allows displaying agents' representation view in which each agent is represented by an adequate icon related to the played role as well as a step by step simulation view.

— The *KERNEL* has two roles. It generates the agents with the specific role they play based on user's inputs and it launches the simulation executions. The agents functioning and interaction to deal with the crisis are simulated according to our specified organizational model. Finally, when the simulation ends, results are displayed to the user on the *output GUI*.

— The *output GUI* displays the simulations results on a log file. Graphs are used in order to observe the evolution of measured performance metrics during crisis management (the evolution of evacuated people number, snow depth, messages number, etc.).

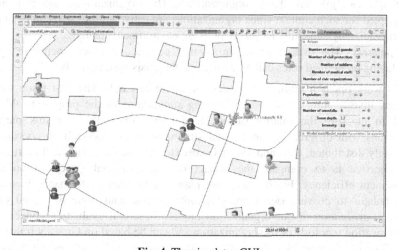

Fig. 4. The simulator GUI

We are currently validating our OM functioning step by step using our simulator. Experimental evaluation in order to measure the efficiency of our OM is ongoing. More comprehensive evaluations would entail simulating different organizational structures (with a centralized coordinator, completely distributed, etc.) with different snow storm crisis scenarios. The objective is to compare the impact of organizational structures on crisis management efficiency and to prove the effectiveness of our model.

4   Conclusion

Crisis systems are made of heterogeneous, distributed and dynamic organizations. Involved organizations have to interact frequently and cooperate at a high level to deal with the crisis. In this work, we have proposed an organizational model (OM) to design and implement a snow storm crisis management system. The organizational perspective, followed in this paper, constitutes a design support and allows structuring the overall functioning through the attribution of roles and interaction rules to which the agents must conform. Our OM presents several advantages including:

- *A possible real application.* Our OM is proposed in order to model and simulate snow storm crisis management in the delegation of Ain Drahem. This work is considered as a first step towards simulating this crisis management. Running experiments with different scenarios can help decision makers to be prepared to such crisis, to establish well defined management plans, to evaluate the defined plans and to optimize their response strategies.
- *Dynamicity.* Crisis environment is most of the time dynamic and evolves in an unpredictable way. Different organizations under the auspice of different authorities are involved. The more the crisis increases, the more the number of involved organizations increases as well. The participants are also dynamic as people can join and leave organizations. The organizational model is well-adapted for such context since organizations are active entities that can be able to reorganize dynamically and to adapt to the environment changes.
- *Openness.* The use of an organizational perspective eases openness: agents playing predefined roles can enter or leave the crisis system freely.

This work opens a number of issues for future research. The first issue we are currently investigating is related to *ongoing simulations* of the proposed OM. We intend to measure the quality of our model experimentally. For this purpose, simulations with different organizational structures (with a centralized coordinator, completely distributed, etc.) and various snow storm crisis scenarios will be realized. The objective is to compare the impact of organizational structures on crisis management efficiency. Furthermore, we plan to add other performance metrics to our simulator to provide richer analysis tools. The second issue is related to the *structural evaluation* of our organization model. Structural evaluation concerns the communication topology of the organization and can be based on Grossi's framework [22]. Grossi's framework allows to proof organizational qualities such as the flexibility (the capacity to adapt easily to changing circumstances), the robustness (how stable the organization is in the case of anticipated risks) and the efficiency (the amount of resources used to perform its tasks). In our case, we will evaluate these qualities and measure the efficiency of our OM. Finally, a *comparison* of our OM with other approaches can be made in order to prove its efficiency.

References

1. Quillinan, T., Brazier, F., Aldewereld, H.M., Dignum, F.P.M., Dignum, M.V., Penserini, L., Wijngaards, N.: Developing agent-based organizational models for crisis management. In: Proceedings of the 8th International Conference on Autonomous Agents and Multiagent Systems (Industrial Track) (May 2009)
2. Aldewereld, H., Tranier, J., Dignum, F., Dignum, V.: Agent-Based Crisis Management, Collaborative Agents. In: Guttmann, C., Dignum, F., Georgeff, M. (eds.) CARE 2009 / 2010. LNCS, vol. 6066, pp. 31–43. Springer, Heidelberg (2011)
3. Jennings, N.R.: An Agent-based Approach for Building Complex Software Systems. Communications of the ACM 44(4), 35–41 (2001)
4. Jennings, N.R., Wooldridge, M.: Applications of Intelligent Agents. In: Jennings, N.R., Wooldridge, M. (eds.) Agent Technology, Foundations, Applications and Markets, pp. 3–28. Springer (1998)
5. El-Korany, A., El-Bahnasy, K.: A multi-agent Cooperative Model for Crisis Management System. In: 7th WSEAS Int. Conf. on Artificial Intelligence, knowledge engineering and data bases (AIKED 2008). University of Cambridge (2008)
6. Byrski, A., Kisiel-Dorohinicki, M., Carvalho, M.: A crisis management approach to mission survivability in computational multi-agent systems. Computer Science 11 (2010)
7. Edrissi, A., Poorzahedy, H., Nassiri, H., Nourinejad, M.: A multi-agent optimization formulation of earthquake disaster prevention and management. European Journal of Operational Research 229, 261–275 (2013)
8. Skinner, C., Ramchurn, S.: The RoboCup Rescue simulation platform. In: Proceedings of the 9th International Conference on Autonomous Agents and Multiagent Systems, Toronto, Canada, pp. 1647–1648 (2010)
9. Hawe, G., Coates, G., Wilson, D., Crouch, R.: STORMI: An Agent-Based Simulation Environment for Evaluating Responses to Major Incidents in the UK. In: Rothkrantz, L., Ristvej, J., Franco, Z. (eds.) Proceedings of 9th International Information Systems for Crisis Response and Management (ISCRAM) Conference, Vancouver, Canada (April 2012)
10. Hawe, G., Coates, G., Wilson, D., Crouch, R.: Design Decisions in the Development of an Agent-Based Simulation for Large-Scale Emergency Response. In: 8th International Conference on Information Systems for Crisis Response and Management, Lisbon, Portugal (2011)
11. Van Truong, H., Beck, E., Dugdale, J., Adam, C.: Developing a model of evacuation after an earthquake in Lebanon. In: ISCRAM Vietnam Conference (November 2013)
12. Anh, N.T.N., Daniel, Z.J., Du, N.H., Drogoul, A., An, V.D.: A hybrid macro-micro pedestrians evacuation model to speed up simulation in road networks. In: Dechesne, F., Hattori, H., ter Mors, A., Such, J.M., Weyns, D., Dignum, F. (eds.) AAMAS 2011 Workshops. LNCS, vol. 7068, pp. 371–383. Springer, Heidelberg (2012)
13. Bénaben, F., Hanachi, C., Lauras, M., Couget, P., Chapurlat, V.: A Metamodel and its Ontology to Guide Crisis Characterization and its Collaborative Management. In: ISCRAM 2008 (Information System for Crisis Reduction And Management), Washington, USA, pp. 4–7 (May 2008)
14. Le, N., Hanachi, C., Stinckwich, S., Vinh, H.: Representing, Simulating and Analysing Ho Chi Minh City Tsunami Plan by Means of Process Models. In: ISCRAM Vietnam Conference (November 2013)

15. Markatos, N., Vescoukis, V., Kiranoudis, C., Balatsos, P.: Towards an integrated system for planning and decision support in forest fire management. In: Proceedings of 4th International Wildland Fire Conference (2007)
16. Asghar, S., Alahakoon, D., Churilov, L.: A dynamic integrated model for disaster management decision support systems. International Journal of Simulation 6(10-11), 95–114 (2006)
17. Zerger, A., Smith, D.: Impediments to using GIS for real-time disaster decision support. Computers, Environment and Urban Systems 27, 123–141 (2003)
18. Ferber, J., Gutknecht, O., Michel, F.: From agents to organizations: An organizational view of multi-agent systems. In: Giorgini, P., Müller, J.P., Odell, J.J. (eds.) AOSE 2003. LNCS, vol. 2935, pp. 214–230. Springer, Heidelberg (2004)
19. Dignum, V.: The Role of Organization in Agent Systems. In: Multi-agent Systems: Semantics and Dynamics of Organizational Models. IGI (2009)
20. Aldewereld, H., Tranier, J., Dignum, F., Dignum, V.: Agent-Based Crisis Management. In: Proceedings of CARE@AI 2009 and CARE@IAT 2010 International Conference on Collaborative Agents – Research and Development, pp. 31–43, Springer, Berlin (2011)
21. Gonzalez, R.: Developing a multi-agent system of a crisis response organization. Business Process Management Journal 16(5), 847–870 (2010)
22. Grossi, D., Dignum, F., Dignum, V., Dastani, M., Royakkers, L.: Structural evaluation of agent organizations. In: 5th International Joint Conference on Autonomous agents and Multiagent systems, pp. 1110–1112. ACM, New York (2006)
23. Petri, C. A.: Fundamentals of a Theory of Asynchronous Information Flow. Presented at the IFIP Congress 62, Amsterdam, pp. 386–390 (1962)
24. Zambonelli, F., Jennings, N.R., Wooldridge, M.: Developing Multiagent Systems: The Gaia Methodology. ACM Transactions on Software Engineering Methodology 12(3), 317–370 (2003)
25. Smith, R.G.: The contract net protocol: High-level communication and control in a distributed problem solver. IEEE Transactions on Computers 100(12), 1104–1113 (2006)
26. GAMA Platform, https://code.google.com/p/gama-platform/
27. Gaudou, B., Sibertin-Blanc, C., Therond, O., Amblard, F., Arcangeli, J.-P., Balestrat, M., Charron-Moirez, M.-H., Gondet, E., Hong, Y., Louail, T., Mayor, E., Panzoli, D., Sauvage, S., Sanchez-Perez, J., Taillandier, P., Nguyen, V.B., Vavasseur, M.P.: Mazzega. The MAELIA multi-agent platform for integrated assessment of low-water management issues. In: MABS 2013 14th International Workshop on Multi-Agent-Based Simulation, Saint Paul, Minnesota, USA, May 6-7 (2013)

Agility of Crisis Response: From Adaptation to Forecast: Application to a French Road Crisis Management Use Case

Anne-Marie Barthe-Delanoë, Guillaume Macé Ramète,
and Frédérick Bénaben

Mines Albi – University of Toulouse
Campus Jarlard, Route de Teillet 81000 Albi, France
{anne-marie.barthe,guillaume.maceramete,
frederick.benaben}@mines-albi.fr

Abstract. Crisis situations are unstable phenomena which evolutions challenge the efficiency of crisis responses. The aim of this article is to present a platform that provides agility to crisis response by helping the crisis cell to make decisions. This platform ensures the context awareness by using crisis modelling. It is fed on the fly by data coming from both crisis field and response monitoring. Based on these data, it can (i) detect the moment when the crisis response is not relevant regarding the pursued objectives and (ii) propose adaptation solution of the response to the crisis cell stakeholders. Moreover, the platform offers (iii) a mechanism of crisis model projection in order to help the crisis cell to forecast the consequences of its decisions. A use case based on the 2010 road crisis in the North West of France illustrates the use of the proposed platform.

Keywords: Crisis Management, Collaborative Processes, Agility, Complex Event Processing, Decision Support System.

1 Introduction

In the crisis lifecycle, the response step aims at executing plans and actions to solve (or at least reduce) the crisis situation. But the evolutionary character of crisis situation challenges the response: the crisis itself evolves by nature or due to its environment and/or the actions led through the crisis response. Because of this, the system in charge of the crisis response has to monitor the evolution of the crisis in order to remain relevant to the crisis cell's objectives (i.e. solve/reduce the crisis situation).

This need was underlined in the road crisis triggered by exceptional winter conditions in the North West of France (Brittany and Normandy) during December 2010 and March 2013. The unusual icing rain and hard snow falls caused slick roads and really bad driving conditions all over the road network. The consequences were mainly the following: (i) traffic disruptions with hundreds of kilometres of traffic jam, (ii) drivers and their passengers blocked into their cars all night long and (iii) truck

C. Hanachi, F. Bénaben, and F. Charoy (Eds.): ISCRAM-med 2014, LNBIP 196, pp. 157–164, 2014.
© Springer International Publishing Switzerland 2014

accidents. Moreover, the consequences were also economic as many deliveries were delayed and people were not able to go to work.

In this kind of situation, the West CRICR (*Centre Régional d'Information et de Coordination Routière*, French regional traffic coordination and information center) sets up a crisis cell in charge of managing the road crisis situation. This cell has (i) a decision maker role in managing traffic (allow circulation, store trucks...), (ii) has to ensure the coordination between the crisis cell actors and (iii) has to give information and advices to road users. The crisis cell follows an established response plan called PIZO [1]. The feedback made on the December 2010 road crisis [2] underlines some dysfunctions in the crisis management of such situations: (i) lack of information for decision makers, (ii) lack of coordination between the stakeholders and (iii) lack of visibility on taken decisions.

Crisis response involves numerous and heterogeneous stakeholders and their services. This implies an interoperability issue, considering interoperability as "the ability of a system or a product to work with others systems or products without special effort from the customer or the user" [3]. The Information System (IS) in charge of the crisis response has to support the coordination of the organizations through their visible part, i.e. their ISs [4]. In order to overcome the issue about the lack of information and visibility, this IS should also ensure information gathering, analyse this information and support the decision-making. In other words, this IS has to be an Information Decision Support System (IDSS).

The specificity of the French administrative procedures in such situations adds a requirement to the IDSS. Write a bylaw, obtain the validation by the National Authority... all of these steps take about two hours between the moment when a decision is made and the moment when the decision is really effective. So, in order to remain efficient, the crisis cell shall anticipate the future situation in order to balance this latency. The IDSS has to provide a description of the situation considering various forecasts (mainly weather and traffic forecasts).

Regarding these needs, the main issue is *How to define an agile Information Decision Support System (IDSS) for road crisis situations by anticipating states of the future situation?* In the remainder of this paper, we aim at providing a methodology to detect and anticipate the future crisis situation. Section 2 deals with a brief literature review, Section 3 exposes the global mechanisms of agility for collaborative processes. Then Section 4 presents the main principles of the model projection and Section 5 ends with a use case.

2   Agility and Forecasts

Many definitions of agility were given in the literature. They mostly concern agility as a general concept or applied to organizations, to software development methods, to supply chain and even humanitarian supply chain, to process or to collaboration. But no one fits with the notion of agility of collaborative processes. The adopted approach of agility in our research work is given by the formula below [5] (which is close to the definition given by Charles [6]):

$$\text{Agility} = (\text{Detection} + \text{Adaptation})*(\text{Reactivity+Efficiency}) \qquad (1)$$

- *Detection:* it consists in detecting an evolution of the situation that could not be solved by the ongoing collaborative processes or challenging the relevance of the running processes,
- *Adaptation:* if a significant evolution is detected, the adaptation step is executed to modify the on-going processes in order to make them relevant to the current situation,
- *Reactivity:* detection and adaptation steps have to be done as fast as possible (and real-time if possible). This is the time dimension of agility,
- *Efficiency:* the performance dimension of agility. Detection has to be correct and the adaptation has to be relevant.

To face evolutions, the crisis cell has to be aware of the future events that will happen. In our context of road crisis management, we are only interested in weather forecasts and traffic forecasts. Meteo France (the French National Weather Forecast Service) produces accurate weather forecasts within a two hours delay.

Concerning the traffic forecasts, many simulation models are depicted in [7]: as we are interested in a macroscopic approach of the modelling of a motorway traffic network, we decided to focus on METANET simulation [8]. We complete this model with an empirical study made on traffic and showing the impact of bad weather conditions on traffic flows [9]. Weather and traffic forecasts are really interesting to design various scenarios in order to foresee the future crisis situation.

3   Mechanisms of Agility

In this section, the methodology to provide agility to collaborative processes (such as crisis response) is presented.

3.1   Modelling the Crisis Situation

Gather and organize knowledge about the considered collaborative situation is the first step to deal with. For this purpose, a collaboration meta model was defined by [10]. This meta model is structured as a central core surrounded by layers. The core represents the general concepts related to any collaborative situation between organizations: environment, partners, goals.

The surrounding layers are domain specific and allow defining concepts related to these domains. These concepts inherit the ones from the core of the meta model. Here, we focus on the layer dedicated to road crisis management [10]. This characterization is done thanks to (i) the data gathered about the business and technical abilities of the crisis cell's stakeholders during the preparedness step of the crisis lifecycle; (ii) the data allowing the description of the crisis itself (response step): environment, goods, people, risks, consequences, complexity factors, etc.

The instantiation of the considered concepts allows characterizing the collaborative situation. These instances are used to populate the collaborative ontology whose structure (i.e. concepts and relations between the concepts) follows the previously defined meta model. Thus, it is possible to gather and analyse the data describing the context, the partners and the objectives of the collaboration.

3.2   Detect the Mismatch

Following the meta model presented in Section 3.1, the model of the crisis situation at time t_0 is created. This called initial model is then duplicated into:

- The *expected* model: it represents the crisis situation, *as it should be*. Only the data emitted by the monitoring of on-going response process is used to update this model,
- The *field* model: it captures the crisis situation "as is". It is a picture of the reality as only data coming from the field is used to update this model.

At any time during the execution of the response, the difference (or distance) δ between the field model and the expected model is automatically measured. Technically, a comparison is made on the whole set of points of both models [5]: δ is the sum of each detected atomic difference δ_i (see Formula 2).

$$\delta = \sum_{i=0}^{n} \delta_i \quad \text{with} \quad \delta_i = w_i * m_i \tag{2}$$

$$\text{where } w_i \in \mathbb{N}^* \text{ and } m_i \in \mathbb{R}, 0 < m_i \leq 1$$

Where:

- w_i is the *weight* of the detected difference δ_i. The weight is used to indicate the impact of a {concept-operation} tuple, as presented in Table 1. An operation represents the kind of difference: addition, deletion, update. For example, the *deletion* of a *partner* (*risk*) has more *negative* (*positive*) impact than the *addition* of a new *partner* (*risk*).
- m_i is the *importance* of the detected difference δ_i. It is used to sort the instances of a same concept by order of importance. E.g. *risk of icing snow* is more important than *risk of snow*. Example of importance values are given in Table 2.

Table 1. Sample of the weight matrix

Concept	Added	Deleted	Updated
Partner	1	4	2
Risk	3	2	2
Goods	1	2	1

For the moment, all the w_i and m_i values are arbitrary defined by the partners of the collaboration during the preparedness step of the crisis management lifecycle. If the calculated δ is over a threshold, the adaptation step is triggered. The crisis cell defines this threshold.

Table 2. Sample of the importance matrix

Concept	Instance	Importance
Partner	MeteoFrance	1
	SAPN	1
Risk	Icing snow	1
	Snow fall	0.6
	Icing rain	0,8
Goods	Animals	1
	Cereals	0.1

3.3 Suggest Adaptation Solutions

The adaptation proposal is based on an analysis of the calculated δ. Patterns were defined to describe the major possible evolutions of the whole system (i.e. the crisis situation, the crisis cell and the environment of the crisis) implying an adaptation of the current behaviour to fit with the goals of the collaboration, as detailled in [11].

Some patterns advice the crisis cell to lead an adaptation in order to fix the current crisis response (corrective adaptation), others advice adaptation for improvement. If a pattern fits with the calculated δ, its corresponding advice is proposed to the crisis cell. It is very important to note that the final choice is let to the users. The IDSS has only a role of supporting the crisis cell's decisions, it never makes the final decision of which adaptation to run.

4   Anticipating the Future

Based on the methodology detailed in the previous section, and in order to prevent the crisis response to not reach the defined goals, a mechanism of model projection is proposed. The idea consists in helping the crisis cell to make decisions by anticipating what it is going to happen. It can be done using a projection of the field model in the future, the projected model. This projection can be achieved by (i) the simulation of the on-going processes on the field model and (ii) taking into account scenarios created through both weather forecasts and traffic forecasts. This methodology follows four steps:

In the very *first step*, the reference model is defined in order to fit with the reference universe (as described by [12]). The crisis management cell models it before the crisis breaks out, during the preparedness step. This reference model represents the target objectives of the crisis response in order to start the recovery phase. In a few words, it is the model of the expected situation after the end of the crisis response.

The aim of the *second step* is to make a projection of the crisis situation. For this purpose, the crisis cell defines scenario that fits with the expected weather and traffic forecasts. But forecasts are not the only events contained into the scenario. It also embeds the processes' events such as activity statuses, duration of activities, etc.

The scenario may be provided by external systems supporting crisis management like software dedicated to forecast weather or to simulate the traffic. We can note that these scenario data can be classified as (i) the field events (weather and traffic forecasts) and (ii) monitoring events (begin, start, in progress, etc. states of activities).

In the *third step*, the current field model (i.e. the model of the crisis situation at time *t*) is projected according the scenario defined during the second step (Section 4.2). The scenario is played —it simulates the real behaviour of the system— and the model evolves according the scenario.

This is made possible by using a similar method than the one developed in [5]: field events of the scenario acts like sensors spread on the crisis field and enable to calculate the field model. In the meanwhile, the monitoring events calculate the "should be" model by taking into account the update of activities' statuses and check the completion of all the activities chosen to solve a given risk. If all the activities related to a risk are completed, then the risk is considered as solved and so it can be deleted from the situation model. As a result of this third step, we obtain the projected model that takes into account both forecasts and on-going response processes.

The *fourth and final step* is the exploitation of the projected model. The result of this exploitation is to determine if the projected model is acceptable from the point of view of the crisis cell. To reach this goal, the comparison mechanism presented in Section 3.2 is used. In this case, the δ calculus is made between reference model and projected model (instead of expected model and field model).

If a significant difference (i.e. over the threshold) is detected, then the ongoing processes should be designed again as they are no longer relevant to the crisis situation.

5   Road Crisis Use Case

The road crisis use case presented in this paper is inspired by the French December 2010 road crisis. At 8:00 in the morning, December 8th 2010, the French National Weather Forecast Service Meteo France announces an « orange alert » (level 3 by 4) for snowfalls. Meanwhile, the motorway manager SAPN (Société des Autoroutes Paris Normandie) announces difficulties to circulate on A84 motorway (level 2 by 4).

A collaborative process involving the crisis cell and two actors is set up. The A84 operator is in charge of cleaning the road (duration: 2 hours) and the Information Cell is in charge of keeping the drivers informed about the situation (duration: all day long). On the weather and traffic forecast side, Meteo France predicts falls of icing snow within the next two hours ; the traffic simulation predicts a normal traffic on A84.

As described in Section 4, the *reference model* is done before that the crisis breaks out. Considering the presented use case, here the reference model is a model of the situation where there is no longer important risk of overturned truck on the motorway.

Traffic and weather forecasts and the process have to be taken into account in this step. Knowing the duration of the « Clean the road » activity (i.e. 2 hours), the end event for this activity should appear at 10:00 a.m. In the meanwhile, an other event representing 10 cm of snow falling shoud be emitted at 10:00 a.m. So, the *scenario* is defined by setting the two following parameters:

{(End:CleanTheRoad)(10:00a.m.);(IcingSnow)(10:00a.m.)}

The *projected model* is made by using the events defined into the scenario step. Considering the first event (End:CleanTheRoad)(10:00a.m.), the expected situation on the crisis field is that the driving conditions evolve in a better way, i.e. there is no longer snow on the road. Now, regarding the icing snow event, it constitutes a gravity factor for the risk of overturned truck. This increases the probability of occurrence of this risk. The projected model of this road crisis situation contains a new risk of overturned truck.

Detection of the mismatch between the reference model and the projected model is done using the mechanisms described previously in Section 3. The difference between both models is identified as an important risk of overturned truck that can occur. This difference shows that the projected model is not acceptable for the crisis cell. Thus, the ongoing crisis response should be redesigned in order to avoid the existence of an overturned truck risk in the projected model.

For this purpose, the crisis cell might decide to open a truck zone (where trucks are parked) in order to forbid truck circulation on A84 motorway. A new process is designed on the basis of this new decision. The projected model is deduced again and it is now closer to the reference one than the previous projected model.

6   Conclusion

A new framework to detect and anticipate future crisis evolutions is proposed. It is based on forecasts of future events and on the monitoring of the on-going processes. By using the results of previous work on providing agility for collaborative processes in an unstable environment, this proposal allows to identify potential differences and adapt the run processes to fit the current situation on the crisis field. This is mainly feasible by comparing two models of the crisis situation, each seen on a particular point of view: the reference (the "should be") model and the projected (the "could be") model.

The main contribution is to use runtime agility to forecast over crisis and avoid it by taking into account the results provided by the projected model. In this case, adaptation of the crisis response is made *before* the process are not relevant anymore considering the evolution of the context of the crisis, the network of partners and services or the failure of an activity of the processes.

Further works includes (i) the assessment of the presented mechanisms by the West CRICR in the next months, and (ii) the definition of a framework to choose wisely the threshold, the weight and importance values used into the δ calculus. Then, the presented use case will be implemented on the enhanced prototype of IDSS (for the moment, it can achieve agility without forecast).

Acknowledgments. The authors would like to thank the French Research Agency project SocEDA and French PREDIT project SIM-PeTra partners for their advices and comments regarding this work.

References

1. CRICR Ouest: Présentation du plan PIZO (2012),
   http://www.ille-et-vilaine.pref.gouv.fr/Actualites/
   Archives/Archives-Annee-2012/Novembre-2012/
   Presentation-du-plan-PIZO-Plan-Intemperies-de-la-zone-de-
   defense-et-de-securite-ouest
2. Panhaleux, J., David, D., Labia, P., Picquand, J.-L., Rivière, D., Terrié, F., Leyrit, C.: Retour d'expérience à la suite de l'épisode neigeux survenu le 8 décembre 2010 en Ile-de-France. Conseil général de l'Environnement et du développement durable (2011)
3. Konstantas, D., Bourrieres, J.-P., Leonard, M., Boudjlida, N.: Interoperability of Enterprise Software and Applications. Springer London (2006)
4. Morley, C., Hugues, J., Leblanc, B., Hugues, O.: Processus métiers et systèmes d'information: évaluation, modélisation, mise en oeuvre. Dunod, Paris (2007)
5. Barthe-Delanoë, A.-M., Truptil, S., Bénaben, F., Pingaud, H.: Event-driven agility of interoperability during the Run-time of collaborative processes. Decision Support Systems 59, 171–179 (2014)
6. Charles, A., Lauras, M., Wassenhove, L.V.: A model to define and assess the agility of supply chains: building on humanitarian experience. International Journal of Physical Distribution & Logistics Management 40, 722–741 (2010)
7. Barceló, J.: Models, Traffic Models, Simulation, and Traffic Simulation. In: Barceló, J. (ed.) Fundamentals of Traffic Simulation. pp. 1–62. Springer New York (2010)
8. Kotsialos, A., Papageorgiou, M., Diakaki, C., Pavlis, Y., Middelham, F.: Traffic Flow Modeling of Large-scale Motorway Networks Using the Macroscopic Modeling Tool METANET. Trans. Intell. Transport. Sys. 3, 282–292 (2002)
9. Rakha, H., Farzaneh, M., Arafeh, M., Hranac, R., Sterzin, E., Krechmer, D.: Empirical studies on traffic flow in inclement weather. Virginia Tech Transportation Institute (2007)
10. Mace Ramete, G., Lauras, M., Benaben, F., Lamothe, J.: A collaborative information system supporting decision and coordination in transport crisis context. In: Proceedings of MOSIM 2012, Bordeaux, France (2012)
11. Barthe, A.-M.: Prise en charge de l'agilité de workflows collaboratifs par une approche dirigée par les événements (2013),
    http://tel.archives-ouvertes.fr/tel-00991683
12. Lagadec, P.: La gestion des crises. Ediscience International (1992)

The Dewetra Platform: A Multi-perspective Architecture for Risk Management during Emergencies

Italian Civil Protection Department[1] and CIMA Research Foundation[2]

[1] Italian Prime Minister's Office - Department of Civil Protection – Via Vitorchiano 2, Rome, Italy
[2] CIMA Research Foundation, Via Magliotto 2, 17100 Savona, Italy

Abstract. DEWETRA is a fully operational platform used by the Italian Civil Protection Department and designed by CIMA Research Foundation to support operational activities at national or international scale. The system is a web-GIS platform aimed to multi-risk mapping, forecasting and monitoring. Using the tools of the platform it is possible to aggregate data both in a temporal or spatial way and to build scenarios of risk and damage. Two case studies are presented: the synthetic design of a risk scenario for the catastrophic rainstorm occurred on October 25th, 2011 in the easternmost part of Liguria and north-western Tuscany, and the contribution to emergency management of Emilia Romagna 2012 Earthquake. The usefulness of the platform has been proved also with a very short-notice deployment due to sudden crisis in Pakistan and Japan, by instance, and with full implementations nowadays operational at Lebanese, Albanian and Bolivian national civil protection, in addition to Barbados and the Organization of Eastern Caribbean States (OECS), in the framework of the ERC Project (Enhancing Resilience to Reduce Vulnerability in the Caribbean). On March 25th, 2014 The World Meteorological Organization (WMO) has signed a cooperation agreement with the Italian Civil Protection Department in order to install and deploy Dewetra in countries requesting it through WMO: so far, Philippines, Ecuador and Guyana have gone for it.

Keywords: web-GIS, emergency management, real-time data, civil protection.

1   Introduction

Establishing a viable forecasting and warning system for communities at risk requires the combination of data, forecast models, real-time observations and trained teams. In each operational centre of civil protection these components should exist and be organized in a network to exchange information, procedures and expertise. The DEWETRA platform[1] (hereinafter DW) is a fully operational platform used by the Italian Prime Minister's Office - Italian Civil Protection Department (ICPD) – "Centro Funzionale Centrale". The system has been designed by CIMA Research Foundation

---

[1] If not stated differently, the authors refer to the official DW suite, fully operational at the Italian Civil Protection Department.

C. Hanachi, F. Bénaben, and F. Charoy (Eds.): ISCRAM-med 2014, LNBIP 196, pp. 165–177, 2014.
© Springer International Publishing Switzerland 2014

on behalf of ICPD with the task of developing a flexible and robust tool to support both operational activities of Civil Protection in Italy and International Cooperation initiatives abroad.

The system was born for prediction of meteorological events and hydrological evaluation of impacts. Over the years many applications have been investigated and added to the system, as a result of needs expressed by users and new findings obtained from research models.

"Sharing information and experience for the purposes of public information and all forms of education and professional training are important for creating a safety culture. Equally, the crucial involvement of local community action can be motivated by the acceptance of shared responsibilities and cooperation".[2] This assertion of UNISDR is basic in DW: the platform is designed to be harmonized with techniques aimed to promote a common understanding of disaster risk procedures and to assist the disaster risk reduction efforts of authorities, practitioners and the public, as recommended in the strategic plan of UNISDR Hyogo Framework for Action 2005-2015. The complexity of environmental systems and the interconnections among weather, climate and related hazards are an increasing challenge to improve the quality and accuracy of information and products. Agencies that play a role at large scale need to establish partnerships and collaborate effectively with national and regional stakeholders to address the global societal needs.

On these bases DW has been endorsed by the World Meteorological Organization (WMO), since the platform is perfectly in line with the strategic plan 2012-2015 which emphasizes the importance of improving delivering services, to advance scientific research and applications, as well as developing technologies, strengthening capacity-building, partnerships and good governance.

The effectiveness of an instrument directed to activities of civil protection and crisis management is based, generally, on the rapid availability of data. The coordination between service providers and data sharing can significantly reduce response times. In addition, the availability of layers at different temporal and spatial scales allows to build profitable multi-perspective scenarios for different users. After many years of development, test and usage, today DW offers the experience of a complete and flexible use of information inside an environment compliant with international standards (INSPIRE[3] and ISO categories).

Moreover DW allows links between various categories of researchers and professional, disaster managers, public officers, technicians, volunteers, even wide

---

[2] "Living with risk: a global review of disaster reduction initiatives", United Nations Office for Disaster Risk Reduction (UNISDR), 2004 - ISBN/ISSN: 9211010640, p.14.

[3] INSPIRE (Infrastructure for Spatial Information in the European Community) is the name of the 2007/2/EC Directive of the European Parliament, published on April 25th, 2007 and entered into force on May 15th, 2007. The complete implementation is fixed for the 2019. The goal of the Directive is to establish an infrastructure for spatial information in Europe to support community environmental policies and to enable the sharing of environmental spatial information and the public access to spatial information.

public. Key points for taking decisions and coordinate operations are: the knowledge of updated real time information; an efficient communication that flows in both directions; an effective use of resources. Decision support encompasses all the actors of emergency cycle, spanning from forecasters to decision makers to the Mayor of a flood prone community or the manager of a flood-control structure. In a similar way, the archive of historical records can be useful to detect the most critical areas of a territory. DW deals with all these aspects and offers a common base of operations for various users.

2   Description of the Structure and Usage of the System

The web-GIS platform DW is ultimately aimed to multi-risk mapping, forecasting and monitoring. It allows the collection and archive of automatically or manually recorded data, and produces value-added elaborations. Forecast models, remote and ground observations can be integrated with data concerning territorial elements as well as data from operators and citizens. The system can be used in real time, but also in deferred time for the study of historical events or forecasting. The architecture of DW is flexible and allows a specific customization for users with different needs. It relies on a hybrid architecture which combines a client-server middle-ware (to ensure robustness and data local back-up), with a web-based application (to guarantee capillary distribution of information). The system is developed by adopting BATs (Best Available Technologies) according to the Client-Server paradigm and is "three tier architecture" compliant (see Fig. 1): the architecture is based on three levels where between the most extreme ones (Presentation and Repository) an intermediate one is added, namely "middleware".

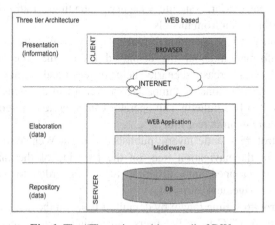

Fig. 1. The "Three tier architecture" of DW

This kind of architecture is widely used for client/server applications: it guarantees the best performances in "net-centric information systems" where the aim is the sharing of information furnished by different providers to a huge amount of users.

The middleware allows to get the entire logic of the system in the server side. Contemporaneously the installed modules can share the whole set of information.

Furthermore the system is compliant with WSA (Web Service Architecture) standards defined by the Open Geospatial Consortium. The principle is that layers have to be published on the web as web services and then linked by the browsers by the simple knowledge of the corresponding URLs.

According to this principle, information in the Repository and every map furnished by specialized providers (Google Maps, MS aerial earth, etc.) can be used by the System. The key points of DW platform can be listed as follow:

- the tool has been developed with open source libraries;
- the system is web based;
- it is compliant with international standards;
- it allows real time data management.

The main characteristic of the system consists in the management of data that can vary in time and in space. The design of DW is based on six main areas of control :

- Area of control #1 - Google maps search engine and static layer search: the first provides the official worldwide toponyms recognized by Google and the second allows a quick search of available static layers;
- Area of control #2 - backgrounds layers: satellite maps, hybrid (satellite/cartography) maps provided and updated by Google; a geopolitical boundary map has been added as well;
- Area of control #3 - dynamic layers: real time and nearly-real time observations (weather stations, radar, satellite imagery, soundings, radio GPS, webcams), prognostic information from models;
- Area of control #4 - operational tools: "query tool" allows users to obtain additional information about the displayed layers; the tool "distance" allows measuring lines and areas; "scenario" helps to select and extract information from the territory; the functionality "impacts" can record in different ways events and damage; with "on-line bulletin", an operator can compile in a semi-automatic way reports and share them in real time;
- Area of control #5 - static layers: published using a Web Map Service (WMS), they appear in the navigation tree, on the left side of the map window. The information is grouped into different topics in order to be organized for emergencies management purposes;
- Area of control #6 - time range: by default, it is set on the last 24 hours before the current instant in UTC time, but users can navigate into a specific window and select time range to reanalyze past events.

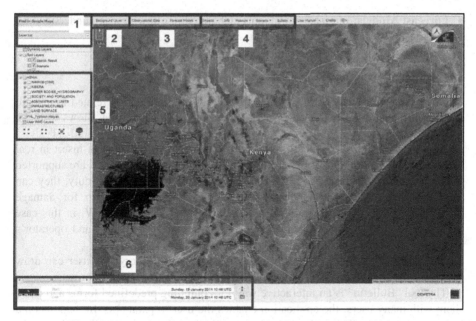

Fig. 2. DW user interface with the six main areas of control in evidence

2.1   Static Layers

Static Layers are spatial data collected and catalogued in themes to describe the territory and elements that belong to it. The "Static" attribute means they don't change frequently, even if they need to be periodically updated. Static data selected for publication on the DW platform are organized according to a logic that is useful in emergency management and for the study of issues related to natural hazards. Spatial layers come both from institutional sources and open data generated from the community. Usually they derive from an analysis phase and a subsequent publication on a local Geoserver. They have been published with standard legends customized to put in evidence categories and attributes useful during an emergency. Moreover, DW can manage direct links to external WMS services, so multiple sources can be added if necessary.

2.2   Dynamic Layers

Dynamic layers are data that normally change in time with different periods: for example data from a weather station can change every minute while data from a forecast model can change once a day. In DW, Dynamic Layers have been divided in two main categories:

- **Observational Data**: data that came from weather station, radar, satellite imagery but also webcams and radio gps. Data can be shown in their native resolution, but customized elaborations are provide, too. By instance, DW recognizes fixed thresholds for rainfall and generates both rainfall maps and warnings if requested.

- **Forecast Models:** output from models elaborated to allow an easy understanding and usage for users.

2.3   Operational Tools

The basic tools of the system are "Info", to get all the information related to a static layer or a dynamic layer loaded in the system, and "Measure", that allows to make linear or areal measurement of an object.

An advanced tool is "Impacts", that allows operators or citizens to insert in real time records from the territory. Two different ways of inserting impacts are supported by the system: the former is referred to reports made by officers on duty, they can save new records into the internal database using a specific form for damage description; the latter is a customized version of USHAHIDI for DW, in this case even private citizens can add impacts using the web site or Twitter, and operator's validation enables the assimilation in DW.

The usage of "Scenario" application activates a spatial query: the user can draw polygons, investigate layers of interest and extract data in text or table formats.

The tool "Bulletin" is an interactive way for compiling predefined forms and share them with many users: the application enables the user to paint specific regions on a map, colors being coded, and to write messages to be published on the bulletin.

3   Case Study n.1: Designing a Synthetic Risk Scenario

Generally, a pre-disaster phase is mainly devoted to design a reliable risk scenario using all the information available to the end user. The assessment of the impending risk level is provided by the classic formula $R = H \times E \times V$, where:

— H stands for the 'hazard', the natural or anthropic forcing triggering a crisis
— E is the exposure, i.e. the population and/or the goods subject to suffer damage of any severity
— V is the vulnerability, i.e. the degree at which E will be affected depending on the magnitude of H

In the following the Authors will give an example of how a risk scenario may be designed by means of DW in case of a severe flood.

3.1   October 25th, 2001: The Event in Nutshell

On October 25th, 2011 the easternmost part of Liguria and north-western Tuscany were ravaged by a catastrophic rainstorm that claimed 13 lives: in little more than 6-8 hours, half of the total yearly precipitation (above 500mm) fell over a an area of about 50x50km^2. Besides the victims, flood and mudslides swept away bridges, highways, railways and dozens of houses for an estimated total toll of more than 1.5 billions of euros.

3.2   The Assessment of Potential Hazard

In this case, H is the potential flooding triggered by the rainfall brought in by a severe storm impacting a definite part of the country: the assessment of its potential severity is the foremost task for a civil protection officer. To this end, DW offers a full range of atmospheric forecast models provided at national and local scale by different institutions. Expanding the Forecast Models drop-down menu, the officer is offered the capability of evaluating - at a broader resolution (continental / synoptic scale) - the needed atmospheric variables are provided by the global numerical weather prediction model IFS operated by ECMWF.

Though its outcomes are valuable, often its space-time resolution (25km, 6-hourly) is not consistent with the very local scale of the most intense mostly-convective phenomena that usually affect mediterranean countries. In this case, the event is expected to hit with almost the same severity Liguria and Lombardy, Veneto and Trentino (not shown).

Operational limited area models (LAMs) try to tackle these issues with a more detailed forecast (5-10km, 3-hourly): COSMO-I7, the NWP model operational at DPC, runs twice a day offering a 72-hour forecast time range. The figure below displays the forecast issued on October 24th: eastern Liguria appears to be threatened far more severely than any other part of the territory. For the present case study, forecasts proved to be effective and reliable since two days before the event eventually took place.

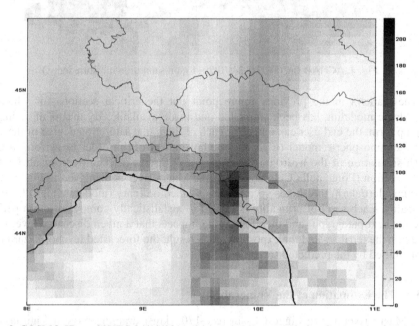

Fig. 3. COSMO-I7 run 00UTC 24/10/2011 (24-hr rainfall accumulation forecast for Oct. 25th)

Furthermore, forecasted rainfall is the main input of hydrologic models, either event-scale and continuous, used to compute the discharge levels for the critical river sections of each catchment to be possibly impacted. The antecedent moisture conditions also are one of the main component of a hydrologic forecast: the Observational Data menu on DW allows the end user to visualize four different sources for this kind of information: three models (ACHAB, AMC, Cancelli-Nova) and one observational dataset (HSAF-derived moisture products). For the sake of brevity, only the output of the ACHAB model is displayed in the following figure. The very last available run issued before the occurrence of the event showed that, in addition to the forecast, the eastern Liguria was already almost completely saturated (light grey / black) by the rain fallen in the previous days.

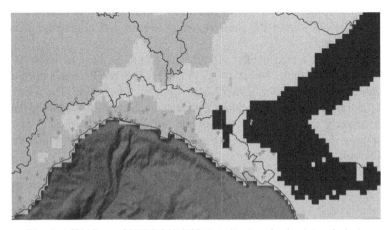

Fig. 4. ACHAB run 00UTC 24/10/2011 (soil saturation/moisture index)

The markers in the previous figure point out the critical sections for which a hydrologic modeling has been calibrated and made available. By means of a simple pop-up form, the end user can enter, for each of them, the saturation degree of the soil and the atmospheric model to get the rainfall input from in order to perform a fast Nash simulation of the hydrograph and the peak discharge. The hydrograph for the outlet section (Ponte della Colombiera) of the Magra river is displayed in Fig. 5. The warning/alert/alarm thresholds specify the so-called ordinary (moderate/high) level of criticality. Each level of criticality is related to a statistically-computed return period (see the next paragraph) and therefore to the impacts that a given discharge level may cause on the territory and the exposures. As a result, the forecasted level of hazard (H) is quantified by the predicted severity of the flood.

3.3   The Estimation of the Vulnerability

The Magra river is the biggest basin (ca. 1700 km²) draining eastern Liguria and north-western Tuscany. Its main course runs through a densely populated area and its outlet has been frequently affected by floods in recent years (Jan. 2009, Dic. 2009, Jan. 2010): for these reason amongst others, the Interregional Basin Authority has carried on during the years an assessment of the hazard and the related risk level that has been constantly updated. The result of the studies has been translated into a flood-prone areas mapping. The synthetic maps report the boundary delimitation as a function of the statistically-computed different return periods (20, 50 and 200 years) displayed in Fig. 6: the higher is the return period the lower is the vulnerability (V) of the exposures.

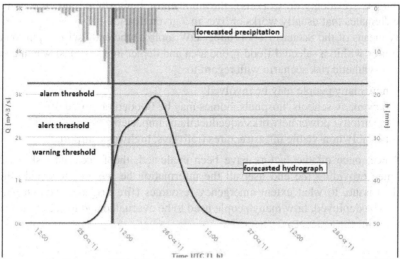

Fig. 5. Hyetograph (forecasted precipitation, upper part of the figure, provided by COSMO-I7 24/10/2011 00UTC run) and the corresponding discharge (forecasted hydrograph) provided by the Nash model for Ponte della Colombiera (outlet section of the Magra river)

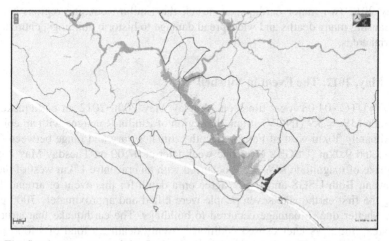

Fig. 6. The flood-prone areas of the final stretch of the Magra river. The shades of grey point out respectively the 20-year (dark grey), the 200-year (light grey), and the 500-year (black) return period perimeters.

3.4   The Exposures

The exposures (E) are the combination of all the quasi-static information about population, goods, infrastructures et c. that can be possibly affected by a given hazard (H). Generally speaking, this kind of information is classified and have to be provided by Administrative or Governmental bodies: one of the most valuable, for instance, is the Census Tracts layer (not shown) which prompts the end user the number of inhabitants (residents or workers), the number of homes/buildings, the number of males/females that usually works or lives in a given district.

By means of the Scenario Tool (upper DW toolbar) the end user can pull on all the exposures within a selected flood-prone area and depict in a very fast way a complete though synthetic risk scenario with regard to:

— how many people may be involved
— how many schools, hospitals, homes may be flooded or closed off
— electricity/ power networks/aqueduct/dams impacted
— possibly non-viable infrastructures (railways, highways, airports)

Hence, once all the factors have been evaluated, the forecasted risk level R is designed providing the end user all the information he requires to decide the alert level to issue, to what extent emergency resources (fire brigades, volunteers, et c.) have to be deployed, how many people need to be evacuated and to set up shelters and supplies for the evacuees.

4   Case Study n.2: A Contribution to the Emergency Management

In May 2012 two major earthquakes struck the Emilia-Romagna region, Northern Italy, causing many deaths and widespread damage to historic buildings, churches and industrial areas.

4.1   May, 2012: The Event in Nutshell

At 02:03 UTC (04:03 local time) on Monday May 20th, 2012 an earthquake with magnitude MW = 5.9 (INGV) struck the region of Emilia Romagna with an epicentre approximately 30km west of Ferrara. Depth estimates vary and range between 6.3km (INGV) and 9.0km (USGS). Over one week later at 07:00 on Tuesday May 29th, an earthquake of magnitude MW = 5.8 occurred with an epicentre 15km west of the first main event. Both USGS and INGV agree on a depth for this event of around 10km. During the first earthquake seven people were killed and approximately 7000 people needed shelter due to damage occurred to buildings. The earthquake that struck the same area nine days later caused additional twenty deaths, a total of 14000 people homeless and further damage to structures already weakened by the previous shock. Following these events, the Italian Council of Ministers declared the state of emergency on May 22nd for the Provinces of Modena, Ferrara, Bologna and Mantova, with a duration of 60 days. On May 30th the state of emergency was extended to the Provinces of Reggio Emilia and Rovigo.

4.2   The Emergency Resources Management

On this occasion, the DEWETRA platform became one of the Italian Civil Protection devices for monitoring damaged areas.

As a good practice, the analysis of affected areas usually relies on a wide dataset of information: results describe the framework necessary to the organization of emergency activities during the post-event management. In the case of Emilia Romagna 2012 Earthquake, the complementary sources to geospatial elements normally available in the platform (such as rivers, transport networks, strategic buildings and so on), were the maps created with fast detecting and detailed analyses from GIO services.

One specific GIO product that has been used, consists in the delineation of affected buildings on target areas, based on visual interpretation of post-event satellite imagery. Damage classes were assigned to building blocks according to the percentage of affected buildings versus the total number of buildings in the building block, specifically: not affected (0-5%), moderately affected (5-50%), highly affected (>50%).

The usage of this source of information in pair with official hazards maps produced by the local authorities let disaster managers to create new layers that study residual risk on the basis of the ongoing situation. In this case flood hazard maps help in the detection of areas useful for the placement of temporary emergency camps. The Fig. 7 describes the final assessment in Sant'Agostino.

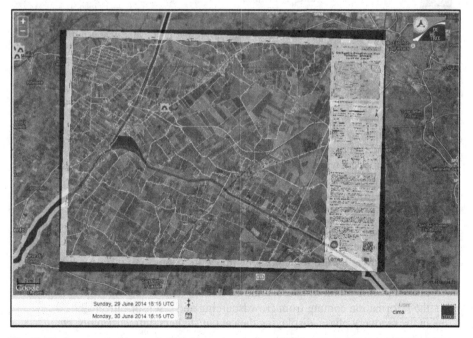

Fig. 7. Displacement of camps in Sant'Agostino during the post event emergency management phase: in the picture, satellite imagery from GIO overlaps flood-prone areas of river Reno

4.3   The Analysis of Residual Risk

Dynamic outputs from meteorological models have been added to the maps to understand the degree of residual risk on constantly changing exposure. At the bottom, the output of a meteorological forecast model evidences cumulative rainfall from June 2nd to June 4th 2012 near the recovery camp.

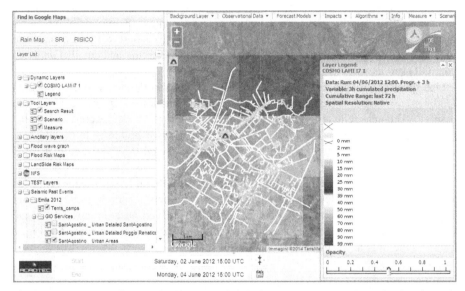

Fig. 8. Displacement of camps in Sant'Agostino during the post event phase: in the picture is visible the forecasted amount of rain from the 2nd June 2012 to the 4th June 2012.

5   Conclusion

DW is fully operational at the prime Minister's Office – Italian Civil Protection Department since 2007. In the following years, each regional civil protection authority (20 independent administrative bodies) has been provided with at least one DW access, equipped with: the regional full observational dataset; forecast models; all the operational tools tailored for specific local needs.

The DW platform proved itself to be effective in the full cycle of emergency management:

— in the preparedness phase, supplying the end user with all the available information needed to assess a complete risk scenario, from the characterization of an incoming hazard to its possible impact to people and infrastructures;
— in the response phase, with the most updated data provided by the real-time or near real-time monitoring tools, the GPS radio locator and webcams visualizer[4], the information coming from crowdsourcing and "'sensor-citizens'";
— in the recovery phase, displaying data about shelters, infrastructures, etc.

---

[4] DW implementation operation at CIMH (Caribbean Institute of Meteorology and Hydrology, central hub for the ERC Project: http://63.175.159.26/erc/home/)

- in the mitigation phase, updating the risk/hazard maps, making possible to overlay impacts, human activities, historic data for climate change assessment, etc.
- DW is a versatile platform and its usefulness has been proved also with a very short-notice deployment due to sudden crisis, such as:
- The 2010 Shkoder (Albania) flood. By the end of 2009 and the beginning of 2010, the Drin-Buna basin suffered a terrible flood. During this event, DW served the ICPD to access and visualize –amongst other products– the satellite imagery of flooded areas, developed in the framework of the OPERA Project (www.operaproject.it).
- The 2010 Pakistan flood. The July-August extra-ordinary rainfall triggered a devastating flood (>2000 casualties, >35 billions € total economic impact) in the lower Indus course. Flooded areas assessment and sheltering/recovery facilities/viable infrastructures were addressed by means of DW.
- Japan 2011 earthquake/tsunami. Satellite-retrieved flooded areas were (see the previous points for OPERA Project) made available through a DW customization tailored on EU/UN requirements to the ICPD.
- Beside these occasional deployments, DW abroad implementations have become quite frequent during the last 5 years as ICPD was asked to install the system tailored on local civil protection needs. DW is nowadays operational at:
- Lebanese national civil protection since 2010, with a special focus on wildfires risk assessment (Al-Shouf Cedar Nature Reserve)
- Albania, operational at the national civil protection since 2011
- Bolivia, operational at the national civil protection since 2012
- Barbados and the Organization of Eastern Caribbean States (OECS), in the framework of the ERC Project (Enhancing Resilience to Reduce Vulnerability in the Caribbean)

Finally, on March 25th 2014, the World Meteorological Organization (WMO) has signed a cooperation agreement with the Italian National Civil Protection Department (which is the owner of the system) to make DW available as an open source to other countries requesting it through WMO. So far, The Philippines, Ecuador and Guyana have recently sent requests for its implementation.

References

1. "Living with risk: a global review of disaster reduction initiatives", United Nations Office for Disaster Risk Reduction (UNISDR) (2004) ISBN/ISSN: 9211010640
2. "Hyogo Framework for Action 2005-2015: Building the Resilience of Nations and Communities to Disasters" (A/CONF.206/6) UN/ISDR-07-2007-Geneva
3. WMO Strategic Plan 2012-2015, WMO-No. 1069 (2011) ISBN 978-92-63-11069-5
4. The 20th May 2012 Emilia Romagna Earthquake – EPICentre Field Observation Report, No. EPI-FO-200512, UCL Department of Civil, Environmental and Geomatic Engineering, University College London
5. Earthquake in Emilia-Romagna and Lombardy,
   http://www.protezionecivile.gov.it/,
   Home > Risk activities > Seismic Risk > Emergencies > 2012 Emilia Earthquake
6. Directive 2007/2/EC of the European Parliament and of the Council of 14 March 2007 establishing an Infrastructure for Spatial Information in the European Community (INSPIRE) (March 14, 2007)

Decision Support for Disaster Risk Management: Integrating Vulnerabilities into Early-Warning Systems

Tina Comes[1], Brice Mayag[2], and Elsa Negre[2]

[1] Centre for Integrated Emergency Management (CIEM)
University of Agder, Serviceboks 509
NO-4898 GRIMSTAD Norway
tina.comes@uia.no
[2] LAMSADE, University Paris-Dauphine,
Place du Marechal de Lattre de Tassigny
75775 Paris cedex 16 France
{brice.mayag,elsa.negre}@dauphine.fr

Abstract. Despite the potential of new technologies and the improvements of early-warning systems since the 2004 Tsunami, damage and harm caused by disasters do not stop to increase. There is a clear need for better integrating the fragmented landscape of researchers and practitioners working on different aspects of decision support for disaster risk reduction and response. To demonstrate and discuss the advantages of integrated systems, we will focus in this paper on vulnerabilities and early-warning systems. While vulnerabilities are mostly used to allocate risk management resources (preparedness), early-warning systems are designed to initiate the response phase. Indicator models have been used as a part of disaster risk reduction frameworks, and in the design of early-warning systems. In this paper we analyse the commonalities and differences between both, and outline how an integrated system that understands vulnerability assessments as part of both risk reduction programs and early-warning shall be designed in future.

Keywords: Disaster Risk Management, Decision Support, Early-Warning Systems, Vulnerability Assessment, Resilience.

1 Introduction

In the year 2012 alone, the global community invested nearly 18 billion US$ to assist those affected by natural and man-made hazards [10]. The impacts of disasters quickly propagate via global supply chains to affect us all, irrespective of where we are [7]. A growing number of professionals and volunteers strive to help [15], yet it seems that we do not learn to manage and mitigate disaster risks: the consequences of disasters in terms of number of lives lost, economic damages, or number of people affected do not stop to increase. Despite the growing number

C. Hanachi, F. Bénaben, and F. Charoy (Eds.): ISCRAM-med 2014, LNBIP 196, pp. 178–191, 2014.
© Springer International Publishing Switzerland 2014

of publications on risk, vulnerability, resilience, and early-warning systems, scientific knowledge has not resulted in changing practices of disaster management [9, 36].

Both the preparation for and the response to disasters requires well aligned communication and information flows; decision processes; and coordination structures [28]. Yet, they are most often considered and discussed separately. To address the problem of the transition from preparedness to response in this paper, we propose an integrated framework that highlights the interplay between different performance measures and discusses the interplay between vulnerability assessments (preparedness phase) and early-warning systems initiating the response. Methodologically, we focus on indicator frameworks for vulnerability assessment and in the design and use of early-warning systems. We highlight the respective interdependencies on both indicator and aggregated levels to derive recommendations for an integrated disaster management framework.

This paper starts from a review of the state of the art in disaster risk management, vulnerability analyses and early-warning systems (Section 2). From there, we discuss the use of indicators, and highlight the commonalities and differences (Section 3) and derive recommendations for how to integrate vulnerabity for more efficient early-warning systems (Section 4). The paper concludes with a discussion and recommendations for future research.

2   Decision Support for Risk Management

In this section we outline the context of our work, and discuss how risk management, vulnerability assessments and early-warning systems (EWSs) are designed that provide support to decision makers in the preparation for and the response to disasters. In the past decades, research has been fragmented into several disciplines and domains such as disaster risk reduction; sustainable development; climate change adaptation; technology development [33]. From a methodological standpoint - despite the many calls for transdisciplinary work - approaches and methods today are still largely situated within disciplines as different as geography or ethnography mathematical approaches in decision analysis have been developed. Here, we aim at comparing different developments in the context of the transition from preparedness to response, and use the perspective of decision-makers as focal point to set the stage for our integrated approach.

2.1   Managing Disaster Risks

The most common *definitions of risk* refer to a combination of an event and its consequences [20, 29]. Risk R of an event e is typically modelled as $R(e) = \int_{x \in \Omega} P(e, x) \cdot C(e, x)$: risk is understood as the aggregation of probability of an event, $P(e, x)$ times its consequences C for all possible states x of the environment Ω. In complex situation, it is however impossible to predict all events e or all possible states x of the environment, their likelihood and consequences. To support decision-makers dealing with complex risks, another concept has been introduced, which focuses on the degree of control that can be exerted (or not).This definition considers the risk for a system s (e.g., a community, a region, a company, ...): $R(e, s) = h(e, s) \cdot v(e, s)$, where $h(e, s)$ denotes the likelihood and severity of the hazard event e to hit the system s, whereas the vulnerability combines the exposure (value of assets at risk) and the fragility of the system against e [3, 22].

We propose to understand risk *management* as a exerting control to prevent damages now or in future. By monitoring the current state of a system, mitigation measures aim at ensuring that its performance remains within an acceptable range (e.g., that service levels are maintained) [35]. Both EWSs and vulnerability assessments should ultimately be designed to enable decision makers to better manage risks. Figure 1 illustrates how EWSs and vulnerability assessments are embedded in the risk management and governance cycle (the latter adapted from [30]).

Fig. 1. The Risk Management Cycle - and relation to Decision Support, Vulnerability Assessment and Early-Warning Systems

2.2 Vulnerability Assessment in for Decision Support in Disaster Management

In general, vulnerability is understood as the characteristics of a system that make it susceptible to the damaging effects of a hazard [17]. One of the most prominent aims of vulnerability assessments is improving preparedness and allocating risk management resources in an efficient way. The diversity of applications - from better planning to sustainable development - has given rise to several types of assessment, ranging from technical vulnerability, focussing on specific systems or infrastructures (e.g., vulnerability of ICT) [17] to social [6], economic or financial [22] vulnerability. Other concepts acknowledge that vulnerability depends on the specific event - and define according vulnerability frameworks for different types of hazards (e.g., earthquakes vulnerability) [33]. Table 3.1 highlights the impact of the different understanding and concepts of vulnerability on the focus of analyses - and henceforth also on assessing, modelling and measuring vulnerability.

Table 1. Perspective on Vulnerability and impact on Measuring and Modelling Vulnerability

	Natural hazard	Social systems	Resilient systems
Perspective	Identification of (possible) hazards, including place and time; determination of consequences	Susceptibility: comparison of impact on population and organizations in different contexts, coping and adaptation capacity	Drivers of system change and underlying cause-effect chains and processes
Measured by...	Exposure to physical threat and sensitivity	Coping capacity, sensitivity, exposure	Thresholds for key variables, adaptation and learning capacity
Exposure of...	Geographical region, assets and activities	Individuals and communities	Socio-economic-environmental systems

In the context of disasters, vulnerability assessments serve to determine hotspots (such as the most vulnerable communities, regions, population [23]) *classification problem* - typically following a traffic light system or a Liekert scale - or for a *ranking problem* determining a relation of nations or communities that are sorted according to their vulnerability, such as in [4]. While there is a growing understanding that the concepts of vulnerability is highly dynamic and can only be understood in its context, there is currently hardly any literature that covers the dynamics of the development, the time scales and geographical scope. Moreover, a clear definition of vulnerability and its relation to risk and crisis management is still missing.

2.3   Early-Warning Systems

Early-warning (EW) is *"the provision of timely and effective information, through identified institutions, that allows individuals exposed to hazard to take action to avoid or reduce their risk and prepare for effective response."* [14]. EWSs are specific to the context, for which they are implemented. However, eight general EWS principles have been defined [11]: continuity in operations, timely warnings, transparency, integration, human capacity, flexibility, catalysts, apolitical. According to [34] and [27], a complete and effective early warning system comprises four elements: risk knowledge, monitoring and warning service, dissemination and communication, and response capability. Failure of any part of the system will imply failure of the whole system.

1. Risk knowledge: prior knowledge of the risks and planning of the control system in terms of sensors, measures, scales, thresholds, ... (assessment and risk mapping helps to prioritize the needs of the early warning system and guide the preparation of intervention and prevention of disasters. This risk assessment may be based on economic, social and historical human experience and environmental vulnerabilities);
2. Monitoring and warning service: a sound scientific basis for constant monitoring and predicting the potential risks faced by communities, economies and the environment. The system has to generate accurate warnings in timely fashion;
3. Dissemination and communication: understandable to persons at risk, organizations and all those who must respond to these alerts. Warnings must reach their addressees by the best diffusion channel(s) (adapted to the addressee) by choosing the good information to disseminate (not to cause panic but to ensure that people act);
4. Response capability: It is essential that persons at risk understand their risks; they must respect the warning service and need to know how to react.

Figure 2 is an example presenting an EWS checklist along of these four dimensions in the context of establishing a local EWS in the Philippines. Typhoon Haiyan that hit the Philippines in November 2013 highlighted, however, the lack of effectiveness of current EWSs: although it had been clearly understood that

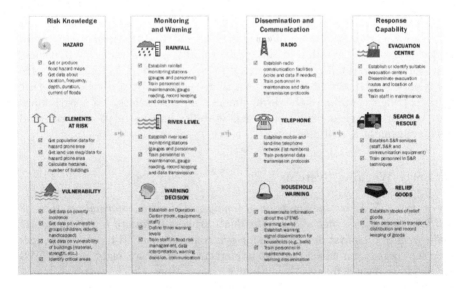

Fig. 2. Checklist Local Flood Early Warning System on the Philippines [24]

the damages caused by Haiyan would be massive some days before the Typhoon made landfall[1], the lack of safe shelters and problems with communications of the storm surge resulted in high exposure of the population and the death of hundreds [13]. It also makes transparent that vulnerability is understood as a part of EWS - but it remains unclear how the vulnerability assessment process needs to be designed to ensure that it provides a solid foundation for an EWS.

Moreover, it is important to take into account current and local information [21] but also past knowledge from past events or grown structures [32]. To be efficient in emgercencies, EWS need to be relevant and user-centered and allow interactions between all tools, decision-makers, experts and stakeholders [12, 14]. As disasters can typically not be predicted or managed on a local or national level, international collaborations [18] and information sharing mechanisms that respect the different requirements of the involved organizations and actors [12] have to be set up.

EWSs are designed to send warnings prior to a disaster. But particularly the case of Typhoon Haiyan highlights that simple warning about the nature of the hazard event are not sufficient. Rather, the warning should reflect the context and go along with solutions, i.e., a sequence of actions to implement or decisions to make [19, 34]. That means EWS cannot any longer be understood as a binary decision problem, where the decision consists in issuing an alert (or not). Rather, the integration of recommended emergency management actions, or the choice of appropriate dissemination channels make the design of EWS a complex problem.

In this paper, we focus on the design phase of EWSs. We do not discuss the process of sending an alert at run-time when a hazard event is upcoming. Rather we discuss the steps necessary to define indicators, establish communication channels, or derive recommendations for actions such that effective warnings can be sent.

3   Indicators

In this section, we provide an overview on the purpose and use of indicator models for vulnerability assessments and EWS, and outline similarities and differences in definition and use.

3.1   Indicators for Vulnerability Assessment

Vulnerability indicator models are designed to turn the abstract concept of vulnerability into a for a measurable, comparable and quantitative concept. Owing to the abstract nature and ambiguity of the concept, indicators in many cases have defining character, and coin our understanding of what vulnerability actually is instead of merely measuring it. In this sense, vulnerability indicators are different from metrics that are closer linked to technology or natural sciences. Typically, composite indicator frameworks are used, which combine qualitative

---

[1] The Philippines' National Disaster Risk Reduction and Management Council issued a first Severe Weather Bulletin on November 6, http://www.ndrrmc.gov.ph/.

and quantitative aspects [3, 6]. Depending on the perspective on vulnerability (see Table), different indicators are selected. For instance, indicator systems that focus on the vulnerability of a region or community typically comprise the following dimensions [8]

- Environmental conditions;
- Economic capacity;
- Social conditions; and
- Institutional and organizational capacity.

Due to the variety of different indicators, measured on different scales and units, a normalization process turning the data into comparable information is required. Most commonly, an indicator s_i will be normalised using a fragility function f indicating if and in how far the value of the indicator $v(s_i) \in [s_i^l, s_i^u]$ will increase or reduce the vulnerability in a given dimension (e.g., social or infrastructure vulnerability, see Figure 3) - and to which extent. $f(v(s_i))$ is typically in $[0, 1]$, where 1 represents total complete vulnerabilty, whereas 0 indicates that there is no contribution to the vulnerability within this dimension. To model how indicators on different dimensions contribute to the overall vulnerability, they are aggregated first intra-, and then inter-dimensional. The most common approach is using a linear aggregation function. However, other methods have been proposed to develop composite indicator models, for an overview see [16].

Most frameworks use static indicators derived from statistical data on a national or broader regional scale. This approach assumes that vulnerability is a sufficiently stable concept, which is not prone to sudden changes and shifts. Communities or societies are, however, complex systems and characterised by dynamic behaviour, non-linearity and emergence. Procedures for indicator selection follow two general approaches, one based on a theoretical understanding of relations between the different indicators [22], or based on statistical relations between indicators [8].

The dynamic character of vulnerability leads to complexity, in terms of processes interacting at several temporal and geographic scales. Because vulnerability cannot be measured directly, indirect measurements should focus on *processes and trends* that shape and influence vulnerability need to be integrated both in the use of deductive or inductive research [1]. To perform an accurate vulnerability assessment that also represents the shock and its (potential) consequences correctly, these different levels of information need to be respected and combined. Structural and trend information will mostly come from official databases and be available on a national or state level. The characteristic information, however, will mostly be available from local sources, referring to specific places or events.

3.2   Indicators for Early-Warning Systems

Early-warning indicators are fundamentally different from vulnerability indicators, for they serve a different purpose: forecasting and predicting the occurence and level of severity of a hazard event. By tracking the evolution of an indicator's value over time, and correlating it to past cases and events, it is the aim to

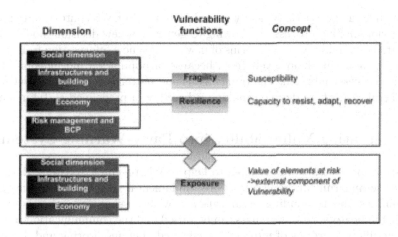

Fig. 3. A typical indicator model to assess disaster vulnerability

understand the implications of an indicator value v_{s_i} exceeding a given threshold level v^*.

To illustrate this, we refer again to our flood example: a common aim of risk management in coastal regions is protecting population against floods. A typical early-warning indicator for flooding is *river level*, where the river level values are measured at time t_1, t_2 and t_3 and so forth. The elapsed time between t_1 and t_2 corresponds to few hours and the one between t_1 and t_3 is few months. Assume that the sensors for measuring the river level are located in different regions: s_1 is located in an arid region and s_2 in a non-arid region downstream. Decision-makers need to interpret the values $v_{s_1}^{t_1}$, $v_{s_1}^{t_2}$, $v_{s_1}^{t_3}$, $v_{s_2}^{t_1}$, $v_{s_2}^{t_2}$, $v_{s_2}^{t_3}$) in a given context. Assume that a city will be flooded, when the river level rises above 4 meters. The interpretation depends on absolute values and thresholds and trends in terms of a *Delta* between two points of measurement:

- If $v_{s_1}^{t_1}$ =1 meter, there is no (immediate) flood risk, since $1 << 4$.
- If $v_{s_1}^{t_1}$ =1 meter $v_{s_2}^{t_2}$ =2 meter, we can consider this value as an outlier[2].
- If $v_{s_1}^{t_2} - v_{s_1}^{t_1}$ =1 meter, then there is a flood risk. Measures need to be taken to collect further data and start the mitigation proces.
- If $v_{s_1}^{t_1} << 4$ meters and $v_{s_1}^{t_3} - v_{s_1}^{t_1}$ =1 meter, no actions are necessary.

This example also highlights the importance of considering decision alternatives: the longer it will take to initiate preventive action or to engage in flood mitigation, the earlier a warning needs to be issued. In larger sensor networks or with a higher temporal resolution, the interplay between indicators becomes even more important, highliighting the need to understand trends and patterns among different sensors, and indicators. Moreover, it is important to remark that, despite the fact that early-warning indicators require interpretation, the

---

[2] This is true if we consider only natural risk.

decision making process is typically data-driven, i.e., in EWS context, data guide the decision making process by allowing to generate a new decision model when new data is available system in terms of new sensors, new information from given sensors, or new threshold levels (e.g., because of population movements). This adaptive process embracing emerging tredns and patterns is quite different from the general case where decision making is based on a predefined static model.

4   Integrating Vulnerability into Early-Warning Systems

Early-warning systems are designed to help people preempt disasters. Both design phase and run-time operations are fundamental components to empower communities and responding organizations: by discussing aims, thresholds, or selecting indicators, risk awareness can be raised and the communication process between different groups of interest is facilitated. The monitoring and decision-component at run-time shall initiate the response, and as such enable a more effective and efficient response to disasters as they unfold. To achieve these aims, EWS need to be integrated into the overall risk management process and respect the local context. Our aim in this section is to show how the vulnerability can be integrated in each step of early warning system described previously.

4.1   Risk Knowledge

As it is indicated in Figure 1, vulnerability assessment is a part the risk management cycle, which informs the Risk Knowledge part of EWSs. Thus, the design of an EWS for a disaster should start from the relevant vulnerability dimensions, such as economic conditions or social capacity (see Section 2.2). The vulnerability in this case can be assessed as a composite index. Figure 4 shows that, in this context, vulnerability is be viewed as result of a hierarchical aggregation process. Each dimension is an aggregation of some specific vulnerability indicators. Analogue to protection priorities and threat ratings, we categorize the composite vulnerability level as *very high, high, medium, low* or *very low*. We propose using the multi-criteria decision making methodology AHP (Analytical Hierarchy Process) [31] to elicit the relative importance of dimensions and establish a hierarchical decision model to assess vulnerability [25, 26].

4.2   Monitoring and Warning

The aim of monitoring and predicting capabilities of EWSs is to provide timely estimates of the potential risks to the people and organizations who need to respond should a hazard occur. This comprises warnings to emergency management organizations, public authorities, critical infrastructure providers or the general public. To ensure that warnings respect also the preparation times (from an alert to completed preventive action), we propose to elaborate a decision model combining vulnerability indicators and early-warning indicators. Such a

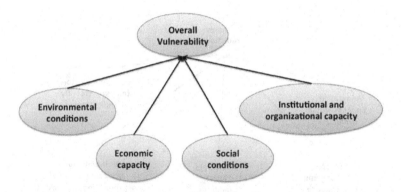

Fig. 4. A hierarchical decision model aggregating four dimensions of vulnerability

model can again be established by a hierarchical aggregation such as presented in Figures 5 or 6. For instance, in an EWS for floods, indicators such as rainfall (in mm) or river level (in m) are considered to model the *hazard* component, whereas the vulnerability indicators measure the severity or potential impact should such a hazard occur. Care should be taken for the question how such indicators can be combined, and what the assumptions underlying the aggregation are, particularly since the vulnerability dimension is mostly relevant to target and inform the warning, whereas for the hazard component prior to a disaster, the temporal dimension is much more important.

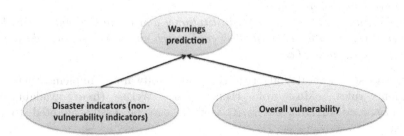

Fig. 5. A hierarchical decision model for monitoring and warning by aggregating a composite vulnerability index and hazard indicators

4.3   Dissemination, Communication, and Response Capability

Finally, vulnerability also needs to be integrated in the last two steps of EWSs. Vulnerability assessments can help to establish the best and most robust communication channels, but also inform where to allocate response resources. To integrate vulnerabilities, we propose to elaborate an association model based on

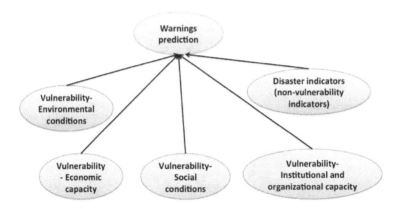

Fig. 6. A hierarchical decision model for warnings prediction of warning by aggregating four dimensions of vulnerability and hazard indicators

simple association rules. An association model consists of a series of itemsets and rules that describe how those items are grouped together within cases. The concept of association rules is frequently used in Data Mining [2, 5]. The items of vulnerability (or of each dimension of the vulnerability) to consider here will be its different levels or categories (very high, low, ...). For instance, we can define the following rules:

- *If the vulnerability concerning economic capacity is very high then it will be difficult to establish radio or telephone facilities during the dissemination and communication phase.*
- *If the vulnerability concerning institutional and organizational is very high then it will be difficult to establish good search and rescue services during the response capacity phase.*

There exist several algorithms and softwares implementing association rules. Most of them, like Weka (free available at http://www.cs.waikato.ac.nz/ml/weka/), can be easily adapted to our context.

5   Conclusion and Perspectives

In this paper, we provided a link between two fundamental concepts in decision support forrisk management and disaster response: vulnerability assessment and early-warning systems (EWSs). Vulnerability assessments typically aim at identifying structural weaknesses and prioritising resources for preparedness and planning. EWSs are designed to support decision-makers to monitor the environment and respond to risks as they emerge.

Despite most often being considered separately, we emphasised throughout this paper that both topics are closely interlinked. EWSs are positioned at the transition from preparedness to response phase, and need to be linked to the planning and risk assessment as well as to the decision-making and mitigation options in the early response.

We focused on one of the most popular methods in both vulnerability assessments and EWSs to demonstrate the need for an integrated perspective: indicator frameworks and composite indices. In vulnerability assessments, typically a composite index is established by using quantitative and qualitative indicators representing different dimensions. This index is most often used to categorise regions, or sectors. Information is largely considered static, particularly when the indicators are meant to capture the features of a system. EWS indicators emphasise the importance of trends, and the dynamic nature of the information landscape.

Although they are fundamentally different in nature, we have shown that it is possible to integrate the vulnerability component in each step of an EWS, such that more targeted action and better informed decision-making can be achieved. At the same time, redundancies in the assessment of vulnerabilities, or the forecasting of damages can be avoided by re-using information about indicators that are already available.

This work lays the conceptual and theoretical foundations for ongoing work, in which the details of an integrated system will be further detailed in terms of indicator selection, interpretation / normalisation, aggregation and link to decisions to be made. Future work consists in developing a comparative framework for vulnerability and early warning indicators related to specific hazards such as floods. Using those indicators we will specify our proposed hierarchical decision models, test them with real data, and evaluate them with decision-makers from policy-making and emergency management authorities.

References

1. Neil Adger, W., Brooks, N., Bentham, G., Agnew, M., Eriksen, S.: New indicators of vulnerability and adaptive capacity, vol. 122. Tyndall Centre for Climate Change Research, Norwich (2004)
2. Agrawal, R., Imielinski, T., Swami, A.: Mining association rules between sets of items in large databases. In: Proceedings of the ACM SIGMOD International Conference on Management of Data, Washington D.C, pp. 207–216 (May 1993)
3. Birkmann, J.: Risk and vulnerability indicators at different scales: applicability, usefulness and policy implications. Environmental Hazards 7(1), 20–31 (2007)
4. Brooks, N., Neil Adger, W., Mick Kelly, P.: The determinants of vulnerability and adaptive capacity at the national level and the implications for adaptation. Global Environmental Change 15(2), 151–163 (2005)
5. Coenen, F., Goulbourne, G., Leng, P.: Tree structures for mining association rules. Data Mining and Knowledge Discovery 8, 25–51 (2004)
6. Cutter, S.L., Boruff, B.J., Lynn Shirley, W.: Social vulnerability to environmental hazards*. Social Science Quarterly 84(2), 242–261 (2003)
7. Bono, A.D., Chatenoux, B., Herold, C., Peduzzi, P.: Global Assessment Report on Disaster Risk Reduction 2013: From shared risk to shared value-The business case for disaster risk reduction. UNISDR, New York (2013),
   http://www.unisdr.org/we/inform/publications/33013

8. Eriksen, S.H., Mick Kelly, P.: Developing credible vulnerability indicators for climate adaptation policy assessment. Mitigation and Adaptation Strategies for Global Change 12(4), 495–524 (2007)

9. Gaillard, J.C., Mercer, J.: From knowledge to action bridging gaps in disaster risk reduction. Progress in Human Geography 37(1), 93–114 (2013)

10. GHA. Global Humanitarian Assistance Report 2013. Development Initiatives, Somerset, UK (2013)

11. Glantz, M.H.: Early Warning Systems: Do's and Don'ts. Usable science. The Center (2004)

12. Hall, P.: Early warning systems: Reframing the discussion. Austral. J. Emergency Manag. 22(2) (2007)

13. Heydarian, R.: Little preparation for a great disasters. Inter Press Service Report, Manila

14. Hyogo Framework for Action. 2005-2015: Building the resilience of nations and communities to disasters. Extract from the final report of the World Conference on Disaster Reduction, UN ISDR (2005)

15. Harvard Humanitarian Initiative et al. Disaster Relief 2.0: The future of information sharing in humanitarian emergencies. HHI; United Nations Foundation; OCHA; The Vodafone Foundation, Washington, DC (2010)

16. Jacobs, R., Goddard, M.: How do performance indicators add up? an examination of composite indicators in public services. Public Money and Management 27(2), 103–110 (2007)

17. Johansson, J., Hassel, H.: An approach for modelling interdependent infrastructures in the context of vulnerability analysis. Reliability Engineering & System Safety 95(12), 1335–1344 (2010)

18. Engel, B., Quansah, J.E., Rochon, G.L.: Early warning systems: A review. Journal of Terrestrial Observation 2(5) (2010)

19. Lavoix, H.: Developing an early warning system for crises, pp. 365–382. From early warning to early action? The debate on the enhancement of the EUs crisis response capability continues. European Commission, Brussels (2008)

20. Lodree Jr, E.J., Taskin, S.: An insurance risk management framework for disaster relief and supply chain disruption inventory planning. Journal of the Operational Research Society 59(5), 674–684 (2008)

21. MEA (Millennium Ecosystem Assessment). Ecosystems and human well-being: A framework for assessment. Island Press, Washington DC (2003)

22. Merz, M., Hiete, M., Comes, T., Schultmann, F.: A composite indicator model to assess natural disaster risks in industry on a spatial level. Journal of Risk Research 16(9), 1077–1099 (2013)

23. Moser, C.O.: Confronting crisis: a comparative study of household responses to poverty and vulnerability in four poor urban communities (1996)

24. Neussner, O.: Manual - local flood early warning systems - experiences from the philippines. Deutsche Gesellschaft für Technische Zusammenarbeit (GTZ) GmbH, German Technical Cooperation Environment and Rural Development Program, Disaster Risk Management Component (2009)

25. Ozyurt, G., Ergin, A., Baykal, C.: Coastal vulnerability assessment to sea level rise integrated with analytical hierarchy process. Coastal Engineering Proceedings 1(32) (2011)

26. Panahi, M., Rezaie, F., Meshkani, S.A.: Seismic vulnerability assessment of school buildings in tehran city based on ahp and gis (2013)

27. Public Entity Risk Institute (PERI). Early warning systems - interdisciplinary observations and policies from a local government perspective - four elements of people centered early warning systems. Public Entity Risk Institute (PERI) Symposium (2010)
28. Quarantelli, E.L.: Disaster crisis management: A summary of research findings. Journal of Management Studies 25(4), 373–385 (1988)
29. Rasmussen, J.: Risk management in a dynamic society: a modelling problem. Safety science 27(2), 183–213 (1997)
30. Renn, O., Klinke, A., van Asselt, M.: Coping with complexity, uncertainty and ambiguity in risk governance: a synthesis. Ambio 40(2), 231–246 (2011)
31. Saaty, T.L.: The analytic hierarchy and analytic network processes for the measurement of intangible criteria and for decision-making. In: Multiple Criteria Decision Analysis: State of the Art Surveys. International Series in Operations Research and Management Science, vol. 78, pp. 345–405. Springer, New York (2005)
32. Schrodt, P.A., Gerner, D.J.: The impact of early warning on institutional responses to complex humanitarian crises. In: Paper presented at 3rd Pan-European International Relations Conference (1998)
33. Thomalla, F., Downing, T., Spanger-Siegfried, E., Han, G., Rockström, J.: Reducing hazard vulnerability: towards a common approach between disaster risk reduction and climate adaptation. Disasters 30(1), 39–48 (2006)
34. United Nations. Global Survey of Early Warning Systems: an Assessment of Capacities, Gaps and Opportunities Toward Building a Comprehensive Global Early Warning System for All Natural Hazards: a Report Prepared at the Request of the Secretary-General of the United Nations (2006)
35. Van de Walle, B., Comes, T.: Risk accelerators in disasters. In: Jarke, M., Mylopoulos, J., Quix, C., Rolland, C., Manolopoulos, Y., Mouratidis, H., Horkoff, J. (eds.) CAiSE 2014. LNCS, vol. 8484, pp. 12–23. Springer, Heidelberg (2014)
36. Weichselgartner, J., Kasperson, R.: Barriers in the science-policy-practice interface: Toward a knowledge-action-system in global environmental change research. Global Environmental Change 20(2), 266–277 (2010)

Integration of Emotion in Evacuation Simulation

Van Tho Nguyen[1], Dominique Longin[2], Tuong Vinh Ho[1,3],
and Benoit Gaudou[4]

[1] IFI, Vietnam National University in Hanoi, Vietnam
[2] Toulouse University, CNRS, IRIT-LILaC Group, France
[3] UMI UMMISCO 209 (IRD/UPMC)
[4] Toulouse University, UT1, IRIT-SMAC Group, France

Abstract. Computer simulation is a powerful tool for planning real evacuation scenarios during a crisis. In such context, emotion is a major factor that influences human decision making process and behavior. In this paper, we present our multi-agent simulation through the mathematical formalization of its main components: emotion and its dynamics, an heuristics for evasive actions of agents, the scenarios for tests and the results of theses tests. We show that on one hand, emotions increase the chaos of simulation which leads to an increase of collisions between agents, and on the other hand the evacuation time decreases because agents are more hurry to leave the place of the crisis.

1 Introduction

Simulations of crisis scenarios are very important tools for an optimal evacuation process of people during a real crisis in a public place. Crisis are difficult to model because many factors affect the results (large number of people, chaos, obstacles, *etc.*). In this article, we propose to take into account emotions felt by agents during a crisis because a lot of works have shown that they have an impact on decision making and behavior of people [17, 11, p. 2]. In particular, catastrophic situations often trigger fear[1]. One of the emotions often cited in case of crisis is panic but in fact, panic does not appear in real situations [5, 6].[2] Thus, our simulation is based on the emotion of fear[3] that is more realistic in such situations [15].

Emotion in computer sciences often relies on the model of Ortony, Clore, and Collins (OCC model for short) [12]. In previous works we have already formalized

---

[1] As in [12, pp. 112–118], we use fear, fright, scare, *etc.* as synonyms because they all refer to the same type of emotion in the sense of [12, pp. 15–17].

[2] Panic would *just* be an individual psychiatric disorder that does not spread among a crowd during a crisis situation... except in disaster movies.

[3] Certainly, we feel several emotions in crisis situations. Here, we only manage fear for several reasons: i) it is certainly the most predominant emotion in crisis situations; ii) every emotion influences both the behavior of an agent and its other emotions and thus, it becomes hard both to model such complex interactions and to analyze the results of the simulation; iii) some secondary emotions could be added later in the simulation (there is no technical barrier).

C. Hanachi, F. Bénaben, and F. Charoy (Eds.): ISCRAM-med 2014, LNBIP 196, pp. 192–205, 2014.
© Springer International Publishing Switzerland 2014

a lot of the emotions defined in the OCC model [1]. We focus here on fear and we use these finely grained results to model its properties. Moreover, emotion can be spread in crowds [8, 4] (this is the "emotional contagion" phenomena) and this property must be taken into account. Thus, the spreading process we use here is based on the model of [4].

Each phenomena (emotion, emotional contagion, behaviors of agents, *etc.*) has been been implemented in our simulation with the GAMA multi-agents architecture [7]. We have also implemented and simulated the scenarios of an emergency evacuation in a burning shopping center.

Simulations using emotion management present at leat two difficulties. First, crisis situations are hard to reproduced during artificial experiments because it would be necessary to induce in subjects some strong negative emotions without really putting them in danger. Second, it is hard to describe behaviors associated with emotions because emotion is very subjective. Nevertheless, our definition of emotions are based on previous researches following some psychological works [12, 9]. We expect it is sufficient for guaranteeing a realistic process.

After a brief review of related work (Section 2) we present the mathematical model of the main featurs of our simulation (Section 3) and the obtained results (Section 4).

2   Related Work

There is a considerable amount of research in integration of emotions into evacuation simulation. (See [16] for instance.) Most of the existing work concentrate in simulation of pedestrians in case of fire in a public location. Agent-based simulations are often used because they allows modelings of each pedestrian as an autonomous entity. In [10] a model of emotion with two dimensions (intensity and time) in an evacuation simulation of pedestrians is presented. This is a simplification of the four dimensions of [19] and includes emotional decay during time.

With the help from the framework ESCAPE, Tsai et al [16] simulate an evacuation scenario from airport to train. They model several kinds of agents: family members, visitors, security policies authorities. The agents interactions are one of the main aspects of the simulation. Evacuation knowledge and information events are propagated among agents. Authorities share their knowledge about the positions of exits with people which do not know the place. They also model emotional contagion using the Hatfield et al's theory [8]. In the simulation, only fear is considered. In this model, emotion does not have ability to decay. However, authorities are able to calm other agents which decrease their fear level. The scenario with the emotional contagion (without authorities) shows that the representation of emotional contagion increases the number of collisions at high speed. The scenario with emotional contagion and authorities show that the level of fear of people is lower (and thus, results are better).

3   Simulation Description

The environment of our model is represented by GIS (Geographic Information System) files which enable the simulation to know the topographical plan of the scene of the crisis. (We suppose in the following that the crisis happens in a store.) Fig. 1 shows a screenshot of the simulation: obstacles are represented by the sixteen gray rectangles, exits are represented by the three small green rectangles on the left side and on the bottom side of the figure, and human agents by small circles. These circles have different colors that represent the fear intensity degree of each agent (no fear, weak fear, medium fear and strong fear). The crisis may have several seats of fire that are represented by flames.

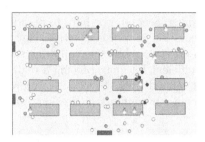

Fig. 1. Snapshot of the screen of the simulation

All the agents have the ability to avoid both obstacles and other agents while moving. In a non-evacuation situation the agents move slowly and in random directions whereas in evacuation situations, the agents try to escape from the store by moving to the nearest exit. As detailed in the following, emotion influences the behavior of agents. Thus at the highest fear level for instance, the agents move at top speed and in a random direction.

In the following: AGT_h is the set of all the human agents i, j...; AGT_f is the set of all fire agents f, f'...; $AGT \supseteq AGT_h \cup AGT_f$ is the set of all the agents. We note x, y... the terms of AGT.

3.1   Emotion Modeling

Fear intensity. Fear intensity is modeled as a floating point number depending on time. Thus, $Int_{Fear_i}(t)$ represents the fear intensity felt by agent $i \in AGT_h$ at time t and $Int_{Fear_i}(t) \in [0,1]$. We are rather interested by values ranges than a particular value: $Int_{Fear_i}(t) \in [0, 0.2[$ means that agent i has no fear; $Int_{Fear_i}(t) \in [0.2, 0.5[$ means that agent i feels a weak fear; $Int_{Fear_i}(t) \in [0.5, 0.8[$ means that agent i feels an medium fear; $Int_{Fear_i}(t) \in [0.8, 1]$ means that agent i feels a strong fear.

The initial value of $Int_{Fear_i}(t)$ for every $i \in AGT_h$ is fixed before the execution of the simulation. (It is a variable of a scenario; see Section 4 for more details.)

Fear decay during the time. Fear intensity varies over time with respect to its initial value (that is a variable of the simulation). The intensity can increase thanks to emotions of others (due to an emotional contagion process) or to external stimuli perceived by agents (emotional appraisal process following events or actions of others and perceived by agents). Moreover, emotions reflect short-term affect and usually decreases and disappear of the individuals focus [14]. The decay of emotion is a complex process [18] which depends on many factors like initial intensity of emotion, characteristic of agent, time, type of stimuli, *etc.* Finding a good function that exactly reflects the decay of emotion is not an easy task. In this work, we use a simplification of the emotional decay which has been proposed by Le et al [10]: for every $i \in AGT_h$,

$$Dec_{Fear_i}(t) \overset{def}{=} -\kappa.Int_{Fear_i}(t)$$

where $0 < \kappa < 1$ is a decay coefficient.[4] $Dec_{Fear_i}(t)$ means that the fear intensity decay for agent i at time t is equal to some percents of the fear intensity at this step of the simulation (at time t). If κ is close to 1 the decay of the fear will be very quickly whereas it will be very slow if it is close to 0.

Fear intensity increase by emotional contagion. Emotional contagion process is a complex phenomena where a lot of parameters may play a role. An important criteria in this case concerns the distance between agents [12, Chap. 4].

In a first step, we need to define what is a neighborhood. Let ρ_i the agent i's perception radius that determines the circle in which agent i can perceive emotions of others. Thus, the i's neighborhood is defined as the set of agents in AGT such that the distance between these agents and agent i is lower or equal to i's perception radius. Thus, if we note $\delta_{i,x}$ the physical distance between agent i and agent x, we have the following formal definition: for every $i \in AGT_h$,

$$Neighborhood(i) \overset{def}{=} \{x : \delta_{i,x} \leq \rho_i \text{ for every } x \in AGT\}$$

The value $\delta_{i,x}$ is computed dynamically at each step of the simulation. ρ_i is a variable of the simulation and is fixed at the initial state of the simulation (at time t_0). For technical reason, we impose that $\delta_{i,i} = \rho_i$ for every agent i at every time.[5] It follows from this definition that $Neighborhood(i)$ cannot be empty because x may be i and $\delta_{i,i} \leq \rho_i$. Thus, $i \in Neighborhood(i)$ for every agent i. Note that the neighborhood of a human agent may contain any kind of agent (human, fire, *etc.*).

Moreover, we must take into account that each individual expresses his/her emotions in a different way. In accordance with our character, we will express our emotions with varying degrees of intensity. Thus, let ε_i be the emotional expression power of agent i. It is a variable of the simulation that is initialized

---

[4] It is an oversimplification because, as many as cognitive processes, emotion decreases in an exponential manner. (For a theory of mind, see [2, 3] for instance.) In future works, we will use an exponential decay and we will be able to compare the results.

[5] It would be more intuitive that $\delta_{i,i} = 0$ but this value has no effect on the simulation. By contrast, it allows that $\theta_{i \to i}(t) = 0$ (rather than $Int_{Fear_i}(t)$): thus, it means that fear of an agent does not spread on itself (see below).

for each agent in a random manner at the beginning of the simulation such that $\varepsilon_i \in [0, 1]$. This value characterizes which quantity of the intensity of an emotion felt by an agent i is expressed by this agent during an emotional contagion process. For instance, the value 0 means that agent i does not express any emotion (even if it has emotions with a hight level of intensity) and the value 1 means that agent i expresses its emotions with the same degree of intensity as the degree of intensity of the emotion that it feels.

Thus, we propose to determine now the quantity of intensity emotion spread by an agent i towards another agent j as follows. This quantity depends on the fear intensity of agent i at the previous step of the simulation, the distance between agent i and agent j, the radius of perception of agent j, and the emotional expression power of agent i, as follows: for every $i \in AGT_h$,

$$\theta_{i \to j}(t) \overset{def}{=} \varepsilon_i \frac{\rho_j - \delta_{i,j}}{\rho_j} Int_{Fear_i}(t-1) \tag{1}$$
$$\text{for every } j \in AGT_h : i \in Neighborhood(j)$$

The value of $\theta_{i \to j}(t)$ is normalized and thus it is easy to check that $\theta_{i \to j}(t) \in [0, 1]$. In other words, the quantity of emotion intensity spread from an agent i towards an agent j is inversely proportional to the physical distance between i and j with respect to its own emotional intensity. Moreover, just a part of this intensity is expressed by agent i (thanks ε_i). At each step, the simulation computes each $\theta_{i \to j}(t)$ value. As $Neighborhood(i)$ cannot be empty, it follows from (1) that $\theta_{i \to i}(t)$ exists and is equal to 0 for every agent i. It means that an agent i may not spread its fear intensity to itself. Note also that $\theta_{i \to j}(t)$ may not be defined for some agents j: it just means that agent i is not in the perception radius of these agents j.

But, as the fear intensity is not necessarily entirely expressed by an agent, the fear intensity received is not necessarily absorbed (we are more or less permeable to emotion of others, we have more or less empathy). Thus, let α_i the emotional absorption power of agent i. Similarly to ε_i, $\alpha_i \in [0, 1]$ and its value is initialized for each agent in a random manner at the beginning of the simulation. For instance, $\alpha_i = 0.8$ means that agent i absorbs only 80% of the emotion intensity received.

We are now able to define the quantity of fear received through an emotional contagion process by an agent i from other agents j that are in its perception radius: for every $i \in AGT_h$,

$$EC_i(t) \overset{def}{=} \alpha_i \max(\{\theta_{j \to i}(t) \text{ for every } j \in AGT_h\}) \tag{2}$$

This quantity is the maximum between all the quantities spread by the agents in the perception radius of agent i.[6] Only a part of this quantity is absorbed by

---

[6] Note that we do not take the sum here. The reason is that when the number of agents in the perception radius of agent i is substantial, the fear intensity of agent i converges too quickly toward 1 (that is the maximum value). In future works, we will study how a sum-based approach could be integrated to our simulation.

agent i (thanks to α_i). Note that, by (1) the set $\{\theta_{j\rightarrow i}(t)$ for every $j \in AGT_h\}$ contains at least $\theta_{i\rightarrow i}(t)$ and it is thus never empty. If the case there is no agent different of agent i in its neighborhood, this set is thus reduced to the singleton $\{\theta_{i\rightarrow i}(t)\}$ with $\theta_{i\rightarrow i}(t) = 0$ and thus $EC_i(t) = 0$. It means that an agent does receive fear intensity from itself.

Note that $EC_i(t)$ can be greater than, equal to, or lower than, the current fear intensity of agent i ($Int_{Fear_i}(t)$). It remains to determine how this value should update the current level of fear of agents. Two choices have been made here. First, just the difference between $Int_{Fear_i}(t-1)$ and $EC_i(t)$ is taken into account (because we want to slow down the the increase of fear level); second, $EC_i(t)$ is updated only if this difference is greater to 0 (this constraint will be dropped in future works). In other words, the update operation of the current fear level is of the form $\max(Int_{Fear_i}(t-1), EC_i(t))$.

Fear intensity increase by crisis perception. Typically in our simulation, crisis is caused by fire. When an agent perceives fire its emotion intensity increases. Similarly to the computation of emotional propagation, we define: for every $f \in AGT_f$,

$$\theta_{f\rightarrow i}(t) \overset{def}{=} \frac{\rho_i - \delta_{f,i}}{\rho_i} Int_f(t-1) \tag{3}$$

$$\text{for every } i \in AGT_h : f \in Neighborhood(i)$$

$Int_f(t)$ is the intensity of fire f at time t. In the simulation, $Int_f(t_0) = 0$ (the fire f is initially put out) or $Int_f(t_0) = 1$ (the fire f is initially lighted). Moreover, $Int_f(t) = Int_f(t_0)$ for every tt (the state of fires does not change during the time).

We propose a function to calculate the portion of fear generated by fires: for every $f \in AGT_f$,

$$Fires_i(t) \overset{def}{=} \alpha_i \sum_{f \in AGT_f} \theta_{f\rightarrow i}(t) \tag{4}$$

This quantity is directly added to the intensity of agent i. For ensuring that the result is lower than or equal to 1, the update function is of the type: $\min(1, Int_{Fear_i}(t) + Fires_i(t))$.

The dynamics of fear intensity. Following the previous decay and increases of fear intensity, we are now able to present the complete equation of the fear intensity during the time: for every $i \in AGT_h$,

$$Int_{Fear_i}(t) =$$
$$\min(1, \max(Int_{Fear_i}(t-1) + Dec_{Fear_i}(t-1), EC_i(t)) + Fires_i(t)) \tag{5}$$

This update function means that in the simulation, the updated fear intensity of agent i is a three steps process:

1. $Int_{Fear_i}(t-1)$ is updated by the decay $Dec_{Fear_i}(t-1)$;
2. the updated fear intensity is compared with the maximum intensity of fear generated by emotional contagion $(EC_i(t))$ and we keep the maximum between these two values (reasons are given above);
3. finally, we add to the previous result the sum of fear generated by fire around agent i $(Fires_i(t))$ and we ensure that the result is not greater than 1 (because 1 is the greatest value of fear) by keeping the minimal value between 1 and the new updated value on fear intensity.

3.2   Behavior of Human Agent

Our behavior is the result of a complex decision making process where many variables are analyzed and integrated with different weights. Emotion plays a crucial role in this process with the help of coping process (see [9], where coping process is viewed as a link between a triggered emotion and the actions following the triggering of this emotion, especially in case of negative emotions). Here, we propose to dynamically compute the behavior of agents with respect to their emotional state (emotion-based model of behavior).[7]

We have defined several behaviors that depend on both the situation and the fear intensity of agents. In the normal state, agents move with a low speed that simulates they do shopping in a store whereas in evacuation situations, evacuees try generally to leave the store. In these situations, we distinguish two kinds of behaviors.

1) As long as its fear intensity is not strong, an agent can find its way out of the store and follows this way. It is able to avoid collisions both with other agents and with obstacles. In order to archive this requirement, we use a heuristic approach that calculates the next position N of the agent which depends on the current position C and the position of the exit E. If there is no obstacle between C and E, the agent go towards the exit by following the direction $\overrightarrow{h}$ (see Fig. 2). As soon as there an obstacle between C and E, we compute the next position N with the help of the vector $\overrightarrow{f}$ such that $\overrightarrow{f} = \overrightarrow{g} + \frac{\overrightarrow{h}}{\gamma}$ where γ is an adjustment factor. When γ is increases (respectively, decreases) the angle between $\overrightarrow{g}$ and $\overrightarrow{h}$ descreases (respectively, increases). [8]

2) As soon as the fear intensity of an agent is strong, it moves both with a very high speed and without target. In the extreme danger case, humans tend to react instinctively [13]. When an agent doesn't know what is the best way out of the store, it tries to evacuate with the other agents who know well the way out. Thus, agents with a strong level of fear can move along with group of agents having a lower level of fear and knowing where the exit is.

---

[7] This is a restriction with respect to other variables that may influence the behavior of agents, but we can argue that emotion is certainly one the most influential variables in these situations.

[8] Our heuristic algorithm does not always provide the shortest path from C to E due to evasive actions.

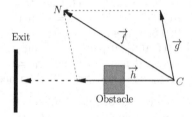

Fig. 2. Evasive action

4   Experiments

4.1   Scenarios

The impact of the emotional agents and of emotional contagion is tested with the help of different scenarios modeled in the multi-agent architecture GAMA [7]. Each scenario describes a supermarket where agents do the shopping. These agents can be emotional agents (that is, agents capable of having emotions) or not. The part of such emotional agents can vary from a scenario to another (0%, 25%, 50%, 75% or 100%). In the initial state, emotional agents can already have (or not) fear with different degrees of intensity (0, 0.2, 0.5 or 0.8 respectively for no fear, weak fear, medium fear, and strong fear) from a scenario to another. In case of emotional agents, an emotional contagion process or emotional decay (or both together) can be enabled or not. (Emotional decay formalizes the fact that emotion intensity decreases during the time. When emotional decay is disabled, every emotion felt by agents are kept during all the simulation.) It can be asked to them to evacuate the supermarket (or not) and the reason for that can be a fire or just the closing of the supermarket.

Let AGT be the set of agents used in our simulation. Our simulation is based on several scenarios. Let be $\mathcal{V}$ the set of the scenarios variables such that

$$\mathcal{V} = \{\varepsilon_0, \varepsilon_{0.25}, \varepsilon_{0.5}, \varepsilon_{0.75}, \varepsilon_1, fear_0, fear_{0.2}, fear_{0.5}, fear_{0.8},$$
$$\varepsilon_{Contagion}, Evac, \varepsilon_{Decay}, fire\}$$

For every $x \in \{0, 0.25, 0.5, 0.75, 1\}$, ε_x is read: there are exactly $x\%$ of AGT that are emotional agents (the remainder of AGT does not contain any emotional agent). For every $x \in \{0, 0.2, 0.5, 0.8\}$, $fear_x$ is read: the initial threshold of fear intensity is x. (It means that every agent will initially have a fear intensity greater or equal to x.) $\varepsilon_{Contagion}$ is read: the emotional contagion process is enabled. $Evac$ is read: the group evacuation is enabled. ε_{Decay} is read: the emotion intensity decreases with time (else, it is a constant). $fire$ is read: there is a fire at the shopping center.

We impose some constraints on these variables because some scenarios do not make sense:

(1) each variable has a boolean value, that is, there exists an assignation function $I : \mathcal{V} \longrightarrow \{0, 1\}$ where 0 names the false and 1 names the true as usual;

(2) there exists $x \in \{0, 0.25, 0.5, 0.75, 1\}$ such that $\varepsilon_x = 1$;
(3) for every $x, y \in \{0, 0.25, 0.5, 0.75, 1\}$, if $\varepsilon_x = 1$ then $\varepsilon_y = 0$ for every $y \neq x$;
(4) there exists $x \in \{0, 0.2, 0.5, 0.8\}$ such that $fear_x = 1$;
(5) for every $x, y \in \{0, 0.2, 0.5, 0.8\}$, if $fear_x = 1$ then $fear_y = 0$ for every $x \neq y$;
(6) for every $x \in \{0.2, 0.5, 0.8\}$, if $fear_x = 1$ then $\varepsilon_0 = 0$;
(7) if ($\varepsilon_{Contagion} = 1$ or $\varepsilon_{Decay} = 1$) and $fire = 0$ then necessarily $\varepsilon_0 = 0$.

(1) means that every variable is true or false (but not both together). (2) means that AGT does not contain any emotional agent ($\varepsilon_0 = 1$) or that exactly 25 percent of AGT are emotional agents ($\varepsilon_{0.25} = 1$) or that exactly 50 percent of AGT are emotional agents ($\varepsilon_{0.5} = 1$) or that exactly 75 percent of AGT are emotional agents ($\varepsilon_{0.75} = 1$) or that every agent of AGT is an emotional agent. (3) means that one and only one of the four above states is true while the others are false. (4) means that there exists at least one initial threshold of fear intensity, and (5) says that there are one and the same. (6) means that if the fear threshold is not zero then there exist emotional agents in AGT. It follows from this constraint together with (5) that: if $\varepsilon_0 = 1$ then $fear_0 = 1$, which means that if there is no emotional agents, then have necessarily no fear at all. Finally, (7) means that if emotional contagion mechanism or emotional decay mechanism are enabled and fire is not presence then there are emotional agent in AGT. (No other particular constraint is given on $fire$ that can happens when there are emotional agents or when there is no emotional agent at all.)

Thus, what the number of possible scenarios? It follows from both (5) and (6) together that if there is no emotional agent then $fear_0$ is true. Moreover, (7) entails that if there is no emotional agent and no fire then necessarily there is neither emotion contagion nor emotional decay. In other words, when there is no emotional agents (that is, $\varepsilon_0 = 1$) only scenarios 1 to scenario 10 in Table 1 are possible. In this figure, $x = 0$, $x = 0.25$ ... $x = 1$ mean respectively that $\varepsilon_0 = 1$, $\varepsilon_{0.25} = 1$ ... $\varepsilon_1 = 1$. Things are similar in the third column. In the fourth column, ✓ means that $\varepsilon_{Contagion} = 1$ (else $\varepsilon_{Contagion} = 0$) and things are similar in the last columns. If we consider now the fact that there are emotional agents (thus, $\varepsilon_x = 1$ for every $x \in \{0.25, 0.5, 0.75, 1\}$), it remains four cases. For each case, the fear threshold can have four different values. And for each value, there are 2^4 possible values for the 4-tuple $\langle \varepsilon_{Contagion}, Evac, \varepsilon_{Decay}, fire \rangle$. That is, there are $10 + 4 \times 4 \times 2^4$ possible scenarios, that is, 266 different scenarios have been used.

For each simulation scenario, we ran 50 times. We measure both the number of collisions and the evacuation time. Simple models without emotion are used as reference (see scenarios 1–4 in Table 1).

4.2   Experimental Results and Evaluation

In this subsection, we show and analyze results of different scenarios. The goal is to examine how emotion and variables (presented in Section 4.1) affect the evacuation efficiency. As presented above, evacuation efficiency is measured by the number of collisions and the evacuation time. Here, the number of collisions is the total number of collisions among agents in each scenario. Evacuation time is the average of every agent's individual evacuation times.

Table 1. Number and parameters of scenarios

Scenario	ε_x	$fear_y$	$\varepsilon_{Contagion}$	$Evac$	ε_{Decay}	$fire$
1	$x = 0$	$y = 0$				
2	$x = 0$	$y = 0$				✓
3	$x = 0$	$y = 0$			✓	✓
4	$x = 0$	$y = 0$	✓			
5	$x = 0$	$y = 0$	✓			✓
6	$x = 0$	$y = 0$	✓		✓	✓
7	$x = 0$	$y = 0$	✓			✓
8	$x = 0$	$y = 0$	✓		✓	✓
9	$x = 0$	$y = 0$	✓	✓		✓
10	$x = 0$	$y = 0$	✓	✓	✓	✓
11	$x = 0.25$	$y = 0$				
12	$x = 0.25$	$y = 0$				✓
13	$x = 0.25$	$y = 0$			✓	
...	...	...		...		
26	$x = 0.25$	$y = 0$	✓	✓	✓	✓
...	...	...		...		
266	$x = 1$	$y = 0.8$	✓	✓	✓	✓

Impact of emotion. To evaluate the impact of emotion on the evacuation, we analyze several scenarios with different rates of emotional agents (ε_x) and fear levels ($fear_y$) while disabling other variables (emotional contagion, group evacuation, emotional decay, fire). We can see in Fig. 3 that when we integrate fear in our agents, the number of collisions increases. However, the increase rate depends on the percentage of emotional agents (ε_x) and of the fear level ($fear_y$). With $\varepsilon_{0.25}$, the number of collisions increases a few with all the values of $fear_y$ while with higher percentage of emotional agents we see a high increase in collisions in scenarios with $fear_{0.8}$ (strong fear). Indeed, at this highest level of fear, the agents run with a higher speed, in random directions, the situation thus becomes more chaotic, the number of collisions increases as a consequence. We also observe that the number of collisions in the scenarios where all agents are emotional (except scenario with $fear_{0.8}$), is the same as scenario without emotional agent. This observation suggests that when agents run with the same speed, collisions occur less often.

The evacuation time, on the other hand, decreases when fear level increases except in case of agents having a strong fear level. At that maximum fear level the evacuation time significantly increases. Indeed, when the fear level increases the agent's speed increases which leads to a shorter evacuation time. However, when agents feel a strong fear, they run in random directions (unless they see an exit) which leads to an increase of the evacuation time.

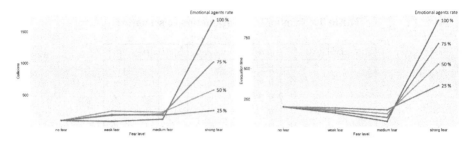

Fig. 3. Summary of scenarios without emotional contagion

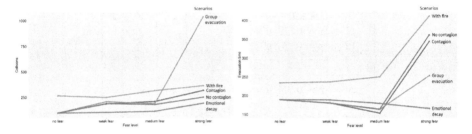

Fig. 4. Summary of scenarios with 25% of emotional agents at beginning, in each scenario one variable is enabled, others are disabled

Impact of emotional contagion. We evaluate the impact of emotional contagion on evacuation efficiency by comparing scenarios with $\varepsilon_{0.25}$, $fear_y \in \{0, 0.2, 0.5, 0.8\}$, $\varepsilon_{Contagion=1}$ and other variables disabled and scenarios with $\varepsilon_{0.25}$, $fear_y \in \{0, 0.2, 0.5, 0.8\}$, $\varepsilon_{Contagion=0}$ and other variables disabled. The results are presented in Fig. 4. In scenarios with emotional contagion, there are more collisions in comparison with the scenarios without emotional contagion. That is, with the emotional contagion, fear is spreading in the crowd; as a result we have higher number of feared agents. This increase of feared agents leads to an increase in collisions. But when $\varepsilon_x > 0.5$ emotional contagion can lead to a decrease in collisions as showed in previous subsection (when the rate of emotional agents is close to 100%, the number of collisions is almost the same as when there is no emotional agent).

As expected the evacuation time decreases slightly when emotional contagion is enabled because the feared agents run with a higher speed.

Impact of group evacuation. As we discussed, the evacuation in group often happens in an evacuation. In reality, the evacuees can help each other and this can reduce the damages of the crisis. To evaluate the impact of the evacuation in group we compare scenarios with $\varepsilon_{0.25}$, $fear_y \in \{0, 0.2, 0.5, 0.8\}$, $\varepsilon_{Group=1}$ and other variables disabled and scenarios with $\varepsilon_{0.25}$, $fear_y \in \{0, 0.2, 0.5, 0.8\}$, $\varepsilon_{Group=0}$ and other variables disabled. Fig. 4 shows that when there are agents

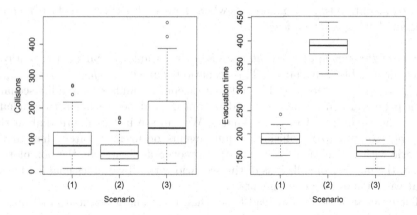

Fig. 5. Scenarios with 0 % of agents feeling fear initially: (1) without emotion; (2) no crisis; (3) with emotional contagion, without group evacuation, emotion decay and fire

have a strong fear, the evacuation in group increases the number of collisions, mainly because evacuation in group leads to a higher density of agents.

However, the evacuation time is lower than in reference scenarios. In fact, the evacuation in group helps the agents having a strong fear to evacuate faster by following other agents and thus decreases the evacuation time.

Impact of emotional decay. To evaluate the impact of emotional decay, we compare scenarios with $\varepsilon_{0.25}$, $fear_y \in \{0, 0.2, 0.5, 0.8\}$, $\varepsilon_{Decay=1}$ and other variables disabled and scenarios with $\varepsilon_{0.25}$, $fear_y \in \{0, 0.2, 0.5, 0.8\}$, $\varepsilon_{Decay=0}$ and other variables disabled.

Fig. 4 shows that when emotional decay is enabled, the number of collisions is two times smaller than the scenarios without emotional decay. As the emotional decay decreases the intensity of emotion, fear subsides and the strong fear of an agent can become a medium fear, its medium fear can become a weak fear, and its weak fear can disappears (it has no fear at all). This reduces collisions among agents.

The evacuation time, on the other hand, increases slightly because at lower level of fear, agents move slower. But in scenarios with both agents having a strong fear and emotional decay enabled, the evacuation time significantly decreases because of the decrease in the number of agents having a strong fear.

Impact of fire. To evaluate the impact of fire, we compare scenarios with $\varepsilon_{0.25}$, $fear_y \in \{0, 0.2, 0.5, 0.8\}$, $fire = 1$ and other variables disabled and scenarios with $\varepsilon_{0.25}$, $fear_y \in \{0, 0.2, 0.5, 0.8\}$, $fire = 0$ and other variables disabled. The presence of fire cause an increase in the number of collisions (see Fig. 4). As we presented, fire is a stimulus that can increase fear level of agents overtime. Especially in the second half of the simulation, when fire propagated everywhere in store, we observe many agents having a strong fear and the situation becomes more chaotic.

The evacuation time also increases when there are fires because of the increase of agents having a strong fear.

Impact of the combination of all variables. We want to analyze a scenario in which all variables are enabled. This scenario begin with ε_0, $fear_0$, $\varepsilon_{Contagion=1}$, $\varepsilon_{Group=1}$, $\varepsilon_{Decay=1}$, $fire = 1$. This ultimate scenario simulates a real life scenario when people are shopping, fire sudden appears and people begin to evacuate. Fig. 5 shows the result of this scenario. We can see in this figure that in this scenario (column (3)), collisions among agents occur more often than in the scenario with no emotion (column (1)). Moreover, as showed by the box plots in Fig. 5, the number of collisions of the scenario with all variables enabled have a great variation among experiments.

The evacuation time is instead lesser than the scenario without emotion.

Scenario of a closing store. In this scenario, we simulate the people to quit the store in a non-crisis manner. Instead of evacuate immediately like in cases of crisis, in this scenario, agents may not quit the store immediately when hearing the closing message. In Fig. 5, we observe that collisions occur less than in scenarios with crisis (both with emotion and no emotion).

The evacuation time is significantly more than in scenarios with crisis because of two reasons: agents do not quit the store immediately and the speed of movement is lower in case of crisis.

5   Conclusion

Integration of emotions in simulation of evacuation is often complex and difficult. In this paper, we implemented a simulation of evacuation with the integration of fear in GAMA language. Ours experiments show that emotion has a great impact on the simulation results. As with emotion integrated, collisions occur more often but evacuation time decreases.

A major difficulty of this kind of simulation is its validation by real experiments. In crisis situations, humans are always disturbed and have a lot of difficulties to explain how was their behavior during the crisis. Sociological works show that panic is a myth, but to feel fear leads to several behaviors.

A limitation of the presented simulation is that evacuees cannot change the exit they want to use, even if this exit is blocked. Thus, dynamic change of exit target seems an interesting perspective.

References

1. Adam, C., Herzig, A., Longin, D.: A logical formalization of the OCC theory of emotions. Synthese 168(2), 201–248 (2009)
2. Anderson, J.R.: The architecture of cognition. Harvard (1983)
3. Anderson, J.R., et al.: An integrated theory of the mind. Psychological Review 111, 1036–1060 (2004)

4. Bosse, T., et al.: A multi-agent model for mutual absorption of emotions. In: Proc. of the 23rd European Conference on Modelling and Simulation. European Council on Modeling and Simulation, pp. 212–218 (2009)
5. Drury, J., Cocking, C.: The mass psychology of disasters and emergency evacuations: A research report and implications for practice. Report. University of Sussex (2007)
6. Gantt, P., Gantt, R.: Disaster Psychology: Dispelling the Myths of Panic. In: Professional Safety, pp. 42–49 (August 2012)
7. Grignard, A., Taillandier, P., Gaudou, B., Vo, D.A., Huynh, N.Q., Drogoul, A.: GAMA 1.6: Advancing the art of complex agent-based modeling and simulation. In: Boella, G., Elkind, E., Savarimuthu, B.T.R., Dignum, F., Purvis, M.K. (eds.) PRIMA 2013. LNCS, vol. 8291, pp. 117–131. Springer, Heidelberg (2013)
8. Hatfield, E., Cacioppo, J.T.: Emotional contagion, Cambridge (1994)
9. Lazarus, R.S.: Emotion and Adaptation. Oxford (1991)
10. Van Minh, L., Adam, C., Canal, R., Gaudou, B., Tuong Vinh, H., Taillandier, P.: Simulation of the Emotion Dynamics in a Group of Agents in an Evacuation Situation. In: Desai, N., Liu, A., Winikoff, M. (eds.) PRIMA 2010. LNCS, vol. 7057, pp. 604–619. Springer, Heidelberg (2012)
11. Loewenstein, G., Lerner, J.S.: The role of affect in decision making. In: Handbook of affective science, vol. 31, pp. 619–642. Oxford (2003)
12. Ortony, Clore, G.L., Collins, A.: The cognitive structure of emotions, Cambridge (1988)
13. Quarantelli, E.L.: The Nature and Conditions of Panic. American J. of Sociology 60(3), 267–275 (1954)
14. Ruttkay, Z.: From Brows to Trust: Evaluating Embodied Conversational Agents. In: Ruttkay, Z. (ed.) .... XD-US.... Human-computer interaction series, Kluwer (2004)
15. Smith, C.A., Ellsworth, P.C.: Patterns of cognitive appraisal in emotion. J. of Personality and Social Psychology 48(4), 813 (1985)
16. Tsai, J., et al.: ESCAPES: evacuation simulation with children, authorities, parents, emotions, and social comparison. In: The 10th Int. Conf. on AAMAS. International Foundation for AAMAS, pp. 457–464 (2011)
17. Vartanian, O., Mandel, D.R.: Neuroscience of decision making. Psychology Press (2011)
18. Verduyn, P., et al.: Predicting the duration of emotional experience: two experience sampling studies. Emotion 9(1), 83 (2009)
19. Zoumpoulaki, A., Avradinis, N., Vosinakis, S.: A multi-agent simulation framework for emergency evacuations incorporating personality and emotions. In: Konstantopoulos, S., Perantonis, S., Karkaletsis, V., Spyropoulos, C.D., Vouros, G. (eds.) SETN 2010. LNCS, vol. 6040, pp. 423–428. Springer, Heidelberg (2010)

Emotional Agent Model for Simulating and Studying the Impact of Emotions on the Behaviors of Civilians during Emergency Situations

Mouna Belhaj, Fahem Kebair, and Lamjed Ben Said

Higher Institute of Management of Tunis
Optimization Strategies and Intelligent Information Engineering Laboratory
Le Bardo, 2000, Tunisia
mouna.belhaj@hotmail.com, kebairf@gmail.com,
lamjed.bensaid@isg.rnu.tn

Abstract. Emotion is one of the major factors that can affect the human behavior, especially in emergency situations. To consolidate this idea, we need to model and to simulate human emotional dynamics and their effects on the behaviors of human civilians in emergencies. This may help consequently emergency managers to better react and make decisions. This paper addresses this challenge by presenting a new emotional agent model. The final goal of this work is to build an emotional agent based simulator of civilians during an emergency situation. The paper describes first the proposed agent model, based on an appraisal theory of emotions. It provides then an implementation and experimentations performed using the RoboCupRescue project.

Keywords: Emergencies, Emotional agent, Human behavior, RoboCupRescue.

1 Introduction

Emergency situations are characterized by their unpredictability and low controllability. Therefore, their occurrence engenders high levels of stress and uncertainty on the humans involved in these situations [1]. This has a major effect on individual and collective human behaviors in such situations. When they are inadequate, human behaviors may contribute in the evolution of the situation into a crisis difficult to manage. This reciprocal effect argues the necessity of the study of human behaviors in order to be able to manage emergency and crisis situations.

Behavioral simulations are necessary in the comprehension of these situations through the study of individual or collective human behaviors. The comprehension of the behavioral dynamics in these situations enables the prevention of their development into crises, through the study of the different scenarios of their evolution. This study contributes to the preparation of intervention plans and/or the enhancement of existent plans. These simulations are also useful in learning and training systems where rescuers are trained to make decisions under time pressure in risky situations [2].

C. Hanachi, F. Bénaben, and F. Charoy (Eds.): ISCRAM-med 2014, LNBIP 196, pp. 206–217, 2014.
© Springer International Publishing Switzerland 2014

In order to reproduce reality-like agent based social simulations of human behaviors, we need to model human-like agents. An important characteristic particular to human is emotion, which has a major effect on behavior, particularly during emergencies where heightened emotional experiences may lead to unexpected behaviors [3]. Therefore, emotions are recognized to be essential to reproduce human-like software agents in simulations. Recent research works, that study human behaviors in emergencies, tend to integrate this psychological factor into artificial emotional agents. Examples include the research works described in [4], [5] and [6].

In our research work, we aim to study the effect of emotions on the behavior of civilians in an emergency situation after a disaster. The objective is to build a human civilian simulator where each civilian is represented by an emotional agent.

In a previous work [7], we have proposed a new computational model of emotions for the emergency situations context. The model explains the process of emotion generation and the parameters (appraisal variables) used to compute emotions intensities. The model is based on a psychological model of emotions named the OCC model [8]. The current article is dedicated to the description of an emotional civilian agent model. The latter explains agent perceptions acquisition and processing mechanisms. It uses the proposed computational model of emotions in order to generate agent emotions that result from perceptions evaluation (appraisal). Moreover, it integrates the effect of the resulting emotional state of the agent on its behavior.

The reminder of this paper is structured as follows. First, we describe the different components of the proposed emotional agent model that will serve for a human behavioral simulator of civilians during emergency situations. Then, we present results of the ongoing implementation of the model. Finally, we provide a conclusion and outline future work.

2   Emotional Agent Model

The emotional agent model is composed of three main components: Perception module, Appraisal module and Behavior module (Figure 1).

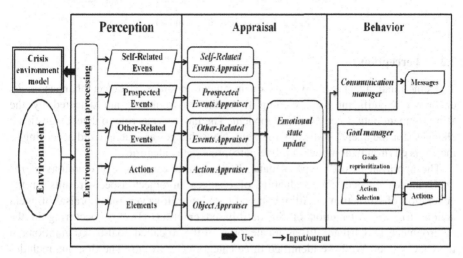

Fig. 1. The emotional agent model

The first module processes perceptual data in order to filter and to categorize significant changes in the encounter of the agent. The second module evaluates the filtered data to generate agent emotions. These emotions are combined with previous ones in order to produce the emotional state of the agent. The last module is responsible for the generation of agent behaviors that are influenced by its emotional state. More details about these modules are described in the following subsections.

2.1   Crisis Environment Model

A crisis environment model is proposed to describe the different entities of the disaster space, and that helps to identify the different objects that an agent may recognize in its environment. These objects cover the different elements in the environment, other agents (civilians or actor: rescue personals), events (related to the agent itself, to other agents or prospected), agent (self of other) actions and messages (Figure 2).

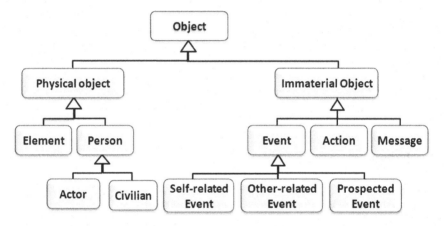

Fig. 2. Crisis environment model

2.2   Perception

The emotional agent perceives its environment in order to detect changes in its encounter. Significant data, coming from the environment, are detected by the "Environment data processing" component. The latter has as role to detect significant changes (for the agent) in the environment. New changes are categorized according to the crisis environment model into five perceptual data categories.

The appraisal of each type of data elicits distinct categories of emotions of the OCC model. Indeed, the evaluation of changes in object aspects results in the generation of Attraction or Attitude-based emotions. However, the appraisal of agent actions triggers Attribution or Standard-based emotions. Events, occurring in the environment, may trigger different categories of the so-called goal-based emotions of the OCC model. We have identified three categories of events. The first one includes events that affect directly the state of a civilian, and named Self-Related Events that trigger Wellbeing emotions. The second class encloses events that a civilian may prospect given its current state; Prospected-Events. The evaluation of this category of events results in Prospect-based emotions. Finally, the events related to other civilians, named Other-Related Events, are appraised to generate a category of Fortune-Of-Other emotions, named Empathetic emotions.

2.3   Appraisal

Agent perceptions are appraised in order to produce civilian emotions. The Appraisal module is composed of five Appraisers: the Self-Related Events Appraiser, the Prospected Events Appraiser, the Other-Related Events Appraiser, the Action Appraiser and the Object Appraiser. Each appraiser receives a category of the processed environment data. Data in input are evaluated using a specific set of dimensions called appraisal variables, defined in the OCC model. Each appraiser uses a different subset of these variables and is responsible of the generation of a particular emotion category. The output of each appraiser is an emotion, whose intensity results from the combination of the values of the appraisal variables relevant to each of the five appraisers.

The computation of the appraisal variables values and intensities of emotions are performed using a computational model of emotions for the emergency management context, that we have proposed in [7]. The latter contains an extensive description of the theoretical foundation of the proposed model, along with detailed definitions of the appraisal variables used, and an explanation of the methods and formula we use in the calculation of their values and in the computation of emotion intensities. In this paper, we are rather concerned with the description of the emotional agent model and its main processes.

Self-Related Events Appraiser. Self-Related Events are events that concern the civilian himself and that affect directly his state by altering his physical or emotional states. This category of events is evaluated by the Self-Related Events Appraiser. The latter uses the *Desirability* appraisal variable in order to assess the contribution/inhibition of the new event on the realization of the current goal of the agent. The output of this appraiser is a positive Wellbeing emotion (*Joy*), if the occurred event is positive and a negative emotion (*Distress*) if it is negative.

We have identified two positive Self-Related Events that are: *Safe (self)* and *InRefuge (self)*. We have also defined negative events recognizable by the agent that are: *Injury (self)*, *HealthStateDown (self)* and *InDanger (self)*.

Prospected Events Appraiser. In an emergency situation, the occurrence of some events (Self-Related) may change the capacity of the civilian to deal with new situations. For example, when a civilian is injured, he cannot move by itself and needs help. Being in that state, a civilian may expect to be helped or to see his health state decreasing. These events, that a civilian may expect, are named Prospected events.

The cognitive appraisal of this category of events results in the Prospect-based emotions of the OCC model (*Hope* and *Fear*).

The appraisal variables of the OCC model, used to evaluate prospected events, are *Desirability, Effort, Likelihood* and *Realization*. The *Urgency* variable was added from the theory of Scherer [9] for the evaluation of these emotions since we think that it is an important variable in the context of emergencies.

The *Effort* is measured through the number of tries that the civilian has made to provoke an event in order to change its current state (number of calls for help when injured, number of tries to escape a risky place).

The *Likelihood* of an event to happen corresponds to the probability of its occurrence given the current state of the civilian and the existence of a helper.

The *Urgency* of the occurrence of an event corresponds to the agent need of a fast reaction to that event when it is in a certain state. For example, the urgency to be rescued is greater when the health state of an agent attains a certain minimum threshold.

The prospect of a positive event: *ProspectHelp (self)* (from another civilian), *ProspectRescue (self)* and *ProspectManageRisk (Element)* (from an actor) elicits a positive emotion (*Hope*). However the expectation of a negative event: *ProspectDeath (self)* and *ProspectInjury (self)*, elicits a negative emotion (*Fear*).

The *Realization* variable is used to model the occurrence of a prospected event (*Realization*=1) or its non occurrence (*Realization*= (-1)). The Realization of a positive (respectively *negative*) prospected event results in a *Satisfaction* (respectively *Fear-confirmed*) emotion. However, the disconfirmation of a *positive* (respectively *negative*) event results in the *Disappointment* (respectively *Relief*) emotion.

Other-Related Events Appraiser. This appraiser is used to generate emotions resulting from the appraisal of events that happen to other agents: Other-Related Events. This category of events is evaluated using two appraisal variables that are: the *DesirabilityForOther* and *Liking* variables.

Assessing the desirability for other of an event needs the capacity of putting oneself on the place of the other, of imagining his current state and goals and to assess the desirability of the event. This capacity is named: cognitive empathy. Therefore, we consider what is called empathetic emotions in the OCC model: Happy-For and Sorry-For.

The *Liking* variable measures the affective link between the empathizer agent (feeling an empathetic emotion) and the target of empathy.

The input of the Other-Related Events Appraiser is the perceived new events that happen to others. This category of events includes positive events: *Safe (other)*, *InRefuge (other)*. It also includes negative events that are: *Injury (other)*, *InDanger (other)*, *HealthStateDown (other)* and *Death (other)*.

The output of this appraiser is a positive (*HappyFor*) or a negative (*SorryFor*) empathetic emotion depending on the valence of the appraised event.

Action Appraiser. Agent actions are evaluated according to their conformity with agent standards. The *Action Appraiser* estimates the *Praiseworthiness* or *Blameworthiness* of the actions of the agent and the actions of other agents in order to elicit the Standard-based (or Attribution) emotions of the OCC model. In the context of an emergency situation, we consider only one standard that is: "helping a person in need is an action that conforms to standards": Help (person). If the civilian is the actor, the appraised action will be Help (Other) and the resulting emotion can be *Pride* or *Shame*. If another civilian is the actor, the appraised action will be Help (self) and the triggered emotion can be *Admiration* or *Reproach*. The distinction of the source and target of the help action enables the agent to generate the right emotion.

Object Appraiser. *Appealingness* and *Familiarity* are the two variables utilized by the *Object Appraiser* to evaluate objects in the crisis environment. The *Appealingness* appraisal variable corresponds to the degree to which the normal aspect of the perceived object. The more the object is seen in the environment, the more it becomes familiar to the agent. Perceiving objects with positive attraction such as refuges may elicit the *Like* emotions: a positive Attitude-based (or Attraction) emotion. However, negatively attractive objects in the crisis environment, such as collapsed buildings, trigger the negative emotion: *Dislike*.

Emotional State Update. An emergency situation evolves quickly. Therefore, different new events, actions or changes in object aspects may appear. Moreover, the states of previously perceived elements may change. Consequently, new emotions may appear and others may be updated. The different appraisers are only concerned with the generation of the new emotions triggered by the appraisal of the altered aspects of the disaster environment. An Emotional State update module is used to handle the potential variations in existing emotions and to integrate new emotions. This module produces the final emotional state of the agent, which is composed of the set of emotions felt by the agent.

2.4   Behavior

Behaviors are action suites that an agent can perform in the environment. The generation of agent behaviors is goal-directed and based on the resulting emotional state. A Goal Manager is used to deal with changes in goal priorities that are influenced by agent emotions. The exchange of messages between agents, which is a particular type of behavioral response, is controlled by the Communication Manager.

Goal Manager . A civilian agent has five goals (Keep safe, Get saved, Escape the risk, Find a family member and Help a person). The agent selects the appropriate action to perform based-on its active goal. Initial importance values are assigned to agent goals. This importance changes when the emotional state of the agent is altered. In fact, the appearance of new emotions reflects the changes of its physical state or the perception of important events. Therefore, agent goals priorities are rearranged when its emotional or physical states are subject to significant changes. The agent chooses the action to perform in the light of the goal with the highest priority and the emotional state of the agent. Civilian agents may perform some actions as behavioral response to their current state, such as Move (environment), Wait (person) and Find (person). They may also have empathetic behaviors as a response to the state of other people in need: Help (person).

Communication Manager. Human civilian agents interact, by communicating, in the crisis environment in order to ask for help or to inform about a fact in the crisis environment. The Communication Manager insures this purpose by handling different information or help messages that an agent may hear or send. Messages, exchanged in an emergency situation, may inform about the emotional state of an agent, so that they may affect the emotions of the receiver and induce empathetic behaviors in it.

3   Experimental Results

A part of the proposed civilian agent model was implemented and integrated into the RoboCupRescue (RCR) simulation system [10]. In the following subsections, we first present the RCR simulation platform. Then we describe the obtained results of the experimentations of the perception module and a part of the appraisal module.

3.1   RoboCupRescue Simulator

RCR simulator is an agent-based urban disaster simulator of an emergency situation after an earthquake. The aim of the RCR project is to support research works on the context of emergency management. It aims at exploring new procedures for emergency management [10] by providing a virtual tool to test different communication, coordination and planning methods.

At the core of this platform, we find the Kernel. The latter is responsible for the coordination and communication between the other components (simulators, agents and viewers). Knowledge about the objects of the environment and their properties are organized as domain objects recognizable by the Kernel. The latter is responsible for providing civilian and actor agents (police forces, ambulance teams and firefighters) with their corresponding perceptual data at each time step of the simulation. These agents process these data and decide about the action to perform. Their actions are interpreted and executed by the Kernel that updates the necessary data in the relevant simulators and displays the result on a GIS (Geographic Information System) viewer [11] (Figure 3). In the current work, we are only concerned with civilian agents of RCR.

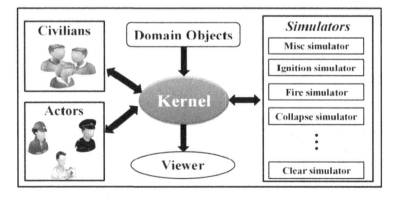

Fig. 3. RCR Simulation System architecture

3.2   Application on the RCR

The simulation of human-like civilian emotions and behaviors in artificial agents needs their integration into a crisis environment simulation that imitates the real crisis situation. Therefore, we choose the RoboCupRescue (RCR) simulation project to test our implementation. On the one hand, we take advantage of the completeness of this system, since it provides a realistic simulation of a disaster environment and where changes in an agent encounter could be collected and processed by the agent. On the other hand, the current civilian agents in RCR have simple behaviors and are not sufficiently involved in the study of the emergency situation [12]. Moreover, RCR civilians do not have emotions. The latter were proved to be necessary to reproduce human-like civilian agent behaviors in emergencies. Therefore, we aim to enhance the civilian simulation by the implementation and integration of the proposed emotional agents into the civilian agents in the RCR simulation system.

3.3   Perceptual Data Acquisition and Processing

At each time step of the simulation, the civilian agents receive perceptual data from the Kernel. These data include visual and auditory information. The first one includes all the entities of the environment in the vision specter of the agent. An agent may perceive buildings, secure agents, other civilians and their properties. The second one includes the messages that the agent can hear. These precepts are processed to detect changes in the agent's context. The detection of a change involves the recognition of a new event, an action or an attractive element.

3.4   Appraisal and Emotions Elicitation

We have implemented two appraisers among the five ones defined in the agent model in order to generate two categories of emotions. The Self-Related Events Appraiser generates Wellbeing emotions. However, the Attitude-based emotions are the output of the Object Appraiser.

Wellbeing Emotions. In RCR, the emotional agents receive information about changes in their own states (health point, location, etc). These perceptions are processed to detect *positive* Self-Related Events, which are: *Safe (self)* and *InRefuge (self)*. The appraisal of these events results on the *Joy* emotion. An agent may also detect *negative* events, which are *Injury (self)*, *InDanger (self)* and *HealtStateDown (self)*. The evaluation of these events elicits the *negative* emotion *Distress*. The death of the agent itself is marked with the event *"Death"* that makes the emotion undefined (Figure 4).

The evolution of the intensities of Wellbeing emotions of a civilian agent is illustrated in the first plot (Plot 1) in Figure 4. However, the evolution of the *desirability* of the causing self related events is shown in the second plot (Plot 2).

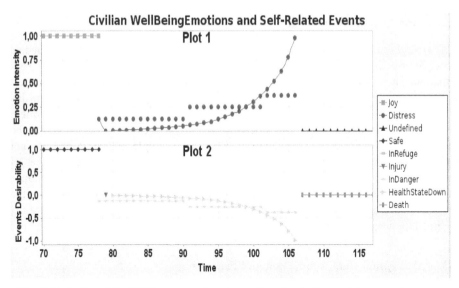

Fig. 4. Evolution of the Wellbeing emotions intensities of a civilian and their causing events

In the illustrative example, the agent is safe (*Safe (self)* event) until the instant 77 of the simulation. Therefore, it has the emotion Joy. At the time step 78, the agent detects the *InDanger (self)* event that is associated to "being in a fiery building" in RCR. At instant 79, the civilian is injured (Plot 2). This is a negative undesirable event with a negative desirability degree (-0.1) and corresponds to a first decrease of the health state of the agent. This causes the appearing of the *HealthStateDown (self)* event (Plot 2). These negative self related events give rise to the emotion distress. Each event is evaluated separately. Therefore, we find two corresponding distress values at each time step in Plot 1. The intensities of this emotion, which corresponds to the absolute value of the desirability of the causing events, will be combined in the *Emotional State Update* phase. More details about emotion intensity and event desirability computation are described in the computational model of emotions we have proposed in [7]. The intensity of the distress emotion and the desirability of the causing events are recomputed at each time step of the simulation. At instant 107, the civilian is dead: (*Death* event in Plot 2) and his emotion becomes undefined (Plot 1).

Figure 5 illustrates the evolution of the number of civilians detecting each type of Self-Related Events (Plot 2) and having the corresponding Wellbeing emotion (Plot 1) over time. We can notice that, the curves of the evolution of the *Distress* (respectively *Joy*) emotion and of the causing *negative* (respectively *positive*) Self-Related Events have similar shapes. In fact, the number of agents having the negative emotion *Distress* corresponds to the number of those facing the *negative* events defined above. Similarly, at each time step of the simulation, the number of agents having the *Joy* emotion corresponds to the sum of the number of agents that are safe (having the event *Safe (self)*) and those that found a refuge (*InRefuge (self)*). For example, we have at time t =140, 41 civilians having the *Joy* emotion, 13 civilians in refuges and 28 civilians that are safe. Finally, the evolution of the number of dead civilians (*Death* in Plot 2) corresponds to those having the undefined emotion (*Undefined* in Plot 1).

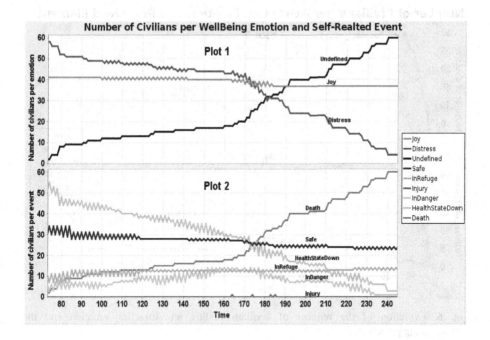

Fig. 5. Evolution of the number of civilians feeling a Joy or a Distress emotion and their causing events

Attitude Based (Attraction) Emotions. RCR crisis environment contains different objects such as buildings (of civilian, Police offices, etc.), refuges, roads and blockades. We have associated, for civilian agents, the *Like* emotion to the perception of a *Refuge* and the *Dislike* emotion to the perception of a *Blockade* or a collapsed *Building* (Figure 6). We consider refuges, blockades and collapsed buildings as the most attractive objects for a civilian in the crisis environment. Civilians, perceiving the different elements of the crisis environment, are safe civilians and are able to move in the disaster space.

Blockades result from buildings collapses. This explains the equality of the numbers of civilians perceiving blockades and of those perceiving collapsed buildings (Figure 6, Plot 2). Consequently, the curves representing the number of civilians seeing blockades or collapsed building are too similar. Note that a civilian may perceive simultaneously several collapsed buildings and blockades. In that case, we suppose that the most negatively attractive building is the one that has the biggest damage. Similarly, we consider that the biggest blockade is the one appraised to generate the *Dislike* attraction emotion.

The number of civilians having a *Like* (respectively *Dislike*) emotion (Figure 6, Plot 1) corresponds to those perceiving a *Refuge* (respectively a *Blockade* or a collapsed *Building*) in the disaster space (Figure 6, Plot 2).

Number of Civilians per Attraction Emotion and Perceived Element

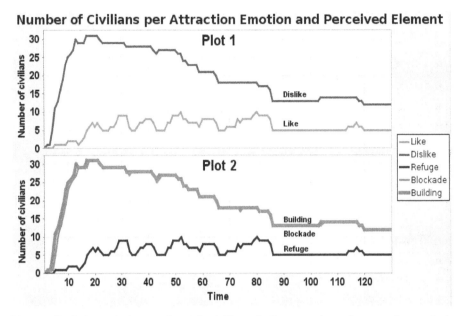

Fig. 6. Evolution of the number of civilians feeling an Attraction emotion and the corresponding perceived element

Some of the blockades may disappear by the action of RCR police force agents whose mission is to clear blocked roads. Moreover, civilians may find and enter inside refuges. Therefore, they don't perceive blockades and collapsed buildings. This explains the decrease of the number of civilians perceiving negatively attractive elements of the environment over time.

4   Conclusion and Future Work

In this paper, we have proposed an emotional agent model for the simulation of human emotions and behaviors in emergency situations. The model emphasizes the role of emotions on the production of realistic behaviors in social simulations during emergency situations. It relies on a process of cognitive appraisal of perceptual data that enables the production of the emotional reaction to what happens in the crisis environment. The implemented part of the model includes agent perceptions acquisition and processing in order to detect relevant changes in the agent context and to generate the corresponding emotions. Future work will include the development of the behavior module that aims to prove the effect of the emotional state of the agent on its behavior. The personality notion will also be integrated on the proposed model. This will complement the proposed emotion generation process by creating more diversified and human like emotional responses. In fact, human personalities define tendencies to feel particular emotions and behavioral predispositions.

References

1. Van de Walle, B., Turoff, M.: Decision support for emergency situations. Inf. Syst. E-bus. Manag. 6, 295–316 (2008)
2. Barot, C., Lourdeaux, D., Burkhardt, J.M., Amokrane, K., Lenne, D.: V3S: A Virtual Environment for Risk-Management Training Based on Human-Activity Models (2013)
3. Aydt, H., Lees, M., Luo, L., Cai, W., Low, M.Y.H., Kadirvelen, S.K.: A Computational Model of Emotions for Agent-Based Crowds in Serious Games. In: International Conferences on Web Intelligence and Intelligent Agent Technology, pp. 72–80 (2011)
4. Jones, H., Saunier, J., Lourdeaux, D.: Personality, Emotions and Physiology in a BDI Agent Architecture: The PEP -» BDI Model. In: IEEE/WIC/ACM International Joint Conference on Web Intelligence and Intelligent Agent Technology, pp. 263–266 (2009)
5. Luo, L., Zhou, S., Cai, W., Lees, M., Low, M.Y.H., Sornum, K.: HumDPM: A Decision Process Model for Modeling Human-Like Behaviors in Time-Critical and Uncertain Situations. In: Gavrilova, M.L., Tan, C.J.K., Sourin, A., Sourina, O. (eds.) Transactions on Computational Science XII. LNCS, vol. 6670, pp. 206–230. Springer, Heidelberg (2011)
6. Zoumpoulaki, A., Avradinis, N., Vosinakis, S.: A Multi-agent Simulation Framework for Emergency Evacuations Incorporating Personality and Emotions. Artif. Intellig.Theo. Models and Appli., 423–428 (2010)
7. Belhaj, M., Kebair, F., Ben Said, L.: A Computational Model of Emotions for the Simulation of Human Emotional Dynamics in Emergency Situations. J. Comput. Theory Eng. 6, 227–233 (2014)
8. Ortony, A., Clore, G.L., Collins, A.: The Cognitive Structure of Emotions. Cambridge University Press (1988)
9. Scherer, K.R.: Appraisal Considered as a Process of Multilevel Sequential Checking., Appraisal processes in emotion Theory Methods Research. Oxford University Press (2001)
10. RoboCup Rescue, http://www.robocup.org/robocup-rescue/
11. Skinner, C., Ramchurn, S.: The RoboCup Rescue Simulation Platform. In: The 9th International Conference on Autonomous Agents and Multiagent Systems, pp. 1647–1648 (2010)
12. Khorsandian, A., Abdolmaleki, A.: RoboCupRescue 2009 – Rescue Simulation League (Infrastructure Competition) Team Description MRL2009 - brave circles (Iran) (2009)

Emergency Situation Awareness:
Twitter Case Studies

Robert Power, Bella Robinson, John Colton, and Mark Cameron

CSIRO
GPO Box 664
Canberra ACT, 2601, Australia
{robert.power,bella.robinson,john.colton,mark.cameron}@csiro.au
http://www.csiro.au

Abstract. The Emergency Situation Awareness (ESA) system provides all-hazard situation awareness information for emergency managers using content gathered from the public Twitter API. It collects, filters and analyses Tweets from specific regions of interest in near-real-time, enabling effective alerting for unexpected incidents and monitoring of emergency events with results accessible via an interactive website.

ESA was developed in close collaboration with users to ensure fitness-for-purpose for the tasks performed by emergency services agencies. ESA processes large volumes of Twitter data and identifies discussion threads, trends and hot topics using language models. A burst detector generates alerts for unusually high frequency words that are filtered using text mining techniques and machine learning algorithms to identify Tweets of interest to emergency managers.

An overview of the ESA platform is presented along with example case studies of its use to detect earthquakes, identify bushfire events and provide all-hazard monitoring in a crisis coordination centre.

Keywords: Crisis Coordination, Disaster Management, Situation Awareness, Social Media, System Architectures, Twitter.

1   Introduction

Effective management of emergency events requires access to timely, authoritative and verifiable information. In Australia, authoritative content is being published on Twitter and other online communication channels by the emergency services to alert the community about incidents, inform them about events underway, reassure the public that a response is underway and provide advice to citizens to ensure their safety.

Emergency managers mostly operate under a command and control structure where only verifiable information from authoritative sources is used for operational decisions. While social media has been recognised as a new data channel to receive public crowdsourced information about emergency events [3,7,12] its adoption is not yet widespread in Australia. This is due to a number of limitations such as identifying relevant information from the large volume of content

C. Hanachi, F. Bénaben, and F. Charoy (Eds.): ISCRAM-med 2014, LNBIP 196, pp. 218–231, 2014.
© Springer International Publishing Switzerland 2014

available, ensuring the veracity of what is being said and reliably determining the location of the event so that resources can be deployed appropriately. These issues are exacerbated by the work practices of crisis coordinators and emergency managers who need to make operational decisions under time constraints while ensuring that these decisions are based on the best available information.

These barriers will be overcome with the widespread and increasing acceptance of social media by the general community and emergency services personnel, so long as this information is appropriately identified. These issues are not solely technical. The policies and procedures used by emergency service organisations need to be revised to accommodate effective communication to the public on social media channels and obtain information from those who are reporting useful content.

To this end we have been exploring information published on Twitter in Australia and New Zealand to determine how best to identify useful content to help emergency managers. Various use cases have been targeted for our investigation, focusing on general 'all hazard' monitoring performed in a crisis command centre, the identification of unexpected events such as earthquakes and bushfires, and the ongoing monitoring of an unfolding event to improve situation awareness.

The use of crowdsourced Twitter content provides emergency management organisations with further information for decision making with the potential for improved community outcomes [2]. Tools currently exist that focus on crowdsourced information to improve the situational awareness of events as they unfold, see for example Twitcident [1] and Tweet4act [4]. Machine learning techniques have also been used to map crisis related Tweets into a disaster-related ontology to find information that contributes to situational awareness [6]. The ESA platform has evolved along similar lines.

The rest of the paper is organised as follows. First we provide background information describing the ESA platform noting how Tweets are collected and processed from Australia and New Zealand and the various interfaces available for users to explore *what's happening*. Then three case studies are presented outlining how ESA is currently used. Based on these case studies, a summary of the operational use of ESA is outlined and the paper concludes with a discussion of planned further work.

2   The Emergency Situation Awareness Platform

2.1   Overview

The ESA architecture is shown in Figure 1 where the red circles indicate the near-real-time processing steps. Tweets are gathered from Twitter and sent to JMS, indicated by the ① in Figure 1. The Tweets are saved in the repository ② for later reference and also processed by the *Burst Detector* ② which generates alerts ③. The alerts are also saved ④ and further processed by the *Event Detector* ④ to target specific keywords which may generate user notifications ⑤. These detector components are processing pipelines and are further explained below.

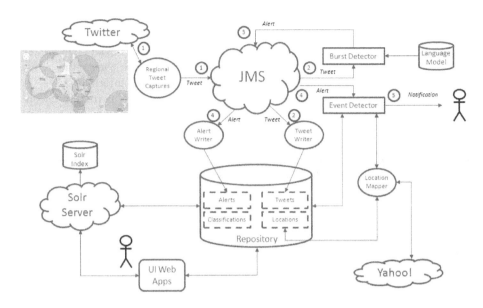

Fig. 1. ESA Conceptual Architecture

JMS provides flexible deployment of new Tweet ② and Alert ④ consumers to extend the system. For example, new language models and burst detection techniques can be easily deployed as can new alert monitors to target different alert words of interest for different users. There are various user interfaces in ESA indicated by the *UI Web Apps* component in Figure 1. They access the *Solr Server* which provides efficient searching over Tweet content and the *Repository* which contains an archive of Tweets, alerts and other derived content. The *Location Mapper* service estimates the user's Tweet location based on their profile using the Yahoo! GeoPlanet API with the derived locations archived.

The following sections briefly describe the core components of the ESA platform, including the backend tasks for gathering and processing Tweets, the various user interfaces available to explore the live Tweet stream and tools used to review previously processed Tweets.

2.2   Tweet Processing

As noted above, Tweets are collected using the Twitter REST Application Programming Interface (API)[1] by providing a latitude/longitude coordinate pair and search radius which returns a collection of matching Tweets. To cover Australia and New Zealand, we have set up nine capture regions. For each of the capture regions, a query is made every 20 seconds which to date has been sufficient to obtain all the published Tweets. Tweets have been collected from the

---

[1] https://dev.twitter.com/docs/api/1.1

whole of Australia and New Zealand since late September 2011 and we have processed over 1.6 billion Tweets at a rate of approximately 1500 per minute.

Originally there were eight capture regions. However in early April 2013, Twitter changed their method of determining a user's location for the Search API which resulted in no Tweets being retrieved when the user's profile location was defined as 'Australia'. The issue was due to the suburb called *Australia* in the Mexican town of Saltillo[2]. The resolution was to configure a specific regional capture to retrieve Tweets originating from this location in Mexico which includes a filter for just the English language Tweets.

2.3   Alerts as Bursting Words

ESA produces alerts every minute by examining word frequencies within a rolling 5-minute window of Tweets. A word is said to be a 'bursting word', representing an alert, when its frequency in the 5-minute window deviates from its typical frequency. A background language model contains typical frequencies for all words and other tokens historically encountered in the Tweet stream. The scale of the deviation gives rise to the colour of the alert, ranging from green to red.

The model is created by processing the Tweets in uniform time periods, currently set to a five minute buffer. All Tweets in the buffer are processed by: extracting the individual words in the text; stemming the words to their common 'root', for example *running, runs* and *run* all have the same stem of *run*; then counting the number of Tweets containing each distinct stem in the buffer. The result is the expected Tweet frequency for each stem which is averaged over all buffers giving the final value used in the language model [13].

As Tweets are collected in near-real-time by the regional captures they are buffered into a five minute window and the same processing is performed as described above to calculate the Tweet frequencies of the stems. When the frequencies in the dynamic buffer are significantly different to those in the historical language model, a burst is found. If the burst is significant enough, an alert is generated. The alert thresholds can be adjusted to target words of interest and place less significance on those not considered of value, such as stop words.

The buffer is advanced every minute creating a sliding five minute 'window' where the oldest Tweets are removed, new ones added, the Tweet stem frequencies for the modified buffer contents recalculated to produce a new set of alerts.

2.4   Alert Monitor

A key component of the ESA platform is the near-real-time burst detector that identifies alerting words using the pre-calculated language model described above. The dynamically generated alerts are stored in a database and presented via the Alert Monitor web page, shown in Figure 2. The main components of ESA are not tailored to emergency events. Politics, sport and celebrity gossip frequently generate alerts within the system.

---

[2] See http://earth-explorer.appspot.com/Mexico/Coahuila-de-Zaragoza/
Saltillo/Saltillo/Australia.

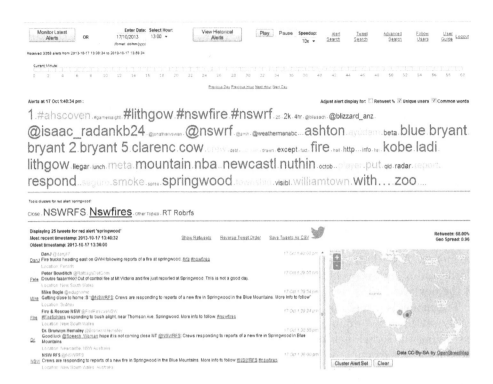

Fig. 2. ESA Alert Monitor User Interface

The Alert Monitor web page has six components: a header consisting of mode settings (to monitor the latest alerts or review historical ones); playback controls (to automatically advance the display of historical alerts at varying speeds); hyperlinks to other ESA interfaces; a time section consisting of a 60 minute slider control with hour and day navigation links; an alert tag cloud of stemmed words; Tweet cluster summaries; Tweet display and the alert heatmap.

The cluster summary, Tweet display and alert heatmap are activated by clicking a stemmed word in the alert tag cloud. The tag cloud can be adjusted to minimise the influence of users who repeatedly Tweet the same or similar content, to minimise alerts that are primarily due to significant retweets and hide common stop words.

The Tweet cluster summary provides a high-level summary of topics from all Tweets contributing to the selected alert word. Topics can be selected to display the Tweets belonging to that cluster. The Tweet display appears on the bottom left of the page and conforms to the Twitter Display Requirements[3]. It includes other features, such as links to the Twitter user's home page and has a means

---

[3] https://dev.twitter.com/terms/display-requirements

of identifying the original Tweet for a retweet. There are also display options to hide all retweets, reverse the chronological order or export the Tweet content to a CSV file.

The screenshot in Figure 2 shows the Alert Monitor web page for 13:40 on 17 October 2013 during the Blue Mountains fires near Sydney. The Springwood fire[4] started approximately 10 minutes before this time, caused by damage to powerlines, and resulted in evacuations and school lock-downs and eventually went on to destroy 193 houses.

The public were Tweeting about this event soon after it began as can be seen in Figure 2. This screen shot shows the Alert Monitor web page after the user has selected the *springwood* alert, which generates five cluster summaries including *Nswfires*. The 25 Tweets contributing to this alert are listed in the bottom left hand corner, accessible using the scroll bar. The alert heatmap provides a visual indication of where the Tweets originated from and includes measures of the retweet percentage and geographic spread. These measures are useful for further analysis of the Tweets and are described further in Section 3.2.

2.5   Alert Search

ESA maintains an archive of all alerts generated, enabling any alert to be revisited and further investigated. The Alert Search page, Figure 3, provides access to the alert archive which can be explored by providing a list of alert words, a date range and minimum alert level.

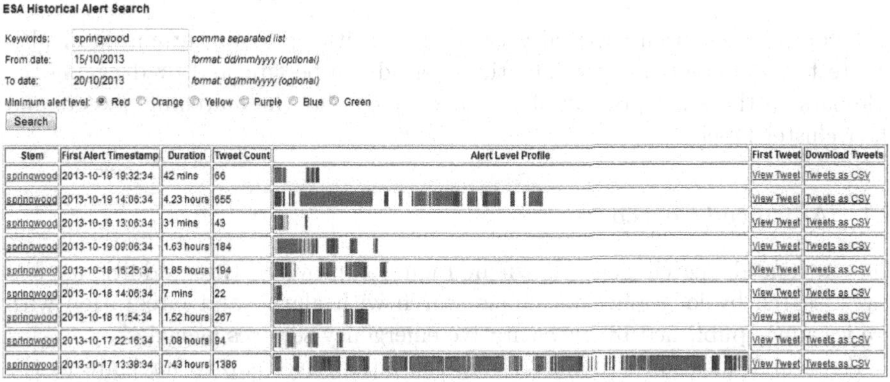

Fig. 3. ESA Alert Search

The example above shows search results returned for the alert word *springwood* with at least one red alert for the period 15–20 October 2013. The result table lists each alert word stem and a summary of the alert profile. The stem is

---

[4] http://en.wikipedia.org/wiki/2013_New_South_Wales_bushfires

hyperlinked back to the Alert Monitor page and will open the monitor page (in historical mode) at the date and time of the first alert. The alert level profile is colour coded and proportional to the alert level and duration. A gap of up to 30 minutes is indicated by the white sections.

2.6   Tweet Search

The Tweet Search page provides keyword search over Tweets from the previous four days using a Solr[5] index. A query consists of keywords optionally combined with conjunction and disjunction operators and using brackets to override default precedence. The screenshot in Figure 4 shows an example of searching for Tweets containing 'fire OR smoke'. The timeline chart on the right shows the volumes of matching Tweets in five minute intervals.

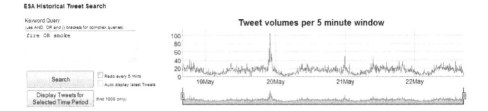

Fig. 4. ESA Tweet Search

A continuous search capability is provided with optional automatic display of latest Tweets and clusters. The time period can be adjusted by dragging the side bars on the lower portion of the chart to display the matching Tweets and their cluster labels.

2.7   Advanced Search

The Advanced Search page shown in Figure 5 provides three additional features: search by location; continuous search with alarm; and integration with fire warnings published by authoritative emergency services agencies[6].

The search location is defined using the interactive map to navigate to the region of interest and Tweets that report to be within this region are returned. This feature uses either the Tweet's geotag, when present, or the user's profile location. To assist with identifying the region to focus on, RSS web feed data from a number of state fire authorities has been integrated and mapped. This has been made available from the Emergency Response Intelligence Capability (ERIC) platform[5].

---

[5] http://lucene.apache.org/solr/
[6] http://eric.csiro.au

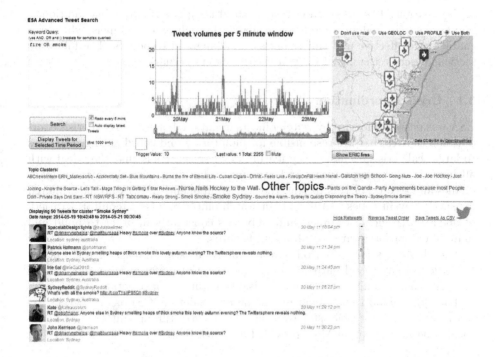

Fig. 5. ESA Advanced Search User Interface

Continuous search is particularly useful in combination with the alarm feature where an alarm sound is activated when the latest search data exceeds a trigger value. In the screenshot of Figure 5, the trigger value has been set at 10 and the red line shows when the Tweet volumes have gone over this threshold.

2.8   Follow Users

The Follow Users page has been configured to display Tweets from around 400 official Australian emergency related Twitter accounts. These accounts are grouped into categories and geographic regions, so that it is possible to focus on accounts that will likely be tweeting about an ongoing event of interest. Tweets from these accounts are specifically gathered via the Twitter Streaming API. Tweets are received almost instantly via the Streaming API whereas there is a delay of up to 20 seconds via our Search API regional captures. It is also useful to have a redundant source of these important Tweets in case one of the Twitter API's becomes unavailable during an emergency.

3   Case Studies

ESA provides the ability for emergency managers and crisis coordinators to use information from the public available on Twitter during emerging and ongoing crisis situations. ESA has demonstrated that it is capable of providing additional, real-time situational awareness not available through other channels, which can enable more effective and timely decision making and responses. The following sections describe the use of ESA in three different scenarios.

3.1   Crisis Coordination Centres

ESA was designed for use by watch officers in national or state based crisis coordination centres that are responsible for monitoring and coordinating responses to large scale crisis events. A key feature of these centres is that they deal with all hazards, including natural and man-made disasters, terrorist attacks, pandemics and so on. For this reason, the core components of ESA are not tailored for specific event types. An important watch officer role is to monitor a variety of open-source media channels and web sites constantly in order to build and maintain situation awareness about all hazards.

The challenges for watch officers are many: to stay abreast of relevant information; analyse and gather relevant metrics from information; and use the analysis results to make consistent decisions about the next action.

The Queensland Department of Community Safety (DCS) has used ESA extensively in the State Disaster Coordination Centre throughout cyclone monitoring operations. Adam Moss provided feedback that:

> ...during TC Oswald (2013), the community tweeted various forms of information from road and bridge closures, river heights, damaged infrastructure, observed weather patterns from the ground, evacuations, and finally detailed community and resilience information. This information provided significant situational awareness thus providing elements of emergency planning when required. ESA also provided images of unfolding incidents informing situational awareness for the high level visits to impacted areas. This provided real time briefing information.

3.2   Earthquake Detection

The Joint Australian Tsunami Warning Centre (JATWC) is operated by Geoscience Australia (GA) and the Bureau of Meteorology. The Centre monitors, detects, verifies and warns the community of potential tsunami impacts on Australia's coastline and external territories. The principle is to provide at least 90 minutes warning of a potential impact on Australia's coastline from tsunami that are generated from earthquakes occurring on plate boundaries in the Indian, Pacific and Southern Oceans.

Recent studies [5,9,10,11] have shown that when an earthquake event occurs in populated regions, reports on Twitter can provide a faster method of detection compared to traditional approaches. The role of seismologists to verify and scientifically characterise earthquakes can be augmented by crowdsourced information that provides both an early warning and evidence of the impact experienced by the community affected.

Geoscience Australia, which provides the earthquake detection capabilities for the JATWC, have been actively using the ESA system extended to provide Twitter earthquake detection capabilities. The ESA earthquake detection process involves: monitoring the output of the burst detector for alerts matching earthquake-related keywords; testing the currency of the alert; determining if the original Tweets producing the alert are geographically close using a geographic spread measure and processing the individual Tweets contributing to the earthquake alert using a machine learning text classifier to determine if the Tweets are first-hand 'felt' reports [9]. The earthquake classifier is able to achieve an accuracy of 91%.

If ESA determines that the alert is related to an earthquake event, a notification email is sent to the JATWC duty officer summarising why the ESA system considers it to be evidence of firsthand earthquake 'felt' reports and includes a summary of the information from Twitter. A example is shown in Figure 6.

yellow 'earthquak' alert detected
Timestamp: Mon, 6 Jan 2014 08:58:32 +1100
View in the ESA Alert Monitor: https://esa.csiro.au/aus/index.html?date=2014-01-06&time=08:58&alert=earthquak

Statistics
Number of tweets (including retweets): 16
Retweets: 0%
Geographic spread: 1.56

Classification Results
Classifier used: Firsthand earthquake 'felt' reports
Percentage of tweets classified as positive: 93.75%
Geographic spread of positively classified tweets: 1.62

Location Summary (excluding retweets)
Adelaide (-34.926102,138.599884) - 12 tweets
Australia (-24.91213,133.397537) - 2 tweets
Melbourne (-37.817532,144.967148) - 1 tweets
*unknown location - 1 tweets

Cluster Topics
Earthquake in Adelaide - 9 tweets
Earthquake Just - 8 tweets
Adelaide Just - 4 tweets
Bed - 2 tweets
Sure - 2 tweets
Other Topics - 3 tweets

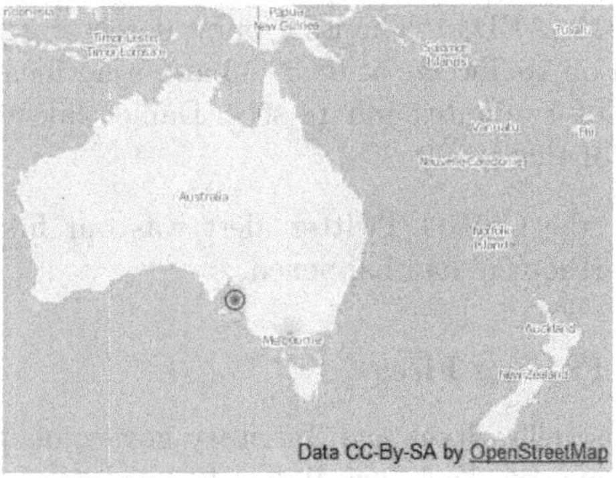

Data CC-By-SA by OpenStreetMap

Tweets (excluding retweets, +/- labels indicate classification result)
+ 06/01/2014 08:55:44 (Adelaide, Australia) Was that an earthquake?
+ 06/01/2014 08:55:56 (Adelaide, Australia) Pretty sure I just felt an earthquake
+ 06/01/2014 08:56:19 (Lemonadelaide) Wooaahh did we just have an earthquake??
+ 06/01/2014 08:56:20 (Adelaide) Did we just have an Earthquake? #adelaide
+ 06/01/2014 08:56:30 (Adelaide, Australia) Was that just an earthquake in Adelaide or did I drink too much coffee this morning?!
+ 06/01/2014 08:56:33 (Adelaide, South Australia) Was that an earthquake just rolled through the #adelhills #feltlikeit #shookthehouse
+ 06/01/2014 08:56:56 (Adelaide, Australia) Earthquake in Adelaide??
+ 06/01/2014 08:56:57 (Australia) Alright I'm out of. Bed now, I think an earthquake just come though @.@

Fig. 6. Example Earthquake notification email

When the notification email is received, the duty officer can then assess if the alert is genuine and gain a quick overview of the intensity of the earthquake with reference to the number of Tweets reported and by reviewing their content. This provides an additional means of early warning to JATWC complementing the information arriving from their existing system based on seismic stations.

During its initial five months of operation the system generated 49 notifications of which 29 related to real earthquake events. The average time delay between the earthquake origin and when ESA sent a notification email was 3:03 (minutes:seconds) [9]. These notifications may also be the first electronic indication of the earthquake, arriving ahead of the seismic information.

Figure 6 shows the contents of the email that was sent for an earthquake that occurred near Adelaide on the 6th January 2014. The stemmed yellow alert 'earthquak' can be seen at the top of the email followed by the timestamp of when it was detected. The remainder of the email is structured to help the reader decide if the alert describes an actual earthquake event. This information includes: summary statistics; a link to the web interface to explore the Tweets; a summary of the probable locations of the Twitter users including the heat map; the cluster topics; and a list of the source Tweets highlighted after processing them through a classifier trained to determine the likelihood that the Tweets are evidence of first hand 'felt' reports. Note that not all Tweets are shown to save space.

According to Geoscience Australian's earthquake database[7] the earthquake corresponding to this event had a magnitude of 2.7 (ML) with an origin time of 08:55:15 (AEDT). The ESA burst detector generated a yellow 'earthquak' alert based on 16 Tweets at 08:59:13 and a notification email was sent at 08:59:29; a delay of 4 minutes and 14 secs. Daniel Jaksa from Geoscience Australia noted that for this event:

> . . . the CSIRO Twitter alert was our first digital notification that an earthquake had happened.

3.3   Finding Fires

In Australia, State and Territory governments have responsibility for bushfire management. Each jurisdiction has its own agency that coordinates community preparedness and fire fighting activities such as the Rural Fire Service (RFS) in New South Wales (NSW) and the Country Fire Authority in Victoria. They conduct activities such as fire fighting, training to prepare communities to protect themselves, land management hazard reduction burns and search and rescue.

During the Australian disaster season, early October through to the end of March, these fire agencies continuously monitor weather conditions in preparation for responding to events when they occur. They also inform the community about known incidents[8].

The NSW RFS comprises over 2,100 rural fire brigades with a total volunteer membership of approximately 72,000. In addition, over 900 staff are employed to manage the day to day operations of the service. To assist with their ability to detect and monitor fires, they have been actively using ESA and we have received the following feedback of their use of the tool from Anthony Clarke:

---

[7] http://www.ga.gov.au/earthquakes/getQuakeDetails.do?quakeId=3461047

[8] See for example the NSW RFS Current Fires and Incidents page:
http://www.rfs.nsw.gov.au/dsp_content.cfm?cat_id=683.

...ESA enabled users to see minute by minute the latest topics relating to the fires, evacuation centres, communities and shows individual Tweets as they come in on these topics.

To enhance ESA's fire detection and monitoring capabilities, the earthquake event detection software was reconfigured to look for fire related alerts from the burst detector and a new fire Tweet classifier was developed to help determine if a Tweet containing a fire related keyword refers to an actual fire event. As discussed in [8], automatically determining if a Tweet is referring to an actual fire is far more difficult than for earthquakes as the word 'fire' and its derivatives are commonly used with other meanings. The ESA fire classifier has an 80% accuracy, which has proved to be helpful in filtering out the non-fire related Tweets.

A review of the historical alerts associated with fire related keywords found that the fire detection email service is expected to perform better during the non-fire season. This is due to the large number of fire events simultaneously occurring around the country during periods of high fire danger. The detector has difficulty identifying new fire events since fire related discussions are popular topics in Twitter and ESA's burst detector produces fire alerts almost continuously. Refining the fire detection process is an area of ongoing research

This review also found that when fire related alerts are present, the names of the affected towns or regions are also alerting. An example of this is the Springwood fire shown in the alert monitor of Figure 2. As noted previously, this fire started just before 13:30[4] and ESA received its first Tweet mentioning 'smoke' and 'Springwood'[9] at 13:34 and generated its first *springwood* alert at 13:39. NSW RFS issued its first Twitter Emergency Warning at 14:10[10]. If ESA had been able to combine the alerts 'springwood' and 'fire' or 'smoke' and was able to determine that 'springwood' was the name of a town, this further location context could be used to improve the fire alerting process. This is also an area of current investigation.

4   Operational Experience

The ESA tool is deployed on a cloud infrastructure using the JMS messaging service platform to connect components. Tweets are gathered from Twitter and published to the messaging middleware and consumers process the Tweets for different purposes (identifying burst words, event detection, Tweet classification, database caching, archiving) where identified events are published back onto the messaging service platform and reprocessed. This allows a messaging chain to be easily integrated into the tool for incremental processing and filtering to identify high value Tweets.

ESA currently has over 140 registered users from more than 50 organisations Australia wide. The system has been in continuous 24/7 operation for over 18

---

[9] See https://twitter.com/RJMajik/statuses/390666952571510784.
[10] https://twitter.com/NSWRFS/status/390676200387276800

months with only minor outages occurring. These have primarily been due to Twitter downtime and electrical maintenance of the data centre supporting the CSIRO cloud infrastructure.

In addition to earthquake detection at JATWC, ESA has proved to be invaluable in bushfires, floods, and cyclones, and has been in use in this context by the Queensland Department of Community Safety and NSW Rural Fire Service (RFS). ESA has provided the ability for emergency managers and crisis coordinators to use information from the public available on Twitter during emerging and ongoing crisis situations to enhance their response.

ESA was developed in close collaboration with potential users to ensure its fitness-for-purpose for the real tasks people in various government emergency services agencies are performing and the challenges they are facing. The tools are user-focused and integrate into their existing work practices providing an alert monitor interface to easily determine what is 'unusual' combined with text mining techniques, machine learning algorithms and advanced visualisations.

ESA processes large amounts of Twitter data and, using pre-calculated language models, it identifies the topics of discussion, trends and hot topics. The burst detector will alert on any unusually high frequency words, so the technique is readily applied to other non-emergency related domains.

Tweets are grouped by discussion to enable the user to have the whole context of conversations. This is especially useful for social media monitors enabling them to obtain overviews of what is being discussed on Twitter and to drill down to specific discussions and individual Tweets. All Tweets are cached allowing historical review of content and forensic analysis.

5   Conclusions

The ESA system provides all-hazard situation awareness by using content gathered from the Twitter social network. It collects, filters and analyses Tweets from specific regions of interest in near-real-time, enabling effective alerting for unexpected incidents with results accessible via an interactive website.

ESA is used in a number of ways to support different emergency management tasks. We have presented its use as an all-hazards monitoring tool, a notification system to identify earthquakes and fires and for ongoing monitoring of bushfires. In all cases, ESA has demonstrated that it is capable of providing additional, real-time situational awareness not available through other channels, which can enable more effective and timely decision making and responses.

Planned future work includes improvements to the process of maintaining the currency of the background language model, better alert filtering, incremental machine learning training based on user feedback, deployment to other regions, and investigation of an ontology of alerts and cluster topics to help categorise and summarise the information content. We are also investigating the use of photos referenced on Twitter as further evidence to support the decision making process. For example, in the first four hours after the *spingwood* alert, 23 unique photos of smoke from the Springwood fire were tweeted (and retweeted), providing further information about the ongoing fire.

Acknowledgements. The authors thank the contributions of our colleagues Sarvnaz Karimi, Andrew Lampert, John Lingad, Peter Marendy, Saguna, Brooke Smith, Gavin Walker, Allan Yin and Jie Yin. There have also been numerous collaborators from agencies supporting this work, especially Anthony Clarke (NSW RFS), Jim Dance and Andrew Grace (AGD), Daniel Jaksa (GA) and Adam Moss (Qld DCS).

References

1. Abel, F., Hauff, C., Houben, G.-J., Stronkman, R., Tao, K.: Twitcident: fighting fire with information from social web streams. In: Proceedings of the 21st World Wide Web Conference, WWW (Companion Volume), pp. 305–308 (2012)
2. Anderson, M.: Integrating social media into traditional management command and control structures: the square peg into the round hole. In: Australian and New Zealand Disaster and Emergency Management Conference, pp. 18–34 (2012)
3. Bruns, A., Burgess, J., Crawford, K., Shaw, F.: #qldfloods and @QPSMedia: Crisis Communication on Twitter in the 2011 South East Queensland Floods (January 2012)
4. Chowdhury, S.R., Imran, M., Asghar, M.R., Amer-Yahia, S., Castillo, C.: Tweet4act: Using Incident-Specific Profiles for Classifying Crisis-Related Messages In: Proceedings of the 10th International ISCRAM Conference, Baden-Baden, Germany (May 2013)
5. Earle, P., Bowden, D., Guy, M.: Twitter earthquake detection: earthquake monitoring in a social world. Annals of GeoPhysics 54(6), 708–715 (2012)
6. Imran, M., Elbassuoni, S.H., Castillo, C., Diaz, F., Meier, P.: Extracting Information Nuggets from Disaster-Related Messages in Social Media. In: Proceedings of the 10th International ISCRAM Conference. Baden-Baden, Germany (May 2013)
7. Lindsay, B.: Social Media and Disasters: Current Uses, Future Options, and Policy Considerations (September 2011)
8. Power, R., Robinson, B., Ratcliffe, D.: Finding Fires with Twitter. In: Proceedings of the Australasian Language Technology Association (ALTA) Workshop, Brisbane, Australia. pp. 80–89 (2013)
9. Robinson, B., Power, R., Cameron, M.: An Evidence Based Earthquake Detector using Twitter. In: Proceedings of the Workshop on Language Processing and Crisis Information (LPCI), Nagoya, Japan, pp. 1–9 (2013)
10. Sakaki, T., Okazaki, M., Matsuo, Y.: Earthquake Shakes Twitter Users: Real-time Event Detection by Social Sensors In: Proceedings of the 19th World Wide Web Conference. WWW, Raleigh, NC, USA, pp. 851–860 (2010)
11. Sakaki, T., Okazaki, M., Matsuo, Y.: Tweet Analysis for Real-Time Event Detection and Earthquake Reporting System Development. IEEE Transactions on Knowledge and Data Engineering 25(4), 919–931 (2013)
12. Verma, S., Vieweg, S., Corvey, W., Palen, L., Martin, J., Palmer, M., Schram, A., Anderson, K.: Natural Language Processing to the Rescue?: Extracting 'Situational Awareness' Tweets During Mass Emergency. In: Fifth International AAAI Conference on Weblogs and Social Media (ICWSM), Barcelona, Spain, pp. 49–57 (July 2011)
13. Yin, J., Lampert, A., Cameron, M., Robinson, B., Power, R.: Using Social Media to Enhance Emergency Situation Awareness. IEEE Intelligent Systems, vol 27(6), 52–59 (2012)

Author Index